PRAISE FOR
Jumping the Job T

D1007436

"Peter Brown continues to be full of fresh ideas and has a real writer's gift."
—**William C. Norris,**
founder of Control Data Corporation

"Highly literate and thought-provoking. Invaluable insights. A skillful blend of style and substance."
—**Phyllis Dunnam, Ph.D.,**
Senior Vice President, Drake Beam Morin, Inc.,
the world's leading corporate outplacement company

"This book offered me a systematic way of thinking about something I have done intuitively for twenty-five years. The suggestions are practical and the cautions important."
—**Howard H. Stevenson,**
Professor of Entrepreneurship, Harvard University
Graduate School of Business Administration

"An excellent guide to creating a new career out from under the corporate security blanket. Down-to-earth and practical."
—**John A. Rollwagen,**
former chairman and CEO of Cray Research, Inc.

"A survival manual. I highly recommend it to anyone leaving the corporate womb to venture out on their own."
—**Margaret M. Blair,**
research associate, Brookings Institute

"A very practical and usable guide, spiced with interesting anecdotes, relevant insights, and irreverent humor. Opens up new career and lifestyle possibilities."
—**Thomas R. McBurney,**
management advisor, former chairman of Pillsbury U.S. Foods

"A 'must read,' not just for those embarking on the consulting path, but for those who are dissatisfied or downright unhappy in their jobs."
—**Bret B. Baker,**
ad hoc financial officer and former corporate CFO

JUMPING THE

JOB TRACK:

✔ security,

✔ satisfaction, and

✔ success as an

INDEPENDENT

CONSULTANT

Peter C. Brown

CROWN TRADE PAPERBACKS
NEW YORK

Grateful acknowledgment is made to Jody Ray Publishing for permission to reprint lyrics from "Eye of the Storm" by Kris Kristofferson. Copyright © 1984 Jody Ray Publishing. All rights reserved. Used by permission.

Published by Crown Publishers, Inc., 201 East 50th Street, New York, New York 10022. Member of the Crown Publishing Group.

Random House, Inc. New York, Toronto, London, Sydney, Auckland.

CROWN Trade Paperbacks and colophon are trademarks of Crown Publishers, Inc.

Manufactured in the United States of America

Library of Congress Cataloging-in-Publication Data
Brown, Peter C.
    Jumping the job track : security, satisfaction, and success as an independent consultant / Peter C. Brown.
        p.   cm.
    Includes index.
    1. Business consultants.   2. New business enterprises.   I. Title.
    HD69.C6B76   1994
    001'.068—dc20   93-28941
                                                               CIP

ISBN 0-517-88157-8

10   9   8   7   6   5   4   3   2   1

First Edition

From here to the end is what matters, my friend.
You're right at the peak of your form,
Still in the eye of the storm.

Kris Kristofferson

CONTENTS

PART II: SETTING UP SHOP—
Straight Talk About the Nuts and Bolts

CONTENTS

ACKNOWLEDGMENTS

I am indebted to the consultants who were willing to share their stories in this book: David Bjork, Jack Brizius, Louisa Casadei, Don Coyhis, Hal Fisher, Sue Foster, Pattie Garrahy, Dave Hallowell, Alice Lucan, Eric Mitchell, John Niles, Diane Page, Alexs Pate, Skip Pile, Bryan Robertson, Verne Severson, Len Smart, Susan Stevens, Kathy Tunheim, Fran Wheeler. Thanks for your time, and for your trust.

The book is much better than it might have been thanks to the following friends who took time to read and critique substantial portions: Peter Gove, Arlinda Keeley, Carol Moss, Gayle Nordling, Steve Sears, Mark Threlkeld, and Bob Walker.

Thanks to my agent, Liz Darhansoff, and my editor, David Groff, for nurturing this book and its author.

Thanks to Dan Odegard and Sharon Hendry for help with the business of writing, publishing, and marketing.

Thanks to Palmer Cook of Nickleby's Bookstore Cafe, Columbus, Ohio, who helped name the book.

I feel special gratitude for Don Linehan's support and advice as a friend, and for his patience and loyalty as a client.

And to Ellen, whose patience, advice, and unflagging support have made all the difference.

INTRODUCTION

Consultants of All Stripes Are America's Emerging Independent Work Force

The Job Market Has Changed, and So Has Consulting

A large, independent work force is rising from the ashes of corporate downsizing, and it's no wonder. The *New York Times* reported in 1993 that *Fortune* 500 firms had downsized by more than 3.6 million jobs, "and the process seems to have accelerated." The *Wall Street Journal* proclaimed "the end of job tenure." Global economic turmoil has killed job security and rewritten the compact between managers and the executive suite. By the spring of 1993, white collar unemployment exceeded blue collar unemployment by 200,000 jobs, "the first such gap on record," according to the *New York Times. Fortune* magazine has called it "a social transformation as massive and wrenching as the industrial revolution."

The same forces that are closing doors to managers are opening doors to independence: men and women abandoning traditional corporate and government careers to seek their fortunes on the outside, selling services and accumulated know-how back to their former employers, finding new security by spreading their income over half-a-dozen clients or more, and taking responsibility for their own fulfillment and financial well-being. Yet, what may be the fastest-growing segment of the work force doesn't have a name. *Business Week* calls them "corporate refugees." Others call them "the portable work force," "outsourcers," "elite temps," or just plain independent contractors. I count myself among them, and in this book, I call us consultants.

Consulting is an old label that conjures up arcane experts in tweed jackets, or flashy young MBAs from high-buck East Coast firms. But the label is being worn in exciting ways. Today, consultants come in every stripe, and you don't need to be an expert or an MBA to become a hot property in the marketplace. In this book, I use the word *consultant* to encompass a wide range of white collar workers supporting themselves outside of organizations, working alone or in small groups, selling information and intelligence services. Their clients are often the same mainstream companies that once prized the loyalty of managers and looked upon those who left as defectors. These companies now see that it makes better business sense to "buy" rather than "make" a good deal of the staffing, production, marketing, and support services that are essential to their success.

In my mind consultants are distinct from entrepreneurs. Entrepreneurs are bent on starting companies, growing them, taking them public, and reaping the riches of capitalism. This is not a book about getting rich. It is a book about finding fulfillment and financial well-being by going on your own, and enjoying a new life of independence in the bargain.

The Road to Consulting Is Not Always Obvious

In 1980 at age thirty-two I decided I needed serious help with my career. I was a successful manager in a large corporation, but it wasn't as satisfying as I had expected, and I resented the rules that put important decisions about my career into other people's hands. I went to one of those psychology firms that does executive screening and hired myself one of the principals and the full battery of tests to get to the bottom of things. Four hundred dollars.

When I returned for the report, the consulting psychologist showed me to a chair in his office, took his seat behind his desk, and handed me a gray folder. Across the front was written Psychological Evaluation in big black letters. I opened it. "Vocational Assessment, Peter Brown." The page was dense with type. There, in words more penetrating than I might have hoped, was my conflicted self reduced to type. And toward the bottom, this: "You are feeling mildly depressed and lacking a clear sense of direction at the present time." Bingo.

Next, the psychologist unfolded a large chart designed to reveal how my interests compared with the interests of people in about seventy-five different vocations. Asterisks, scattered randomly across the page, picked out my soul mates: musicians, investment fund managers, dentists, professors, photographers, and men in the merchant marine.

So. There it was. We both stared at the asterisks, as if with time they might organize themselves into a revelation. What, he asked finally, did I think I might like to *do*?

I was at a loss and searched his face for a clue. "Consulting?" I said.

"Oh, yes!" he said. He gave me a confident grin. "You'd be great at it."

So I paid my $400 and became a consultant.

In fairness to the psychologist, his tests and interviews really *had* captured me on paper—establishing my dilemma but not pointing to an answer. I had to discover the right direction for myself. That encounter was significant for me not so much in what I learned from the psychologist or the signs from his analysis but that, in going to ask the question, I had taken a first step out of the world of conventional assumptions about jobs and careers.

I jumped the job track into consulting with no more credentials than a bachelor's degree in liberal arts, eleven years' work experience, and the contacts I'd established during those years. I've been on my own ever since, and the psychologist was right: it was a very good fit. I found my focus as a planning consultant, a broad niche that's put me into the path of a wide variety of opportunities. And, importantly, I've made a good living doing it.

How to Tell If the Independent Life Is Right for You

When you discover you can make it in the marketplace all on your own, you find yourself in a new world of opportunity. Suddenly, you have a whole new concept of work, self-worth, and economic security. Being independent means calling the shots, getting the financial benefit of your own hard work, building equity in a business with your name on the door.

More and more people are doing it, and many employers are helping them by providing start-up contracts, referrals, and support. Unlike permanent employees, consultants can deliver results and be gone, helping employers solve problems and meet special needs without adding to overhead.

If you're thinking of jumping the job track to go on your own but the thought raises more questions than answers, I'm here to tell you the risks are manageable and the rewards are great.

To make the decision, you need to know two things: (1) whether the independent life is right for you, and (2) how to make a success of it.

To answer the first question, you need to visualize life as a consultant. This book will help you do that. I've talked to dozens of people around the country who left their jobs to work independently. Many tell their stories in this book—why they went on their own, what went right, what didn't, and the lessons they'd like you to know.

To answer the second question, you need straight talk about the basics:

- What's the risk?
- How do I get clients?
- How much will I make?
- How do I set my rates and price jobs?
- Do I need to incorporate?
- What should I call my business and where should I locate?
- How do I get fringe benefits?
- What about contracts? Record keeping? Taxes?

This book answers all these questions and many more with practical advice to build a successful business and keep it simple and profitable.

Who I Interviewed and How I Found Them

The people you will meet in this book are excited about working independently. Some I have known for years, others I found by networking. To be fair to you, I set some criteria to make sure the people who were whispering into your ear knew what they were talking about. I looked for people who had left traditional jobs to go on their own, had been on their own at least five years, and were making a middle-manager's salary or more, which I defined as $50,000 to $100,000 after business expenses. Almost all of the people you will meet here are at the high end of the range or well above it.

I wanted variety, too. The women and men you will meet range from a circuit board-layout consultant to a First Amendment attorney. From a rural, white husband-and-wife team of national public-policy consultants to an urban, black international pricing consultant. From finance, market research, and telecommunications consultants to a Mohican Indian applying the principles of the Medicine Wheel to teach corporations how to change their cultures. They are turned-on people, doing important work, making it on their own.

I talked with many other consultants. I didn't have room to write a complete profile of each, and some haven't been in business long enough to meet my criteria. Still, their experiences were illuminating and entertaining. You will find them interspersed within the chapters, beginning with Bryan Robertson, who opens chapter 1 with a great story about how he came to throw over a successful corporate career to start his export consulting business.

How the Book Is Organized

The book is in two parts. The first ten chapters contain the more urgent material and the advice from consultants on topics that you won't find in any other book about starting your own business: how to know when it's time to leave your job, how to build bridges to independence, how to figure the risks and rewards, how to set your rates and get clients, how to bill, how to grow without hiring employees, how to keep control of your business, and how to adapt to the natural cycles of consulting.

The last four chapters are full of nuts and bolts: how to pick a name and location, whether to incorporate, how to project your revenues and expenses, how to provide your own fringe benefits, how to protect yourself from liability, how to keep records, and how to keep your nose clean with the IRS.

Each of the first ten chapters closes with a profile of a consultant who meets the criteria set out above, and whose experiences and wisdom help illustrate points in the chapter. There is an eleventh profile following chapter 14 to close the book. In the subtitle for part 1, "What Twelve Successful Consultants Would Like You to Know," I count those eleven and myself.

All of the consultants I talked to were glad to have a chance to share what they'd learned and wished they'd had a book like this to help them get started.

If you're thinking of jumping the job track, meet the people in this book and listen to what they'd like you to know.

PART I

The Independent Life—

What Twelve Successful

Consultants Would

Like You to Know

1   HOW TO LEAVE YOUR JOB

Knowing when it's time, and building bridges to independence

Bryan Robertson Has an Awakening

Bryan Robertson is one of those young fair-haired guys who move up through the corporation so adroitly you wonder what they've got that you haven't. He is tall, has a wide smile, and has been known to sign off a conversation with the admonition to "keep on sweating"—possibly a credo that accounts for more than his athletic build. We met for breakfast at the Ritz Carlton in Boston in the spring of 1992. I wanted to know why a guy like Bryan, who seemed to have had the best of what corporate life could offer, would throw it all over to go on his own.

Bryan had been vice president for US and European marketing at G.H. Bass, the shoe company, a subsidiary of Phillips–Van Heusen Corp. He was part of a team brought in to turn around sagging sales and losses that had grown to $71.5 million by 1987. For his part, Bryan created a new marketing function, and through it he developed a new advertising, positioning, and market segmentation strategy. He directed a new major-account marketing program to reposition Bass in top department stores, oversaw redesign of the entire corporate identity, and conducted a relaunch of Bass in Europe.

The results were excellent. In 1990, Bass reported a $29-million profit on sales of $250 million. And yet looking ahead, Bryan couldn't get excited about his job. In retrospect, he says, he was actually quite unhappy.

"I had everything I'd always wanted. I was head of marketing for a major division of a *Fortune* 500 company, but I wasn't satisfied and I couldn't figure out why. I went to see a career counselor. We had two sessions—not aptitude tests, more like therapy focused on work. The second time we met, the counselor said, 'I've got one simple question. If the president of your company left tomorrow and they came and offered you the job, how would you feel?' To my surprise I answered, 'Awful.' I'd never even considered the question. It really hit me at that moment that I'd always be miserable as long as I continued to put myself into the traditional corporate situation.

"This was a sea change for me. I had always thought my road to happiness was the one leading to the chairmanship of IBM. Now it seemed that the higher I got on the corporate ladder, the worse I felt. *That's* when I knew it was time to try going on my own instead of just finding another job."

Bryan left G.H. Bass and used his knowledge of retailing, marketing, and Europe to create Subsidiary Services International, which would serve as "an export department for hire" for American companies that produce consumer fashion goods and want to enter Europe (see chapter 2). A year later, with SSI in place, two solid corporate clients, and strong momentum, Bryan took a break to reflect on the lessons from his career.

"You have to shake this misconception we have—I don't know where it comes from—that working for a big organization is a *secure* thing. It's almost as if the corporation were a surrogate family, that succeeding in a corporation means you're succeeding in life. I used to think, 'Gee, I'm in this big company and I have this big job and title, I really *must* be good.' Unfortunately, it seems as you get higher up, all those faces around you become less friendly, more adversarial. Everybody's into a jousting game that absorbs an immense amount of energy. What I've discovered is, if you really enjoy your work and you don't thrive on that kind of politics, then you might be a lot happier on your own. Really, all this is just about being happy and making money."

Contrary to conventional wisdom, Bryan says, you don't necessarily have more security being part of a big organization than you do going on your own. "You do at that juncture where you're looking at making the change. You're thinking, 'Oh, my God. I'll be starting from ground *zero*. My income will get cut back, I won't have all the benefits, who's going to pay for my life insurance and health care? But if you look at it not from *this moment* but down the road two or five years, you can see where you'll have *more* security being self-employed." Nobody can lay you off. You've spread your income over four or five clients. If one goes down, it can be replaced.

"But people think about their security in terms of today. My question to them is this: Is it really going to be that secure in your corporation a year, two years or five years from now? The people who call the shots can turn and just say, 'We're consolidating your function at headquarters,' or 'The company has been sold,' or simply, 'You're fired.' The real risk in consulting isn't losing your long-term financial security. It's the fact that you're testing your own limits. When you go on your own and don't cut it, the only person you can point the finger at is yourself. You can't say, 'Well, my boss was an idiot.' *That's* the scary thing."

Succeeding on your own is a real affirmation, Bryan says. "And that poses another internal battle for some people: can you feel comfortable with your own success? If you're accustomed to the constant struggle, the notion of actually 'making it' may not jibe with your self-image."

Bryan certainly hit a responsive chord with me. But there are a lot of other reasons people leave jobs to go on their own, as I soon found out conducting interviews for this book.

Others Who've Jumped the Job Track, and Why They Did It

More and more people are going into consulting, propelled by the changing world economy, public sector budget crises, corporate downsizing, and new patterns of work that are opening so many opportunities for consultants. People are going on their own for personal reasons. Some are discovering what Bryan Robertson found, that the road to happiness isn't the one to the chairmanship of IBM. Others are going on their own because they've hit the glass ceiling, or because their position has been eliminated, or because their employer is willing to set them up in business and buy back their services by the day. Following is a handful of telling stories about people who have reached the conclusion that it's time to go on their own, and their reasons why.

Deciding You Don't Fit

Some people, and I am one, leave secure jobs and go into consulting simply because deep down they really don't fit into the culture of larger organizations, though they may come across as highly successful in the corporation, the university, or the larger government bureau. Or, like Fran Wheeler (see profile in chapter 3), they might have been pegged over the years as undeniably bright but chronically at odds with the world around them, never quite able to sing the company tune.

Fran designs printed circuit boards, laying out the tiny, complex circuitry that runs a variety of esoteric electronic equipment. She started in the early seventies, picking up the skills in a series of cutting-edge jobs at companies in Silicon Valley and Boston's Route 128 technology corridor. She did exceptional work, but whenever she began to rise in the corporate structure, she got crosswise with corporate politics and either quit or was shown the door. Her list of employers reads like the membership roster of a high-tech trade association.

In 1987, Fran got the old familiar feeling that she might be headed for another layoff, and she decided it was time to change the pattern. She went to the company president and offered to quit and work for the company from her home as an independent supplier. He took her up on it, and so began Wheeler Design. She's been on her own ever since, making more money than ever, with a roster of clients from California to North Carolina.

John Niles (see chapter 9) grew up in Detroit during the civil rights riots of the sixties and set out for a career in government to try to make the system work better. Years later, he quit his job in the mayor's office in Washington, D.C., and abandoned his dream of becoming a city manager. He had come to see that the kinds of jobs people moved into when they rose up the government hierarchy—jobs that represented his future—were tied up by politics and bureaucracy.

"I realized that system change is not easy to do as a manager," John told me. "You're too much captured by the ongoing agenda, the daily routine of hiring and firing. You can't focus on a narrow-enough set of projects to make a difference. I decided what I really wanted to do was work *with* line managers to help them make change, not to *be* a manager." He went out on in his own. One Sunday morning fifteen years later, we talked in his Seattle kitchen and John reflected on his years as an independent consultant—the ups as well as the downs. "This being on your own is not something I do because I *want* to," he said. "It's something I do because I *have* to. I couldn't bear the thought of going someplace every day to work."

John's experience reminded me of my own. I was a manager of Control Data when I decided to go on my own in 1980. Although three levels down in the hierarchy, I was considered bright, helped shape new ventures, raced back and forth across the country in a Lear jet with the CEO, and was occasionally invited to contribute to boardroom discussions with visitors. In a sense, working in the corporation gave me an opportunity to define myself, and the more clearly I understood who I was, the more inevitable it became that I would leave.

For one thing, I proved to myself that I could earn the respect of top management, and concluded by inference that if I stuck around long enough I could rise reasonably well through the ranks. For another, I came to see that by staying in the corporation, I was giving over responsibility for my career to others. And third, while I *wanted* to be above the culture preoccupation with rank, I couldn't keep from getting sucked into it, judging my value against all the little measures a company uses to signal stature: title, access to top management, number of windows in your office, where you parked, the dimensions of your desktop, whether your office had a light switch and door lock. I felt flawed for caring, but frankly it was a little too much like all those years I spent trying to outgrow the shadows of four older brothers.

I decided it was a good time to find other ways of testing myself and owning responsibility for my own successes and failures. I burned no bridges on my way out the corporate door; was told, in fact, that if life on the outside got a little too chilly, I would be welcomed back. That simple assurance was worth volumes in self-confidence and peace of mind, and it's one I'm glad I have never needed to test.

Seeking More Freedom

Some people leave jobs for consulting because they envision a better life-style. Dave Hallowell is an example (see profile in chapter 2). In one of his first jobs, Dave was a human resources manager for a seed corn company in Iowa back in the fifties. "I worked alongside two consultants, and the minute they started their assignment, I said 'That's what I want to be.' " He set out to become one by returning to school for an MBA, and getting a job where he could expose himself to a range of management challenges.

By the time I met Dave in his Bellevue, Washington, office in 1992, he had been on his own as a management consultant for twenty-six years. He said he always shudders just a little when he thinks back to what he knew and what he was selling in those early years after leaving his management position at Farmhand Corporation and setting up shop, at age thirty-two, as a consultant. Nonetheless, he says, "six months down the road, it was obvious I had a future in consulting. I was getting business, I enjoyed it, and it was consistent with that original vision I had back in Iowa."

Len Smart (see profile in chapter 4) grew up in Vancouver, BC, got trained as an electronics engineer, found a mentor at his first job out of the university, and decided to follow his mentor into the consulting life at the first opportunity. That opportunity came in the late seventies, consulting in telecommunications, and Len has been on his own since. "Consulting absolutely, unconditionally, ruins a person as an employee," Len says. "It does something to your head, the independence, the latitude that is your own to live or die by. And when I look back on the last fifteen years, there's no way I would do it differently."

Jack Brizius and Sue Foster (see profile in chapter 8) left high-level government jobs in Washington, D.C., for the consulting life because it allowed them to move out to the hinterlands of southern Pennsylvania, run a business, build a house, raise a family, and sink their roots into the fields and woods of northern Appalachia. How did they know it was time? Sue entered consulting first, in 1979, after leaving a job at the Department of Health, Education, and Welfare, where she was deputy undersecretary for intergovernmental affairs. President Carter was appointing a new Secretary of HEW, and Sue faced the choice of making the transition or starting something different. "I had one of those bizarre experiences. I was at a cocktail party and I found myself listening to what I was saying. I was so boring! I thought, I've got to do something else." Sue saw consulting as a way to buy time, maintain her contacts, and sort through her choices. "You do better if you anticipate the turning of the wind and create your own options," Sue says looking back, glad she left when she did despite the uncertainties.

Susan Stevens (see profile in chapter 9) took a sabbatical from her job in a nonprofit agency in 1982 to take a summer course in economics and finance at Cornell University. She returned to Minnesota resolved to do something new with her career. She took a series of short-term assignments with several nonprofit organizations. When she finished one assignment something else would come along, and it was during this period that the notion of going into business for herself took form. "My husband said to me, 'You're a hard worker. You might as well be on your own and get paid for it.' " She had come to feel that no job could ever give her the latitude or opportunities she could give herself. Susan started the Stevens Group to provide financial and management consulting to nonprofit organizations and foundations across the country. That was over ten years ago. Today, the Stevens Group is a stable of seven full-time consults.

Balancing Work and Homemaking

Other people get into consulting as if by accident, leaving their jobs to raise kids, being called at home by former associates and asked to do projects, finding themselves in demand, looking around and raising their rates, and ending up in successful, long-term consulting practices.

That's precisely how Pattie Garrahy (see profile in chapter 7) got into the business. She left a big job as media director for Fabergé, the cosmetics firm, to become a full-time mother, but she was dogged by friends and associates to do projects on the side. She did the projects, found ways to balance the work with the child rearing, and one thing led to another until Pattie realized the time had come to take consulting seriously. Pattie is now president of PGR Media, her own media planning firm.

Diane Page (see profile in chapter 5) left the marketing department of General Mills to join an ad agency, left the ad agency to raise a family, and acceded to calls to handle marketing-research projects in her spare time. Her work was very project focused, so she could fit it into her life where there was room. As her kids grew up, the mothering part of Diane's life took less time and consulting took more. She moved her office out of her home to sharpen the separation between work and family. These days, Diane's consulting practice keeps her busy fifty hours or more a week working for clients like General Mills, Pillsbury, 3M, Coca-Cola Foods, Taco Bell, Helene Curtis, and DowBrands.

Outsourcing

Corporate downsizing has confronted many people with opportunities to leave their jobs and sell their services back to their employers as outside vendors. When Bain and Company, the Boston consulting firm, was downsizing in the late eighties, Louisa Casadei (profiled below) offered to leave her job as a manager of the company's training function and provide training services back to the company under contract. She set her price and negotiated a contract that launched her training and presentation-coaching business.

Kathy Tunheim left Honeywell under similar circumstances. After the company restructured in the late eighties, it no longer needed the full staff of public relations professionals on salary at corporate headquarters. "You could see Honeywell's future, and we weren't all in the picture," says Kathy, who was vice president of PR at the time. So she and four associates approached senior management with a recommendation to consolidate the function and an offer to set up their own shop and sell back to Honeywell as much or as little PR support as the company needed. So began the PR consulting firm of Tunheim Santrizos Company (see chapter 2).

An Alternative Way to Practice Your Profession

For some people, consulting can be a good safety net. Alice Lucan, who appears later in this chapter, is a Washington, D.C.–based First Amendment attorney who left Gannett for the intimacy of a small law firm, then got laid off when the recession hit. Today, Alice commutes to her third floor, where she provides First Amendment consulting to *USA Today* and other newspapers and writes amicus briefs for the US Supreme Court.

Verne Severson (see profile in chapter 6) is an electronics engineer in Minneapolis. When the start-up firm he worked for went belly-up in the mid-eighties, he called around to people he knew in local technology firms who were familiar with his work and started doing design projects under contract. "I was reluctant to put the word *consultant* on my business card," Verne says. "I thought of myself as an electronics engineer. But then one day I figured out that consulting isn't a profession. It just describes the manner in which you practice your profession."

Today, Verne's niche is helping mid- and small-size high-tech companies with new product development. These companies have production and marketing capability, but they can't afford to keep a full-time staff of engineers on board to design new products and keep abreast of technology advances. When these companies have ideas for new products, they call Verne. He helps design the product, builds a prototype, and shows how to make the product perform the way his client's customers require.

Leveraging Your Know-How

Some people go into consulting because they want a business with their own name on the door and a chance to leverage what they've learned into an equity that will help them retire. Bryan Robertson, whom you met earlier in this chapter, belongs in this category. So does Skip Pile, president of Pile and Company (see profile following chapter 14). Skip spent fifteen years with Boston's largest ad agency, the last five as a senior vice president. During his tenure, the agency's billings rose from $10 million to $320 million. When it became apparent that the two owners weren't going to invite Skip into the business as a partner, he decided it was time to take what he'd learned and put it to work for himself. In 1987, at age thirty-nine, Skip set up his own shop to help large corporations get better services from ad agencies and streamline their internal marketing communications functions. In his fifth year, Skip and his two associates billed nearly $900,000 for their consulting services.

Eric Mitchell left Xerox in 1982 after nine years in various management positions. He packaged the know-how he had developed as a pricing manager and corporate controller into a corporation he called the Pricing Advisor, Inc., and set out to market a newsletter on pricing (see profile in chapter 10). When I interviewed him in 1992, he had four thousand subscribers to his newsletter, and some of the biggest corporations in the country as consulting clients. He was running an annual pricing conference and was setting up a trade association for pricing professionals. "Different media, same message," Eric told me, "giving advice to people on pricing. I didn't want to become dependent on one revenue source."

Consulting as a Bridge to Retirement

People are retiring earlier, and consulting is a way for many to make retirement more stimulating and financially feasible.

Hal Fisher, who appears later in this chapter, took early retirement from his position as vice president and portfolio manager for Boston's Keystone Investment Management Corporation. He was very successful, but he felt stale. His clients were spread from Seattle to Appleton to Wapakoneta and Allentown. He was tired of long days in planes, airports, rental cars, and meetings.

He and his wife, Marge, talked it over, and Hal gave eight months notice so Keystone would have time to find a successor. They sold their house in Hingham, where they had raised three kids, and moved lock, stock, and barrel up to Loon Watch Point, a secluded cottage they had built years earlier on a jut of land over Lake Conway in New Hampshire's Washington Valley. There, Hal has found a new way to capitalize on his thirty-odd years of experience in the investment field, doing business as Conway Investment Management Services.

Pursuing Your Personal Vision

For Don Coyhis, who left Digital Equipment Corporation after thirteen years as a rising star on the management track, consulting provides a means to pursue a personal vision—helping Native American youths achieve sobriety and develop their full potential (see chapter 3). Don is a Mohican Indian and founder of White Bison, Inc., a nonprofit corporation based in Colorado Springs. Through White Bison, Don uses the principles of the Medicine Wheel and teachings of Native American elders to help businesses and other institutions create a healing forest within the organization—change the organization's culture—in order to achieve their goals. While he was still at Digital, Don used these principles to restructure his own department, with such success that the program has since been adopted by other parts of the company to drive their quality program. White Bison uses the proceeds from Don's consulting engagements to underwrite its curriculum of programs for Native American youths.

Each of these stories is different. These people made the move to consulting for one or several of the following reasons:

- Didn't fit in a large organization.
- Wanted more freedom.
- Needed a different balance between work and homemaking.
- Had an opportunity to outsource their function.
- Were between jobs and saw consulting as an alternative means to practice their profession.
- Wanted to leverage their know-how into a business with their own name on the door.
- Saw consulting as a bridge to retirement.
- Saw consulting as a means to pursue a personal vision.

Yet despite their differences, these stories are laced with common themes. For example, it's possible to draw some general conclusions from these consultants' experiences about how to tell when it's time to leave your job and go on your own.

It's Time to Leave Your Job and Go On Your Own When . . .

- Being independent seems to hold greater potential for fulfillment than being part of a larger organization.
- You have self-confidence, optimism, and a knack for building relationships.
- You have knowledge or a skill that helps organizations solve problems.
- People will pay you for what you know.
- You can afford to take a moderate financial risk.

In the chapters that follow, you will learn more about each of the considerations on this list, and about other lessons these people have learned in the course of starting and building their businesses.

Assessing the Risks and Rewards

Consulting poses modest risks and rewards to two aspects of your well-being: your finances and your self-esteem.

Financial Risks

Consultants can make a very good living, but they seldom get fabulously rich because there are only so many hours in a day, and time is what they sell. On the other hand, unlike opening a restaurant or producing the next generation of personal computer, it doesn't take a lot of money to give consulting a try. A decision to leave your job and go into consulting is often a decision to put your financial well-being temporarily at risk to gain more independence and fulfillment.

Financial Equities You Put on the Line to Become a Consultant

- Your current salary.
- The prospect of future income (your financial security).
- Employment benefits:
    Health insurance
    Paid vacation
    Paid sick leave
    Disability insurance
    Life insurance

Employer's contribution to your retirement plan if you are not yet vested.

- Your tenure as an employee and accumulated benefits of rank: bonus, stock options, car.
- Savings you draw down to set up an office, fund operating costs, and provide personal income until your revenues can meet these expenses.

But now the good news: You can minimize financial risk and maximize the potential for gain before you even get started. The key is to construct simple financial projections, or "pro formas," which are spread sheets that illustrate your financial position on a month-to-month and cumulative basis.

Questions Financial Projections Enable You to Answer

- How much capital will it take to start my business and hold on until I'm making a profit?
- When will I break even?
- How can I keep my fixed costs to a minimum?
- What will happen to my bottom line if I change the way I do business, for example: have fewer clients but charge them more, or hire an assistant so I can increase my billable hours?
- How will basic choices (like officing at home versus renting professional space) affect my earnings, capital needs, and the number of months to reach break-even?
- What would it cost me to wait out a three-month dry spell with no revenue?
- What will happen if I take a regular monthly draw out of my business to support my personal income needs, before the business is making money?

With the help of a computer program like Lotus or Microsoft Excel, you can easily construct these "what if" models, and in so doing estimate how much money you will risk to get into business and the best ways of reducing risk and enhancing revenue. To illustrate the value of financial projections and how they work, and to help you identify types of costs and revenues to plug into your own projections, I have run pro forma spread sheets in chapter 12 for a starting consultant. They illustrate four alternative expense and revenue scenarios. In these scenarios, the risk capital required to start the business and carry it to break-even varies from $9,150 to $38,550, including a reserve fund sufficient to cover an extra three months without income.

Risks to Your Self-Esteem

Your self-esteem is vulnerable in consulting because you're putting *yourself* on the line when you sell: every time a prospect says, "No thanks," he's not saying it to somebody representing IBM Corporation, or city hall, or First National Bank; he's saying no thanks to *you.*The trick to safeguarding your self-esteem is to take your successes personally, but not your failures. When you do something well, linger over it, share it with others, turn it over in your mind, wonder at how clever you were to do what you did. Consulting can be a great self-esteem builder because you cannot pass your successes off to others.

By not taking your failures personally, I mean simply acknowledging each setback as a cost of being alive in this world, resolving to do better next time, and looking ahead. You can put a lot of the negatives off to circumstances beyond your control: a prospect who clearly didn't appreciate the value you offered, politics, recession, small-mindedness, short-term thinking. Of course, you need to learn to qualify prospects so you don't waste marketing effort on people who are unlikely to buy. You need to learn to sell the prospect what he wants to buy, not what you're trying to sell. You need to learn how to anticipate the pitfalls and navigate around the hazards.

These skills you pick up along the way—every knock you take in the early years is paid-up insurance for the later years. But most successful consultants, no matter how many years they've been at it, have a reserve of self-esteem and know how to replenish it when circumstances draw it down. Most, too, seem to nurse a valuable flicker of doubt, a twinge of insecurity that makes them go the extra mile to please the client and make sure the job is done right, on budget and on schedule. If you get cocky, become inured to the pain of rejection, or steel yourself through cynicism, you will probably lose the edge that made you great in the first place and kept your clients coming back. A little salt makes the sweet much sweeter.

Increased Security:
The Hidden Reward of Consulting

Six years ago, when my wife and I were applying for a mortgage, we had to jump through extra hoops because my being self-employed made us look like a high risk to the mortgage company. I told them they had it backward: Ellen worked for Control Data and could be fired at any moment. The company was laying people off by the thousands. My income came from many sources that were constantly being refreshed. I had direct control over projects, contracts, revenues, and expenses. I was the sales force, I delivered the services, I billed the customers. Now, I don't mean to say I was making us rich, but rich wasn't the issue. The issue was whether our prospects for future income and ability to pay on our mortgage were as good as those of a normal, two-income, corporate-employed household. And I maintain that they were better, because I'd been on my own long enough to prove I could make it, and nobody could lay me off.

If I'd had the corporate job and Ellen had been the consultant, I'll bet the mortgage company wouldn't have flinched, but that's a different issue.

Big is no longer the same as *secure* in our economy, as it probably once was. Ask the former employees of IBM, General Motors, GE, or Bank America. Loyalty and seniority are no longer insurance against layoff, as companies look to trim the ranks of middle and upper management, making cuts where they'll save the most. Expertise is no longer insurance against layoff: companies are learning it is cheaper to buy the services of most experts by the day rather than to keep them on staff twelve months of the year.

So what *is* security? The answer is different for each of us. For me, security means protecting my income and assets and building for retirement. Chapter 13 talks about these in more depth. The point here is simply that through consulting I have more income security than I did in the corporation because I control my own earning power and spread my income among multiple clients. This not only provides a sense of financial safety, it also makes me feel capable, flexible, and alert.

Every consultant I've met who has survived in the business tells me two things about security: they still panic during the slow times—it's a reflex, like grabbing the arms of your seat when your airliner hits a down draft—but they have always managed to get business, and the fact that they can diversify their income over a number of clients causes them, on most days, to feel they have more real income security than most people who work for a single employer. Being able to go out into the marketplace and earn a living without the dressing of a large organization is one of the best forms of security you can have.

Deciding What Kind of Consulting to Sell

Many people have excellent general management backgrounds and broad experience, are quick on the uptake, and have the potential to be effective in any number of capacities. Even specialists have choices when they go on their own: what markets to serve, and what niche to occupy within their specialty.

Most of the consultants you meet in this book who have been on their own for five to ten years or more have made significant shifts in their focus along the way, to better align themselves with the market. Dave Hallowell, who has been consulting since 1966, can chart the evolution of his business against shifts in American management philosophy. Skip Pile, who spent years as business manager for the largest ad agency in Boston, set out to provide consulting services to the agency side of the advertising business and ended up switching to the client side—serving corporations that buy agency services—because that's where he found the strongest demand for what he knows best. I began my consulting practice working with foundations and nonprofit organizations, then changed my focus to work with corporations because I found they also needed what I had to offer and were in a far better position to pay for it.

In any business there's a lot of give and take between what the seller wants to sell and what the buyer wants to buy. Odds are you will need to be out in the market for a while before you discover the greatest value you can add to your clients' businesses and which kinds of clients are your best marketing target.

Tips for Defining Your Focus

- Build on what you know and are good at; you'll be most confident in these areas. But remember, you don't need to know banking or health care to be a consultant to banks or hospitals. (See chapter 2.)
- Focus on customers who have money and are accustomed to spending it on consultants.
- Focus on solving problems in which organizations have a clear fi-

nancial stake, because they will see value in spending money for your help.

- Focus on sectors of the economy that are in turmoil—health care, financial services, retailing, marketing communications, international trade, public services, public finance—because those are areas where organizations need to reinvent themselves in order to succeed.

- Pick a focus that you can describe in simple terms: the problems you're in business to address, how to work with your clients' organizations, how the clients benefit—because focus and simplicity make it easier for you to sell, and easier for the client to buy.

Bridges to Get There Safer and Faster

You can do many things to ease the transition to consulting. Foremost are to get the support of your spouse if you have one, find a mentor, and line up some business before you leave the womb of a salaried job. Here are some thoughts on each of those strategies, and others.

The Spouse Ally

You don't need to have a spouse in order to succeed in your own business, but if you do, making your spouse your ally will make the start-up and early years go more smoothly. Nobody sees your strengths and weaknesses more clearly. And nobody will be more directly affected by your decision to chuck your job and go on you own. A change to the consulting life affects nearly everything you do—from where you work to how you handle your personal finances, how you buy your health care, how and when you take time off, how you plan and fund retirement, and how you feel about yourself. (See chapter 8, "Work, Money, and Private Lives: Consulting Notes from the Interior.")

Leaving a job and going on your own should salve some frustrations, like the need to control your own destiny or leverage the value of your know-how, but it introduces its own set of anxieties, notably those associated with financial uncertainty. You feel them and your spouse feels them. A funny thing about anxieties is that once they've been acknowledged, they lose some of their power and urgency. But ignore them, and you set the stage for your comeuppance. Denied their voice, financial anxieties have a way of erupting at precisely the wrong times—when events appear to confirm their legitimacy: when people aren't returning your sales calls, when a client postpones a job you'd counted on billing this month, when a hot prospect you'd already figured for sold stuns you by failing to sign up.

When you feel yourself sliding into one of consulting's unavoidable slumps, you need a champion, somebody who will share your incredulity over the sheer stupidity of a wayward prospect, somebody who helps you gather yourself once more for the charge. You don't need a spouse who, by not having been a party to your consulting decision, feels hostage to it and leaps on every setback as evidence of your folly. A torrent of feelings roils beneath the surface of most marital conversations over money, security, and the worst that could happen when one partner proposes to upset the domestic equilibrium. But if you don't have this conversation before you embark on the consulting life, you can bet it will come up when you are least able to deal with it objectively.

Recruit your spouse from the beginning into an open appraisal of your consulting opportunity, the risks, the benefits you each hope to gain, the pitfalls you can expect along the way, how you will overcome them. Agree in advance how you will know when the time has come to call it quits. If you do this, your partner will know there's a limit to the line you're willing to play out. The setbacks can be castigated and left behind instead of gathered in as exhibits for the prosecution. On the dark days when you need an ally most, you will have one right on the other pillow.

Special Knowledge or Credentials

If the area you want to consult in requires these, try to get them in advance. When Dave Hallowell decided to become a consultant he went back to school for an MBA. When returning to work after earning the degree, he made a point of getting broad management exposure by taking a wide variety of staff and line assignments before finally making the break to go on his own. Susan Stevens got a foundation grant to take a sabbatical from the nonprofit agency where she worked in order to attend a six-week course on finance and economics at Cornell University.

If you're negotiating your departure from a big corporation, think about what kinds of courses might give you an advantage in the consulting market, and see if your employer will subsidize your attendance as part of their outplacement program.

Credit

Run projections to estimate your financial needs, and if borrowing is in the picture, make the arrangements before you leave your job. A word on this from John Niles: "Everybody has an attitude about credit, and you'd better get your credit position and your attitude toward credit straight. If you think you're going to need it, get it while you still have a job. If you wish you had a five-thousand-dollar line on your gold card instead of two, the time to get it is not after you quit. Credit standards are higher for self-employed people than they are for corporate people. The financial world is oriented toward people with jobs and employers. If getting a second mortgage on your house is part of your plan, don't hold off on applying for it until after you've left your job." Amen.

Mentors

Find yourself a mentor. Begin by asking yourself who you know who's been on his own and succeeded, somebody who will give you straight talk and coach you through the process. A mentor can help you set your prices, qualify your prospects, structure your proposals, and figure out how to work your way out of a jam. A mentor is a model, coach, friend, source of moral support, and an important part of your marketing network.

Mine is a guy named Bob Walker. He's retired now, but he's been my mentor from the day I had lunch with him and said I was thinking of leaving my job and trying consulting. He offered me cheap space in his offices in a creaky old building that was later razed for the new Minneapolis convention center. He'd been in the consulting business for twenty years, and in addition to renting me space on a month-to-month basis, he let me buy into all the support services I needed to get into business without plunking down serious money: desk copier, secretarial and receptionist support, bottomless coffee pot. In the early days, every time I took on a new client, I strutted into Bob's office to announce my victory, and then, half an hour later, went back into his office in a panic to ask him how to do the job.

Bob kept a jar of stale candy on his worktable. When I came in for advice, he'd put down whatever he was working on, step over to his table, pull up a chair, prop his boots on the simulated walnut tabletop, rear his chair back and talk me through the situation while he tried peeling the cellophane off a gummy, half-decomposed Jolly Rancher. I'd relate what the client had told me about the client's situation. Bob, who'd seen it all before and liked me to know as much, would then proceed to set me straight, conjecturing why the client had really called, how screwed up his organization probably was, and how no matter what I did for him it'd more than likely stay screwed up because that's the way organizations are.

While he was saying things were hopeless, I'd start working on his blackboard saying how about if I started out doing this, and he'd say no, better to start by doing this other thing, then we'd talk about what I should do next, and so on. In an hour we'd have concocted a basic game plan for the job, and I'd go back to my office and get to work. A large share of the culpability for my surviving as a consultant falls to Bob Walker, whether or not he'd admit as much to you.

Insurance

You need to have health insurance. In most cases, you can retain the group health insurance coverage you have from your current employer (although you will probably be required to pay the premium) for up to eighteen months from your departure, under the provisions of COBRA (Consolidated Omnibus Budget Reconciliation Act of 1985). Talk to your employer to set this up. Or, if you have a working spouse with employer-paid health insurance, look into signing on as a dependent. Otherwise, you will need to go into the market and buy individual coverage. For pointers on this, see chapter 13, "how to provide your own benefits."

Disability insurance is also something you should consider buying prior to leaving your job. If you don't have it now and think you will want it when you are self-employed, you should look into getting it while you have a salary, because you can only purchase a benefit equal to a fraction of your income (usually no more than 60 percent), and your income will be hard to establish in the early stages of your consulting business. Also, consider the difference between policies that cover you for your profession versus those that cover you for your income. (Again, see chapter 13.)

Portables

Portables is a term lawyers (and others) use to characterize clients whose principal loyalty is to the lawyer rather than the firm with which the lawyer practices. If the lawyer should leave the practice, the client follows. Portables can be found in many service businesses, where expertise and good service forge a tight bond between the client and the employee: advertising, financial counseling, circuit board design. To get a better understanding of the value of portables, consider the experience of Alice Lucan and Hal Fisher.

Alice Lucan left her job as legal counsel at Gannett Co., Inc., in 1988. She was forty-four. She had spent twenty-two years in journalism and law, ten of them at Gannett. She was ready for a change and thought she'd like to set up her own practice, "but I was too scared." She joined a practice in a branch office of a large, established firm, bringing her expertise in First Amendment law to help her new associates provide legal services to newspapers. Two years later, with the recession undermining sales of advertising pages and forcing newspapers to cut costs— including legal services—Alice was laid off.

Fortunately, when she had left Gannett Alice had been able to take some of their legal business with her. When layoff time arrived at the law firm, she told me, "I added up and averaged out all the work I had done for *USA Today* and Gannett as outside counsel over the last two years. Then I figured out what my husband and I needed me to make in order to survive. Between the two figures, I came up with a billing rate, went to my client, and asked for the order. I said, 'Look, this is predictable for you, and predictable for me.' The in-house lawyer said, 'You've got it.' " At that moment, *USA Today* became Alice Lucan's portable. A lawyer with portables has options. So when Alice left the law firm, she took her *USA Today* business with her—changed her letterhead, started commuting to her third floor, and kept right on working for her client.

Hal Fisher is a financial consultant who used his portables to help him take early retirement in 1987 from Boston's Keystone Investment Management Company, after thirty years in the investment business.

When he left, Hal had more assets under management than anyone else at Keystone. "Over the years, I was able to build relationships with certain clients who came to have a lot of trust in me. So when the time came for me to leave, they wanted to come, too." He set up his own financial consulting business at his lake home in New Hampshire.

One of Hal's portables is a family trust he had been advising for twenty years. Another is a client that originally stayed with Keystone and later changed its mind and signed on with Hal. Through family contacts, he picked up a third account in Minnesota, and at the time we spoke he was cultivating another account relationship in his former home town of Hingham. Other of Hal's former clients who chose to stay with Keystone still wanted his input on their accounts, and Hal arranged with Keystone to serve as broker of record for these clients.

Today, Hal is a trim, tanned, sixty-three-year-old. When he and his wife, Marge, aren't entertaining guests who've negotiated their way through the three miles of wilderness along Little Kate Road to their improbable zone of comfort and hospitality, Hal may be fishing or downhill skiing. Or you might find him in his second-floor loft office reading some of his $2,000 worth of financial periodicals. "I'm more knowledgeable sitting up here reading and working on the phone than I was in Boston, where I had fifty accounts to service. I read an article, and then I'm out on the boat sailing and thinking about it. If it makes sense, I'll get on the phone and we'll do something."

The brokerage side of Hal's business has gone dormant. There wasn't enough direct involvement as a broker to maintain those relationships long-distance. The financial counseling relationships are healthy and very satisfying to Hal. They don't generate the kind of income and bonuses he cadged servicing fifty accounts for Keystone, but that's okay, too. When he gets around to it, he might trade off a little of his sailing time to do some marketing. But probably not this week.

Angels from Consultant Heaven

The difference between success and failure in consulting can be as thin as one contract—especially the *first* one, because it jump starts your business with revenues when you need them most, gives you a surge of confidence, diverts you from your darkest anxieties, and provides you with a name to drop when you call on other prospects. Half or more of the people I interviewed in writing this book had a pivotal business relationship that made it possible for them to hit the ground running when they opened their business.

Who are these angels, and how do you find yours? Your angel will turn out to be somebody who knows the quality of your work, wants to see you succeed, and is in a direct position to get you business. Most often, it will be your current employer, whether you're being laid off or leaving on your own initiative. If you have the personality for consulting—good at relationships, strong desire to please, a good performer—the odds are good that your employer thinks a lot of you and is reluctant to see you go.

To turn your employer into an angel, put together a case for transforming your relationship from that of employee to that of consultant: why you're going into consulting, that you are committed to your employer's continued success, that you are familiar with what needs to be done in your employer's business, and how much you would like to continue to make a contribution. By hiring you as an outside consultant, your employer will be buying only your hours directly spent on his problem, free of all the indirect costs associated with employment, including benefits, retirement, and so on.

A company that's downsizing is prime for consulting contracts because they often want to make it attractive for their people to leave, and department managers have head count reduction quotas to meet but no less work to be done. You may not qualify for one of those attractive early-retirement packages many companies are offering, but you could structure a proposal with an attractive one- or two-year retainer that would make it possible for you to more than break even from the get-go, and be attractive to your employer because he'll not only get rid of another body, he'll get valuable services in the bargain.

Anybody who is in a position to use consultants, who knows you and the quality of your work, and who takes a personal interest in your success, is a candidate for a start-up contract. The time to approach them is before you leave your job, unless doing so would be unethical. Above all, be aware of this: *to get a contract, you must ask for one.*

Ideas to Take Away

- It's time to leave your job and go on your own if being independent holds more promise for fulfillment, you have a knack for building relationships, you have an ability to help solve problems, people will pay for what you know, and you can afford to take a moderate financial risk.
- The risks in consulting are not great because it takes little capital to get started. For most people, consulting leads to *increased* financial security because you control your own earning power and spread your income over multiple sources.
- With financial projections, you can minimize risk and increase potential for gain before you even get started.

- Focus your business: on what you know and are good at, on customers who have money and use consultants, on solving problems that cost your clients money, on sectors of the economy that are in turmoil.
- Describe what you offer in simple terms so it is easier for you to sell and for the customer to buy.
- Build a bridge to consulting:
     Make your spouse your ally.
     Get special knowledge, credit, insurance, before you leave your job.
     Find a consultant to be your mentor.
     Take your portables with you.
     Get a contract before you walk out the door.

Louisa Casadei, profiled below, knew it was time to leave Bain and Company when she became a manager and was no longer on the front lines doing what she loved, communication coaching. She negotiated a one-year contract with Bain as her bridge into consulting, and when the contract expired she negotiated release from her noncompete agreement so she could broaden her client base. Bain and Company became Louisa's angel from consultant heaven because she had built a relationship of trust and respect, and had the wisdom to ask for their help.

ASKING YOUR EMPLOYER TO HELP YOU LEAVE
Profile
LOUISA G. CASADEI
Communication Consultant, Rockport, MA

Louisa Casadei is thirty-seven. She looks like a model. She is thin and elegant with creamy skin and dark, Liza Minnelli hair. The day we meet, she sits at her kitchen table in a red blazer, everything else in black: sweater, slacks, shoes. The house she shares with her husband, Eric Johnson, sits high on a rock between Gloucester and Rockport. It's set two streets back from the Atlantic, but looks to the southeast with sweeping views of the ocean and the twin lights of Thatcher Island. Her office, where she looks after her business as a communication consultant, is downstairs.

Louisa coaches business people on how to present themselves effectively in professional situations. One day she may be working with a group of lawyers to improve their client development skills. Another day she may be working with an investment bank, coaching a young entrepreneur on how to pitch his company to potential investors.

Over a cup of strong coffee, Louisa will tell you about the two times in her professional life when the actions she took proved decisive to her consulting success. The first was when she was an employee at Bain and Company, an international management consulting firm based in Boston. Louisa worked in the training department, coaching Bain's consultants on their client presentations and producing videotapes for Bain's training and recruiting functions. She'd gone to Bain out of college to see what it was like to work in an office. She worked her way up from administration, thanks in part to the skills she'd picked up studying acting in college, and to a mentor who ran the training function and saw talents in Louisa that Bain needed.

"I learned how to do training by doing it. Same with video production. What I really took to, though, was coaching. I had the acting background, and I discovered that coaching is a little bit like directing. It's not telling someone what to do, it's helping them figure out how to do it." Louisa holds to a personal philosophy that an effective presentation must be looked upon as a give-and-take dialogue focused on the client's agenda, rather than a performance focused on the presenter's agenda.

She also believes that every way in which one communicates with a client has an effect on the success of the overall client relationship.

"Most people who come to me are seeking presentation skills training. I try to get them to focus on the larger goal—creating good, credible relationships with their audience, whether that audience is a client, colleague, or judge and jury. Presentations are only one aspect of building effective relationships."

When she first started coaching the consultants at Bain, she felt a little bit like a fake. "I didn't have an MBA, but I was teaching MBAs. It took me a while to see I was getting results, getting good feedback. After a two-hour workshop, I'd see the consultants performing a lot better. And people really embraced the idea of dialogue as opposed to performance. Positive results gave me more confidence, and the confidence fed my creativity. I started using acting techniques and letting my instincts take over." Her workshops were consistently among the most highly rated of Bain's training activities.

When Bain and Company ran into earnings trouble in the late eighties and was forced to downsize, it was her mentor who got laid off, and Louisa who was promoted to manager. Seeing her mentor get laid off was hard. And being a manager didn't prove to be what she'd expected. "I thought I wanted to be a boss. It was part of the culture— upward, upward, upward. But when I became one, I found I didn't like budgeting and giving reviews. I liked to coach."

This is the point at which she made her first decisive move. She went to her boss and proposed to change her relationship from that of employee and manager to one of contracted trainer. She showed how she could meet Bain's training needs by working three days a week. She showed how the company could save money by not paying her insurance, ESOP contribution, and other indirect costs.

In preparing her pitch, Louisa had come up with a billing rate, which she'd arrived at by forecasting her own overhead, equipment needs, and insurance costs, adding these to what she needed to earn, and dividing the sum by the number of hours she thought she could bill. Her boss studied her proposal and then gave it back to her. "He asked me to take it home and rethink what I needed to charge for my time. Had I fully considered all the tasks involved in running my own business, everything I'd need to buy to be independent?"

Louisa did a competitive analysis, identifying other trainers and what they offered, where they ranked, and what they charged. When she brought back her proposal, she had increased her hourly rate by half. Her boss took her proposal to his boss, and next thing she knew, Louisa was in business.

"That was a big lesson: you don't get what you don't ask for. I was pretty excited. Here I'd be doing what I liked best, and I'd be making more money than a full-time employee. I had a one-year retainer, and two days a week free to look for other clients."

Asked how she knew it was time to leave Bain, she says, "I sensed I had a unique service. I was not feeling stretched enough. And I wanted the satisfaction of reaching more people."

She also got tremendous moral support from friends and colleagues. One of the video postproduction houses heard she was going on her own and called to offer free office space and the use of their recording facilities in exchange for helping bring them business. "That call was good because it gave me confidence to know someone else believed in me." She pursued the offer but didn't take it in the end for several reasons: the space didn't provide enough privacy, video wasn't going to be a major part of her business, and she discovered she could use her clients' conference rooms and video facilities when she needed them. But she says the conversation taught her some valuable lessons about teaming up that she's since made use of in other situations.

It was only two months into the new arrangement with Bain that she got a call from a Bain client that she'd done some coaching for in the past. He wanted to hire her services. Louisa and her boss at Bain had anticipated such calls and agreed to handle them on a case-by-case basis. This one, they decided, she would serve directly as an independent consultant, rather than through Bain, and thus she had her first non-Bain client. Her second came from a former Bain staffer who had left to start his own business and called Louisa on behalf of a friend who needed training. By the end of her first year, Louisa had billed $100,000.

And then a crisis hit. Bain did not renew her retainer. They had entered a second phase of downsizing, and Louisa was a victim.

"I was overwhelmed," she recalls. "My security blanket was gone, and I really felt like an independent consultant instead of an employee for the first time. Suddenly I needed clients." That's when she took her second decisive step. "I sat down and asked myself, 'Who needs what I do?' I knew I didn't want a lot of one- or two-day projects. I wanted to work with clients who knew they needed ongoing support. I came up with two kinds of prospects, lawyers and consultants. And that posed a problem. Bain had asked me to sign a noncompete agreement, saying I wouldn't work with any of their top ten competitors for the duration of my retainer and for one year thereafter."

A lawyer advised Louisa that noncompete contracts don't hold up if they prohibit a person from practicing her livelihood. But instead of pursuing legal recourse, Louisa went back to the executives at Bain and simply asked to be released from the agreement. "I told them I needed to make a living. They let me out. I was relieved and delighted, but not surprised. They'd been supportive and very fair all along." And once again she came to understand the significance of her earlier lesson: you don't get what you don't ask for.

Looking back, she sees that transition as critical because it forced her to diversify. She marketed primarily by networking with former colleagues at Bain who had gone on to work for other firms. "I asked myself, 'Who do I know at these different consulting firms?' In many cases, there were former colleagues from Bain, and they were in very senior positions. I'd call, meet them for coffee or lunch, see their offices. It was a business that I knew, so it was a relatively easy sell. Then they'd put me in touch with their head of training or human resources. And I found out that's the best approach, to sell the end user first—the executive—rather than coming in through the HR people." Even her first law client was a former Bain connection.

Her second-year billings were half the first year's, but as the client base has grown, her billings have recovered. Today Louisa typically maintains an ongoing client list of six firms, and as many again who come and go. She counts among her current ongoing clients two prominent Boston law firms, two international business management consulting firms, and a nonprofit corporation. All told, by the time of our interview, she had worked for over fifty clients, mostly on the East Coast but as far afield as California and Chicago.

What kind of person does Louisa think would do well in her business? "Consulting is *hard*. You and your process are the product. So it's very personal. Yet, a consultant can't have too big an ego, because it's not about doing things *your way*, it's about discovering *the best way*. Not being an expert, but a facilitator. Asking the right questions. Synthesizing. Drawing conclusions. Asking the *next* right questions. Knowing when to make statements. Knowing how to provide structure, be open and flexible, pull a process back on track."

She calls her business Real People Presentations. "The point," she says, "is just this: in order to be an effective professional, first you have to be an effective *person*."

2 TAPPING INTO HIGH POTENTIAL

Why consultants are getting so much business
when corporations are laying off

Role of Consultants in an Era of Turmoil,
and Why Every Organization Needs Them

Economic turmoil puts capital at risk and forces organizations to reinvent themselves. This opens doors to consultants.

I am not talking about normal cycles of growth and recession. Companies wait out recessions by idling plants, laying off production workers, selling off inventories, and holding their breath. Not good for consultants. I'm talking about long-term global economic restructuring that is changing the shape of our major institutions: the auto industry, banking, telecommunications, government, education, health care.

I'm talking about the integration of Europe into one market with buying power to rival the United States. I'm talking about the push for quality, global competitiveness, innovation, and time compression affecting industries around the world. For example, bankers are trying to discover what it means to become sales-oriented and entrepreneurial. Hospital administrators are analyzing how to maintain the bottom line when managed-care systems are introduced to reduce costs and shorten patient stays.

The organizations that I work with and read about are trying to do more with less—become strong global competitors while they streamline operations and rationalize excess capacity. They are trying to approach zero defects, knock the socks off customers, develop strategic partnerships with suppliers and distributors, consolidate backroom operations, and rediscover their core competencies. They're trying to divest themselves of peripheral operations, leverage brand equity, flatten management. They're trying to shrink inventories, train and motivate their workers, learn how to manage a multicultural work force, and increase the pace and success rate of new product development.

In all this change, two phenomena are of particular interest to consultants in the nineties: downsizing and outsourcing.

Downsizing

There are two fundamental differences between recessionary layoffs that put production workers out of work and organizational restructuring aimed at shrinking the ranks of middle management. In the latter, known as downsizing, middle management gets most of the pink slips. And, second, downsizing is not a short-term strategy to ride out a temporary downturn in the economic cycle, it is a long-term strategy for making the corporation more cost-competitive. The jobs are not idled, they are eliminated.

Headlines tell the story. "No Room at the Top; Opportunities Narrow for 70-Million Baby Boomers," reports the *Los Angeles Times;* "The Ranks of Middle Managers Are Thinning, Jobs Are Getting Harder"(*Industry Week*); "Professionals Join Ranks of Nation's Unemployed" (*Christian Science Monitor*); "Tightening the White Collar" (*Management Today*); "The Baby Boom Generation: Confronting Reduced Opportunities" (*Employment Relations Today*).

Others talk about the "glass ceiling" for women and minorities, about "career gridlock," "career plateauing," flattening of the corporate organization, and even "rightsizing." In it's "Review and Outlook" column of July 20, 1992, the *Wall Street Journal* wrote, "One of the most profound changes taking place across American society today is what might be called 'the end of tenure'—the idea that one's job, whether as teacher or CEO, is somehow protected for life from the forces of change in the outside world." The column goes on to point out that this hard truth, discovered by the private sector in the eighties, now confronts workers in government and public services as well.

US News & World Report wrote in November 1990 that as companies downsized to stay competitive in the eighties, an estimated four million jobs in *Fortune* 500 companies disappeared—jobs that belonged to manufacturing workers and middle managers. GE flattened management from eleven layers to four and reduced its work force by 100,000. IBM downsized by over 100,000 jobs during the period from 1986 to 1992, and reported, in July 1993, another 60,000 to go. From 1984 to 1989, 1.3-million manager and professional jobs were eliminated from the US work force. During the period ending June 30, 1991, 56 percent of firms surveyed by the American Management Association reported job cuts averaging nearly 10 percent of their work force.

Middle managers were hit hardest, taking 16 percent of the cuts while constituting only 5 to 8 percent of the work force. By mid-1993, downsizing had become so accepted as a prerequisite for future success that an article appeared on the front page of the *New York Times* with the headline, "Strong Companies Are Joining Trend to Eliminate Jobs."

These changes spell opportunity for consultants who can help organizations understand what changes they need to make, help them implement those changes, and help them function effectively with fewer employees.

What Will Sell in the Nineties

Any list of consulting opportunities arising from the changes in society and the economy would have to include the following:

Helping Organizations Streamline

- Develop integrated management systems.
- Consolidate redundant functions.
- Eliminate staff specialists whose services can be more efficiently contracted out.
- Integrate systems for information processing and telecommunication.
- Improve efficiency and effectiveness of purchasing, inventory management, manufacturing, marketing, distribution.
- Flatten management.
- Reduce cycle times for product development/manufacturing/marketing.

Helping Organizations Grow

- Better understand changing customer needs and wants.
- Analyze cultural and demographic trends to target marketing messages and growth.
- Improve quality and customer satisfaction.
- Apply technological advances to outmoded products and services.
- Redesign incentive compensation systems.
- Build regional and global brand equity to support sales growth and profit margins in the United States, Europe, Asia, Latin America.

- Get more impact from marketing communications investments.
- Reposition themselves in current markets and enter new markets.

Helping Organizations Reinvent Themselves

- Evaluate market trends, technologies, and competitor strategies.
- Develop a strategic plan for achieving sustainable competitive advantage.
- Raise capital.
- Forge alliances and joint ventures; acquire and divest operations.
- Retrain employees.
- Redesign government services and funding mechanisms (education, health care, affordable housing, inner-city job creation, infrastructure repair).

Helping Organizations Adjust to Societal Changes

- Develop better security systems to protect people and information.
- Comply with environmental regulations.
- Adapt to the growing cultural diversity of the work force.
- Modify employee benefit programs to fit changing needs and values.
- Reorganize production, marketing, and distribution to fit international geo-political realignments.

The list could be longer, but it makes the point: there's a lot of hard, creative work to be done in every sector, and, while organizations are being forced to downsize, they are also being forced to look outside both for *know-how* and for people who have the *time* to figure out what needs to be done and coax it into place.

Outsourcing

Outsourcing is a term for the trend among corporations to go outside for services that traditionally have been supplied inside the company. Outsourcing is not new, but it has become far more prevalent. Among the first functions companies shed and buy back under contract are those performed by specialists: executive compensation, public relations, information systems design, sales training, mergers and acquisitions support.

Hay Management Consultants is an international firm specializing in human resources and organizational effectiveness consulting to middle market firms with sales of $50 million to $ 1 billion. They have 1,200 consultants in offices around the world, and they are familiar with the trends in corporate staffing. David Bjork, a senior consultant in Hay's Minneapolis office, says outsourcing and consulting are on the rise as virtually every industry in this country downsizes. "It's a massive restructuring, including companies that have traditionally been fat and sassy, like pharmaceuticals." Downsizing is most pronounced in staff areas, which is where companies generally hire consultants.

One result of downsizing is an increase in the workload on remaining staff. They inevitably need to do more hiring of consultants, because every time a project comes along, they run up against a capacity problem. "Companies rarely develop all their systems internally anymore," Bjork says. "They buy packages or they farm out programs. It may cost more on a short-term basis, but it's not a permanent cost." Bjork says there's a general understanding that vendors who are specialists in a business like systems are more efficient. Even if they cost more, they have a better capacity to get done on time and the company has better control.

If you're thinking of making a case to your employer to outsource your function and buy back your time as a consultant, here are some benefits such a move might offer.

Potential Benefits to Employer from Outsourcing Your Function

- Reduces fixed costs.
- Reduces headcount.
- Transforming an employee into a vendor creates new incentives for performance.
- Services still available as needed.
- Creates opportunities to redesign the function to better support new strategic directions.
- Frees company to use multiple suppliers.
- Frees company of liability and indirect costs of employment.

Potential Benefits to You

- Clearer performance expectations and focus.
- A business in place of a job, with revenue from the outset.
- An opportunity to transform hard work into profits and assets.

- The potential of serving multiple clients, diversifying your revenue sources, and increasing your financial security.
- An established client to use as a marketing reference to build your business.

To get an idea how outsourcing can be initiated, consider the two examples that follow. Kathy Tunheim left Honeywell to create the independent public relations firm Tunheim Santrizos. Bryan Robertson left G.H. Bass to create Subsidiary Services International, "an export department for hire."

Kathy Tunheim Creates Tunheim Santrizos

One day early in 1990, while Kathy was vice president for PR and internal communications at Honeywell, she sat down with her boss and said she thought it might be time to look at the notion of spinning out the corporate communications function, including Kathy's job.

"My boss was one of those unusual people who can hear a new idea from somewhere out in left field, and immediately see it's worth kicking around," Kathy says. Honeywell had come through several years of turbulent restructuring, redefining itself in its markets, divesting major parts of the business, taking significant financial write-offs, fending off potential predators. During this period much of the communications function had been centralized at headquarters: crack communications managers surrounded the executive suite like so many wagons circled for damage control.

Kathy had built much of the team herself, and they were highly respected. But by 1990, with a leaner corporation embarked on a new course, Kathy and her associates could see it was time for a large part of the function to be pushed out to the operating units, where it could focus on marketing, and another significant part, including crisis management, to be made available on a more flexible basis instead of being kept on salary, waiting for a crisis.

Kathy and four others had been meeting regularly over breakfast to discuss the situation. "Out of all the talking came an idea that we would take the people who provided a good part of that communications mechanism and eliminate it from the company but make it available in a new way," Kathy says, by proposing to go into business and sell as much of their services, or as little, back to Honeywell as the company might need.

"We reached the point where we said, If we're going to make this proposal and Honeywell doesn't go for it, are we still going to go? Everybody wanted to think about that one over night, but we each came back and said 'we have to.' We felt the idea was right for Honeywell, and not doing something wasn't an option. If we didn't define our future together, we'd each have to do it on our own."

In approaching her boss, Kathy started with an informal conversation to let her know what she was thinking about, and why. "I didn't want there to be a sense that I was going away from something, but rather that something new made more sense for Honeywell, and provided opportunities for growth and professional development that some of us didn't think we were going to get by staying on the corporate staff." She gave her boss a copy of a column by Peter Drucker that had appeared in the *Wall Street Journal*. In the article, called "Sell the Mail Room," Drucker says that increasingly there will be people with specialized staff skills who rise to the top of their function on corporate staff and discover there is no obvious next career step. CEOs should be open to the idea of helping those employees go into business and sell their services back to the company.

With her boss's blessing, Kathy and her team put their thoughts down on paper, including financial projections that compared costs of continuing the function as currently organized versus costs of contracting significant portions to an outside vendor. "We did the pro forma assuming the contract could have gone to anybody. It had to be Honeywell's decision first of all to contract out, and second of all to decide who they want to contract it with."

Then Kathy and her boss sat down with Honeywell's chief financial officer. "His question, I'll never forget, was 'I don't understand why you want to do this.' I had to say, 'Because it makes so much sense.' I'm from a middle-class, midwestern family, and I grew up in an environment where if something didn't really make sense and it was expensive, you just didn't do it. Keeping a full complement of PR professionals on staff had made sense through the preceding five years, but looking ahead, it was an expense the company couldn't justify. So we had a nice conversation, and then he looked at the financial projections we'd put together, and, financially, outsourcing made a lot of sense."

Tunheim Santrizos opened its doors in June 1990 with the understanding that Honeywell was acquiring a very considerable amount of Tunheim Santrizos' time to help Honeywell make the transition. "As we went through the first twelve months, we worked with Honeywell to sharpen our role and work the size of the contract down. We have continued to do that for the second year, and the number is now less than half what it was when we started, and that was the original idea, to help them clear the deck, but not to do it with any loss of control in case any crises were to hit."

Meanwhile, the new company went out after other clients. At the end of their second year, when Kathy and I met, their client roster listed more than twenty companies—mostly blue chip. The firm had grown from six people to thirty, and gross and net revenues were significantly ahead of plan.

Bryan Robertson Creates
"An Export Department for Hire"

Leveraging what he learned selling G.H. Bass shoes into European markets as VP of marketing, Bryan Robertson has created Subsidiary Services International.

SSI is a simple concept that solves a very complex problem for American branded consumer fashion goods firms that want to expand into Europe but do not have a European base of operations or established European distributor and retailer relationships. These firms typically have two options for entering Europe: one is to turn their brand over to a European distributor that has the knowledge and marketing infrastructure to take the American brand into the market. This approach involves little investment risk, but the American partner has almost no control over how his brand is priced, distributed, and promoted in Europe.

The American company's second option is to set up a European subsidiary and drive the product launch with its own people. The company retains control of pricing and distribution, but setting up a free-standing European subsidiary is extremely expensive, taking on the cost structure and employment obligations of a European business and putting considerable investment at risk. Bryan's solution offers his clients the best of both options: high control, low cost, low risk.

Operating as SSI, Bryan helps clients like Eastland, the footwear company, enter Europe through a five-step process. In the first step he conducts a strategic analysis and develops a plan for the client's brand in Europe: which markets to enter, and how to enter them. His second step is to help the client identify and evaluate potential distributors in its target countries, and negotiate distributor contracts.

Step three entails setting up operational systems and financial controls for the European market: moving the product from factory to warehouse to retailer; handling payment; handling quality assurance— the details that make up a successful business. Step four is helping set up sales and marketing programs to build the brand in its target markets. Step five is managing and monitoring the business in Europe, and making recommendations on how to help it grow. Bryan manages the business until sales reach a level that justify the client's setting up his own European office.

SSI charges each client a monthly retainer until the client's European sales reach a negotiated threshold, at which point SSI charges on a percentage-of-sales basis. Bryan's target is to have five clients on board at any one time.

A the time I met him in the spring of 1992, Bryan had contracts with Eastland, the footwear company, and B.D. Baggies, the men's ready-to-wear company, and he was well down the road in negotiations with another prominent American branded fashion retailer.

One thing that strikes me about these two examples of outsourcing is the receptivity of corporations to doing important work through start-up, outside shops when the case is well presented. In the fat days of the sixties and seventies, corporations were pretty smug. If a company needed a vehicle fleet for their sales force, they hired a fleet manager and built a fleet. If they needed to train computer technicians, they started a technical institute. If they needed to distribute published material, they set up their own print shop, bindery, and mailing operation. No longer. If you can do it for them better, cheaper, or quicker and be gone, you can get the business.

I believe corporate outsourcing will continue its impressive growth and will flourish eventually in government and quasi-public areas such as academe and health care, where pressures to restructure are coming rapidly to a head. Many successful consultants will find their way into business through this approach, and those who leave the employment fold with a substantial contract in hand will have a ticket past much of the hungry start-up phase experienced by most businesses.

Why You Don't Need to Be an Expert to be a Successful Consultant

Did you study syllogisms in high school? The teacher gave a test containing various propositions of logic, and you were asked to explain which were faulty and why. For example:

Major premise: A consultant is somebody with credibility.

Minor premise: Experts have credibility.

Conclusion: You must be an expert to be a consultant.

Faulty logic, but many people cling to it. If the problem isn't credibility, perhaps it's lack of something to sell, as in: to be a consultant, you need marketable skill or knowledge. Experts have marketable skill or knowledge. Therefore, . . . etc.

If you come to believe only one claim this book makes, I hope it's that you don't need to be an expert to succeed in consulting. Before I elaborate, let me define some terms.

Three Types of Consultants

- *Generalists:* Consultants with expertise and common sense who help a client define its problem so that the *client* can solve it.
- *Specialists:* Consultants with particular know-how who can solve a specific problem or deliver a specific service a client needs.
- *Experts:* (1) Consultants with extensive education and highly specialized expertise who amortize the cost of their education in their billing rates. (2) Specialists whom a client hires and calls experts so their opinions will carry weight. (When I use the term expert in this book, I will be meaning the former.)

Generalists

Because of their breadth, generalists are adept at applying lessons from their own experience to the problems of another organization, whether those problems relate to organizational structure, product development, or marketing. Generalists are comfortable walking into unknown territory, learning the lay of the land, defining what needs to be done, and developing a critical path to achieve results—much the same as an effective manager, but with the added benefits of coming from the outside, having no stake in the organization's politics, and bringing the wisdom earned from their past successes and failures in many different organizations.

Broad experience helps a person sniff out the peculiar. Like therapists and midwives, generalists aren't there to *do* the work, they are there to help define what work needs to be done, point the direction, and provide wise counsel while the client owns the problem and does the work of solving it. This is why somebody like me or David Bjork (the senior consultant at Hay), who has never been a banker, a philanthropist, or a hospital administrator can be a consultant to banks, foundations, and hospitals. The generalist helps reveal the problem, give it definition and legitimacy, draw out the creativity of the client's team, help them outline a plan of attack, and focus on the solution.

Before he became a consultant, David Bjork was a teacher of music history with a doctorate in that field from UC Berkeley. When he decided to enter consulting, he went back to school for an MBA. "The skills I brought to consulting were analytical ability, research ability, and excellent communications skills."

Half tongue-in-cheek, I asked David how a music history background helps him as a consultant, and he gave me a serious answer.

"Consulting is basically all harmony and counterpoint. If you're looking at virtually anything in the corporate environment, there are many competing forces, playing off against each other. An example would be international product line management versus geographic management. In the financial services industry, it's always credit versus growth. In a manufacturing industry, it's product development versus maximizing your margins on whatever product you have. It may be marketing versus sales and engineering. You need to master what these are, and then you need to synthesize them in a way that's a little bit neater than the client can ever do.

A generalist's biggest dilemma is often figuring out how to describe what he offers—defining his services with enough specificity to make the sale, yet with enough flexibility in the execution to discover the right fit between what the organization needs done, and what the generalist can help them do. Clients turn to consultants for solutions. But the more specifically you define your focus in order to be relevant, the more you limit your prospects to people who need that particular kind of help. Generalists do best when they can get paid to become acquainted with an organization, working with the client to define the organization's problem and chart a course to their solution, including the specific role the consultant will play and at what cost. At its best, this is a process of mutual seduction.

If you are a generalist, you will find a way of solving this problem. I solve it by representing myself as a planning consultant. Planning can embrace a multitude of sins, so I have not closed too many doors with that label. While I can adapt my planning skills to many situations, I rely on a methodology I have refined over the years that usually gets me to the end of an engagement without getting too far out of my element.

When I am selling myself to a new prospect, I describe what I believe are the ingredients of a good plan, the steps involved to develop them, the product, the cost, the benefits, and how my approach is different from others. When the client raises hypothetical situations that could come up during the process, I try to describe how I have handled similar situations in other projects. The first phase of most projects that I undertake involves learning considerably more about the client's situation so that we can design the planning process to address the important issues and get the kinds of results the client's team will find most useful.

Specialists

Specialists focus on helping a client solve a particular kind of problem, and while they do provide coaching and direction, more often than not they deliver a hands-on service. Since a specialist is slotting herself into a defined area of expertise, the going rate for people in her field pretty much limits what she can charge, unless she's found a way to add value to differentiate herself and justify charging a premium.

Most outsourcing is performed by specialists. Diane Page is a market research specialist (see chapter 5). She conducts and interprets market research for her clients, helping them make smarter decisions about products and marketing. She prices herself in the midrange of the market-research market, and differentiates herself through her exceptional skills as a focus-group moderator and by staying abreast of changes in consumer attitudes.

Verne Severson is an electronics engineering consultant who specializes in new-product development (see chapter 6). He designs and builds prototypes and provides advice about product features. His target market consists of medium- and smaller-size technology companies that don't have the engineering and prototype production capability in house.

Christelle Langer packages PBS programs and markets them to sponsors from her home in Emmaus, Pennsylvania. Pattie Garrahy is a nationally recognized wizard of media buying from her office in Providence.

From a marketing perspective, specialists have it all over generalists because they have something specific to sell—something a prospective client can clearly see would be a solution to his problem. Specialists can be specific about how they will work with the client, articulate the benefits, and develop patterns and systems to make their costs and successes more predictable.

For example, when Fran Wheeler gets a new client for her printed circuit board design services, she gives the client a seventeen-page booklet she wrote called "PCB User Guide and Checkoff Sheets." The booklet lays out success factors for the job up front, including a description of the client's responsibilities. In effect, with the booklet she is telling her client, "If you do this, you'll get a good product." So in many ways, being a specialist or an expert may make it easier to break into consulting. But having a specialty is not a prerequisite for consulting.

Experts

Experts have a more narrowly defined and deeper set of qualifications and charge more. The justification for this fee, just as you justify the fee of a brain surgeon, is that you are not only buying the ten hours that the surgeon is working on your brain, you're also buying your share of the years it has taken for him to become the kind of expert who can solve your problem. We all bring to each engagement the total sum of our life's experiences and education, but a person who amortizes the accumulated costs and traumas of his personal history in his consulting rates is definitely billing as an expert.

As a rule an expert is not hired to take a client through a discovery process but to serve as a kind of consultant laser beam. Be precise, brief, and totally effective. If the problem costs a lot of money, the solution is worth a lot of money. If you're planning to become an expert, pick a field where the problems are expensive. Conversely, if you want to be seen as an expert, you probably have to charge like one.

Admittedly, the line between specialist and expert is fuzzy. Alice Lucan, who left Gannett where she was legal counsel, is an expert on the First Amendment and provides legal advice to medium and smaller newspapers that cannot afford to have an expert in house.

To a layman, Verne Severson seems like an expert in electronics engineering. But in Verne's eyes, he's not an expert: he keeps abreast of innovations in the application of electronic technology but does not stay up with advances in basic science. Those who do, he says, are the experts in his field. But Verne offers something the experts can't offer; he knows how to take an idea from the marketing people, pull together the latest applications technology from several fields, and build a working prototype, getting his hands dirty in the process. Electronics companies with labs full of experts couldn't compete in the marketplace without people like Verne who can bridge the gulf between science and the consumer. Specialist? Yes. Expert? Depends on where you sit.

There is room in consulting for people at all points along the continuum, from generalist to expert. The further toward generalist you sit on that scale, the harder it is to describe what you do, but a strong generalist has an enormous potential market because he can apply his problem-solving skills to a wide variety of situations.

The further toward expert you sit on the scale, the easier it is to define what you do but the harder it may be to differentiate yourself from others with the same specialty (and, therefore, the harder it may be to price yourself above the midrange in your field), and the narrower the market you can serve.

Except for the small fraction of the market that requires true experts, most clients hire consultants for three reasons: (1) they don't have enough people inside to get the work done (example: engineering, accounting, finance, marketing); (2) they can't afford to keep somebody who is somewhat specialized on staff if they only need her once a year (example: executive compensation, media planning); (3) they need an outsider with objectivity and credibility (example, conducting an audit or building consensus for a controversial decision). To succeed in these assignments you need seasoning, good working skills, and a good consulting methodology. Each of these is addressed in the chapters that follow.

Ideas to Take Away

- Global economic restructuring puts capital at risk and opens doors to consultants.
- Consulting opportunities in the nineties will focus on helping organizations streamline, grow, reinvent themselves, and adjust to societal changes.
- Corporate downsizing is a long-term strategy and fuels the trend to outsourcing.
- Public budget crises will give rise to more outsourcing by government and institutions in quasi-public areas like health care and academe.
- You don't need to be an expert to succeed as a consultant.
- Generalists have a harder time defining and marketing their services but have a broad base of potential clients.
- Specialists have an easier time defining their services and target

clients but have a narrower market and may have a harder time differentiating themselves from other specialists in their field.
- To succeed in consulting you need seasoning, good work skills, and a good methodology.

Dave Hallowell, profiled below, has been on his own as a general management consultant for nearly thirty years, starting out at age thirty-two on the strength of an MBA and the seasoning provided by a mix of management assignments. He has succeeded over the years by staying attuned to shifts in American management philosophy and by constantly improving his methodology to get the right kinds of clients and deliver results.

A CAREER AS A GENERAL MANAGEMENT CONSULTANT
Profile
DAVID A. HALLOWELL
Management Consultant, Seattle, WA

Dave Hallowell runs his business from an office on the ninth floor of an eighteen-story tower at the corner of 110th and Northeast Eighth Street, a commercial district in a section of greater Seattle called Bellevue. He's located in one of those well-done, shared executive suites where one- and two-person professional firms can have first-class space and support services without having to carry all the overhead on their own.

The day we are to meet for the interview, I find my way to his reception area. With its open stairs, sand-and-gravel carpeting, and buff-colored wood-grain appointments this suite seems to be an oasis of tasteful, arid understatement that offsets the unregenerate mists and rabid vegetation draping the homes and backyards and fences, the vistas, cloverleafs, and overpasses of Seattle.

Dave comes down and introduces himself. He is as neat and spare as his native state of Wyoming. Silver hair, tan skin, and a discrete Ted Turner mustache that puts me in mind of a magazine ad for men's shirts. Wearing a beige linen sport coat and umber slacks with a sharp crease, he leads me through the back halls to the coffee room, and then upstairs to his office, where we sit at a table and talk about his career in consulting.

Wyoming, Dave says, doesn't spawn many management consultants. He got into it in the sixties, which, I'm thinking as he speaks, was certainly not an era when people went willy-nilly out on their own without an expert's credentials to back them up. But Dave did, and on the few occasions when he thinks back to what he knew and what he was selling in those early years, he shudders just a little. Now he's crowding sixty. He says he no longer craves client contact. He's looking for associates, working to turn his years of accumulated know-how into an asset that will fund his retirement. To do that, he must make the transition from salesman and hands-on practitioner to product developer and trainer, turning his practice into a business that is not "Dave-dependent," as he puts it—one in which others deliver his products and generate the income.

Dave was born and raised in Ranchester, population 151. He earned a bachelor's degree in business from University of Wyoming and was recruited out of the university by General Mills. He worked variously in Minneapolis and Iowa in production planning and personnel, did a stint in the military, and established a human resource function for a small seed corn company. In the latter capacity, he hired the services of two consultants from Des Moines. They were his first exposure to the consulting way of life, and made a big impression. "The minute they started their assignment, I said 'That's what I want to be.' "

He mustered what resources he could and went west to the University of Colorado for an MBA. He graduated broke and in debt, but he had the degree. He persuaded the seed corn company to ship him and his belongings back to Iowa. He worked there for a year and a half, then went north to Minneapolis, where a friend helped him land a job at Farmhand Corporation.

At Farmhand he got "beautifully broadened" over a three-year period, starting in human resources, assuming responsibility for a parts manufacturing function, becoming assistant to the director of marketing and engineering, and then becoming sales administration manager. He says this was a pivotal period in his training to become a consultant, both because it established his management credentials and gave him a line-management orientation.

Dave left Farmhand and started his consulting company on January 6, 1966, age thirty-two. He set as his focus supervisory training for middle- and first-level managers. He combed through a list of local employers, picked out those with the most employees, sent them prospecting letters, and followed up with telephone calls. One letter went to Chet Hirsh, who was treasurer at Deluxe Check.

"I'll never forget when I called him up. I'd never sold anything in my life. He said, 'There's a 95 percent chance that we won't do business with you, and a 5 percent chance that we will. If you're willing to take the odds, come on out and I'll talk to you.' " Dave went, and so began his first contract and a fifteen-and-a-half-year consulting relationship with Deluxe Check.

"Six months down the road, it was obvious that I had a future in consulting. I was getting business, I enjoyed it, it was consistent with that original vision I had back in Iowa."

Asked how he accounts for that early success, he credits two factors. "I had a passion for certain basic beliefs that I think were infectious. I believed in the importance of participation in a business by its employees, giving people more responsibility for their own work. And I believed in the importance of having a focus in an organization. In addition to my beliefs, I had a facility for systematizing and synthesizing many ideas into a few broad management concepts."

That facility has served him well over the years, and he has accumulated experience and stayed attuned to the sea changes in American management philosophy, enabling him to evolve his consulting products to stay abreast of what the marketplace wanted. For example, it wasn't long after he started consulting that he took an interest in what he calls the job enrichment/job design movement and started incorporating those principles into his training.

"Job design is based on the principle that people are motivated by the nature of the work they are asked to do, and if you can give them a meaningful job that provides for growth, recognition, achievement, and responsibility, they will be motivated." He performed a number of job-design projects for employers in the Twin Cities. Control Data's Institute for Advanced Technology hired Dave to run a number of job-design seminars in Washington, D.C., and Seattle, which gave him national visibility. He says the concepts at work in job design constituted the seeds of the total-quality-management movement that is sweeping through corporate America today.

Dave found that the job-design contracts were causing him to work at lower levels of an organization than he liked because that's where the jobs were in trouble. As a result, he wasn't getting the visibility with senior management that he needed in order to make a broad impact. So in the midseventies he modified his focus to pull many of the job-design concepts together into a larger management system that he could use with senior-level managers. He developed an integrated approach to planning, goal setting, performance appraisal, and budgeting, called it the Integrated Management System, and sold it to such firms as Northern States Power, Boise Cascade, and Milgard Manufacturing.

Since then, Dave has begun taking on associates and has broadened his product still further, keeping it rooted in the same principles that fueled his start. The main elements of what he now calls the Management and Employee Performance System are training, consulting, and monitoring. The focus is on system change within the client's organization—improving customer service, improving the organization's ability to compete, improving internal management communication, and integrating the management processes of planning, goal setting, performance appraisal, budgeting, and compensation into one cohesive management system.

"Most organizations do not look at the power of a management system. I contend that a good system is one of the hidden, powerful dimensions of a good organization. But you don't make major changes in organizations' management process with a video program or by selling workbooks. You do it in a slow, methodical way through a combination of consulting and training and process. It's a three- to four-year effort. If you don't put a consultant with the product, the odds of making real change are nil."

The monitoring aspect of Hallowell Associates' Management and Employee Performance System is one of its more unusual elements. "We ask that the client monitor both the consultant's progress and the client's progress for five years, and we have quite an elaborate evaluation system. In one case, we're getting individual surveys back from 1,700 managers in the client's company to track how well each of the company's major units is doing with each of the components of the system: what's working well, what's not, where they need help, how well Hallowell is doing to support them."

Hallowell Associates' fees depend on the size of the customer, ranging over the life of a project from $60,000 to $75,000 up to $300,000 to $400,000. Before they get involved with a client, they conduct a preliminary study and will turn down organizations when they don't feel they can have a long-term success.

In 1989, Dave moved to Seattle and made the decision to expand his business beyond a one-man shop. Today he is splitting his time among serving clients, marketing, trying to hand pick consultants to join the business, and keeping his products up-to-date. At the time we spoke, he had hired an associate to run a Minneapolis office, and another to join him in Seattle to take over marketing.

How does it feel to be making the transition from hands-on consulting to hiring others to do the client work? "Exciting," Dave says. "It's a natural next phase for me. I've had twenty-six years of doing the consulting. I've walked that road many times. The classroom is a place for younger, higher-energy people."

He says his goal is to establish three or four offices nationally, with three to four associates in each office. These need to be people with a general-management orientation rather than specialists. "They have to be able to live with ambiguity and pull from that ambiguous climate what's happening in an organization."

Judging from his own experience, he feels that being an effective consultant takes a combination of three qualities: "You have to know what you're talking about—have something to offer that is legitimate and needed in the marketplace. You have to be reasonably skillful in relationships. And you have to have a willingness to take significant risk."

Asked what those risks are, Dave says, "Most obvious is financial failure. Less obvious but equally significant is the risk to a person's self-esteem. This is a business where you get rejected a lot. You'd better be secure enough psychologically to handle that.

"The best way to protect your self-esteem is to believe strongly in what you're doing and be able to put disappointment behind you. That's a continuing part of this business, even after twenty-six years. You have to be able to get up the next day and focus on what's going to happen from this point on. And for me, spirituality is awfully important. It gives me perspective. It's awfully easy to get consumed with all the issues that occur in managing a business. It's very important that one not get consumed by them. To remember that life is bigger than these successes and failures."

I ask how a person can evaluate whether he has the ability to take these risks. "I use a worst-case scenario sometimes," Dave says. "What's the worst thing that can happen, and can I live with that? If I can, I'm probably going to be okay."

After all these years, the worst aspects of consulting in Dave's view are the fact that he will never know how he would have done if he had stayed inside the corporate mainstream, and the sheer effort required to sustain a consulting career. "It extracts a great deal of commitment and work to keep riding out the ups and downs. No matter how many years you've been in it, you always panic on the down slope. You never get over that."

The best aspects of consulting? Dave smiles at the question. "The freedom it offers. The recognition. And the feeling that you've done your own thing. Knowing you've survived the test of fire."

3   TRUSTING WHAT YOU HAVE TO OFFER

"(Your name) *since* (the year of your birth)"

Your Know-how

Over the years, a number of friends have taken me to coffee to ask about the consulting life. They're toying with the idea, but when they begin the soul searching they come up asking a fundamental question: What do I have to sell? If you're a specialist, say a commercial real estate appraiser, the answer comes easily: Sell your expertise. If you're a generalist—a problem solver, good with people, results oriented—the answer is elusive. What you have to offer as a consultant consists of what you know, your access to others with expertise, and something I call your performance factor.

What You Know

It's easy to see that a specialist in software systems for convenience stores has valuable knowledge. The value can be described and the benefits can be sold to potential customers. The generalist who can walk into an unfamiliar organization, size up the dynamics, help identify needs, outline a plan to meet them, and get the organization's key employees on board has knowledge, too, and a lot of it. That knowledge is hard to describe yet clearly has value. It is the knowledge that comes from experience.

In a real sense, what you are selling is the accumulated wisdom of all your years. Every time I reprint business cards, I am tempted to have them say, "Peter C. Brown, Since 1948." That's when I entered the school of life, and what I've learned since then is what I bring to every client's job. The useful gray hairs are the ones you earn the hard way. Each time you walk into a troubled situation, feel anxiety well up in your stomach, and find your way through to a successful outcome, you hone your instincts and accumulate know-how.

In consulting, process is the product, and *how* is as important as *what*. David Bjork, the senior consultant at Hay, says much of what he has to offer clients he learned in an earlier career as a teacher. "When I got into consulting, my background teaching music history not only gave me no leg up in trying to market, it was also a little bit of an embarrassment. I'd tell clients I used to teach, but never tell them what I taught. My favorite line was 'theory and methods,' because it's reasonably close to being true, no matter what it is you teach.

"The truth is, what I learned teaching music history was excellent training for consulting, because consulting turns out to be a form of teaching, and the methodology is universal. To be a good consultant, you need good skills in learning quickly—that's research—and being able to size up a situation, as well as good generalist analytical skills—logic, persistence, enough detail to follow through to the end of the question. And most important is having first-rate communication skills to sell your conclusions to the client, which is a blend of entertainment and teaching."

In thinking about what you have to offer as a consultant, it is useful to think about the difference between knowledge of what things are and knowledge of how things work. Architects may know how to design homes, but few could build one. A lot of contractors who know how to build quality homes don't know good design from a dead cat. The more a consultant knows about both the *what* and the *how*, the more she has to offer her clients.

When Diane Page contracts to conduct market research, she knows the difference between quantitative and qualitative research, when to invest in one or the other, what kinds of qualitative research—focus groups versus in-depth individual interviews, for example—are best for different circumstances. That's the market research *what*.

Where Diane really sets herself apart, though, is her ability to carry out the research. She knows how to recruit the right kinds of respondents to participate in a focus group, how to design a discussion guide to get at the important information her client needs to learn, how to moderate the discussion to probe for the real meaning behind participants' comments and opinions, how to interpret respondents' reactions, and how to put the important information into a report so that it helps her clients make the right decisions from what they've heard.

That's the *how* knowledge, which makes the *what* knowledge useful to the client and gives the consultant value.

In my business, the *what* may be knowing the makeup, purpose, and use of a strategic plan. The critical *how* is how to structure the planning team; how to separate strategic issues from operational concerns, and how to focus on the former and leave the latter for another day; how to build a shared vision for the future of the organization; how to deal with surprises in the planning process; how to build buy-in for the plan; how to transfer a long-range plan into specific, achievable steps to be integrated into individuals' work plans; how to monitor progress and update the plan so that it becomes a living, working road map for the organization instead of fodder for the archives.

Consider what Kathy Tunheim has to say about trusting what you have to offer: "It's hard to trust what you're good at when you step into an established industry, and you don't fit the mold. When we left Honeywell, we set out to become part of the PR industry. If you look at the major players, you'll discover that in order to say you're a full-service PR agency, you're supposed to have this long list of capabilities. Well, we're good, but don't have everything on the list.

"But we have something that's not even on the list: an insider's knowledge of corporate life in the nineties. And we're getting business others aren't getting, because we understand the turmoil clients are going through—they make a PR decision in January, and now it's March first and everything's different in the company. All the people who made the decision are in different jobs, everything's all hosed up. We know that environment, we know how to change gears, redefine the job, help the client solve the problem he's got today. A traditional PR agency takes an assignment in January and delivers a promised product in April, but by then the clients can't remember why they asked for it.

"Even though somebody sometime back wrote the book on how to be a public relations agency, it's not healthy, number one, to presume that's a good way to do the business, or, number two, that it's going to stay that way. Part of the reason there's an opportunity for this firm is that the clients have changed, but the consultants out there in our field haven't—at least, not as much as they need to and will."

So, the knowledge that gives you value as a consultant is the knowledge that enhances your ability to perform. People with a lot of *what* knowledge but not much *how* knowledge may be too academic or theoretical to be helpful. Although smart, they're not streetwise, and that means they aren't of much practical value as consultants because they can't help translate what they know into useful action within the client's organization—they can't help the client put their know-how to work to improve his business.

In my experience, it's the *how* knowledge that people most often take for grated in themselves because it's often second nature—intuition and common sense accumulated from years of living. The natural inclination is to discount your own experiences and think you have to be an expert in some or other *what*. Don't underestimate what you know how to do.

The most valuable know-how you bring to consulting may not even be remotely similar to what others are selling. Don Coyhis brought the teachings of the Native American Medicine Wheel to change the culture of his Customer Support Center at Digital Equipment Corporation. Don is from the Stockbridge-Munsee tribe. He was a Digital manager for thirteen years and got involved on his own time working for change in the Native American community. He saw an opportunity to exchange some processes and principles of the corporate culture with some teachings of the Native American culture, and help both sides. "It was kind of like walking two logs across the river," he told me.

"As I was working in the Native American community doing training, I was having a hard time making it stick. So I went to an elder and he said, 'I'll give you four laws about community change.' And it was these four laws that I brought back into Digital.

"The first law is that change comes from within. The elder put a seed in my hand and said, 'What do you see?' I said, 'I see a seed.' He said, 'No, that is a blooming flower. Inside of that seed, everything is contained for the blooming flower.' So the first principle that we put into place is that any change we make in our department at Digital has to come from inside the organization. The leader's job is to help build the desire to change.

"Second, you will move toward and become like that which you think about. In order for development to occur, it must be preceded by a vision. No vision, no development. If that's true, we needed to think about what we were thinking about. Find our vision.

"Third, a great learning must occur. The universe is a system of harmony and polarity: man/woman, boy/girl, up/down. The poles give us balance, and the system is held together with principles, laws, and values. The cycle of life on the Medicine Wheel is in four parts: baby, youth, adult, and elder. In a corporation, the four segments might be shop floor worker, supervisor, manager, executive. If you are to change the system, everyone must be in the learning. The managers can't say, 'Go fix the employees, they need it.' The Medicine Wheel teaches that the system and the individual must change simultaneously. You have to design a process for a great learning to occur for everyone across the organization.

"Fourth, you must create a healing forest. Let's say that you have a hundred-acre forest. In that forest you have a disease. You take one tree to a nursery and nurture it until it is well, and then you bring it back to the forest. This law says that the tree will always take on the nature of what it returns to. In other words, when you make changes, you must have a healing environment that supports the change."

Don helped implement these concepts as part of a change program in the Digital Customer Support Center. He says that in two and a half years, they improved customer satisfaction, broadened managers' span of control, and saved the company over $30 million.

Not surprisingly, the program was adopted by other departments. But Don had a personal vision, and he left Digital to form White Bison, a nonprofit organization in Colorado Springs. Through White Bison, he is applying what he learned in the corporate world to Native American communities, with a focus on helping achieve sobriety among youth. He funds those efforts with money he makes by taking the principles of the Medicine Wheel into corporations, government agencies, and other institutions across the country. But if you want to hire him, get in line. He's often booked six months ahead for consulting, and more than a year ahead for speaking engagements. And you might want to check your budget, because his billing rates *start* at $3,000 a day.

I am struck by the way Don's experience illustrates both the potency of *how* knowledge, and the fact that you don't have to be peddling teachings from the Harvard Graduate School of Business to be a valuable consultant to mainstream institutions.

Access to Others with Expertise

The adage that "it's not what you know but who you know" takes on a twist in consulting. Nobody's accomplished in all the skills required to make an organization work, and when you uncover a gap in a client's capacities, it pays to have a network of other free-lancers you can call on to fill the gap—somebody with a finance background, somebody with expertise in organizational development, or pricing, or program evaluation, or work force diversity, or data communications, or labor relations.

From time to time I find myself working with family-held businesses where difficulty resolving the future focus and direction of the company uncovers deep-seated conflicts among members of the family. In other kinds of businesses, people can be moved out or bought out when doing so seems less onerous than the prospect of working through personal differences—but not so in a family business. So I call on a consulting firm whose specialty is helping families resolve conflict in family-owned businesses. It's a subject that requires special methods—a hybrid of family therapy and management consulting—and the fact that I know somebody very good to call enables me to help a client beyond the help I can provide myself, and may bring me renewed business with the client sometime down the road.

The handle "& Associates," which a lot of consultants put after their names, serves two purposes. The first is to make them sound more substantial than a lonely solo practitioner, the assumption being that prospective clients will figure bigger is better. I don't know whether this is true. I do know that when prospects call me, it's me they want to deal with, and I only use the "& Associates" when I need to make clear that I am a business, for example, in signing a contract or getting past the receptionist who asks "Can I tell him who you're with?"

The other reason some consultants use "& Associates" is to reflect a network of specialists that most consultants can bring to bear on a client's problems—a network of tried-and-true associates who the consultant has come to trust and can bring to the client with confidence that the association will be successful.

Your "Performance Factor"

There are a lot of smart people who'd make lousy consultants. Know-how is only half the formula when it comes to understanding what you have to sell. Know-how, as I've described it above, is your accumulated wisdom, specific expertise, methodologies you have developed to deal with situations, and your access to others with expertise.

The other half of the formula is a combination of attributes that I call your performance factor. Your performance factor is the combined effect of your confidence, comfort with uncertainty and ambiguity, ability to simplify complexities to facilitate decisions, ability to shift the customer's focus from the perceived issues to the real issues, your need to please, and your willingness to accept what you cannot change. These qualities aren't things clients look for in a consultant, but they are qualities that help make you effective and lead to repeat business.

Confidence

You tell a friend that you're consulting. Your friend says, "On what?" You smile. "What do you need?" Your friend smiles back and nods, as if you have confirmed what everybody else knows, that a consultant is some kind of chameleon whose professed expertise changes to suit the circumstance, and consulting is a scam, something people do between gigs, a way to kill time while you look for honest work.

There are three kinds of confidence you need to summon to be a consultant: confidence in your value to the client, confidence in your problem-solving skills, and confidence in your relationship skills.

Confidence in Your Value to the Client   If you believe consulting is basically a scam, you'll approach prospects as if you were asking them to do you a favor by becoming clients. You need to believe in what you're selling. A confident consultant is like a good piece of writing. When somebody lacks confidence in what they're offering, their uncertainty comes through on the page. The piece is weak. You lose confidence in it as a reader. The same holds for consulting. If you don't think you can be helpful to a client, tell him, because he'll read it in your eyes.

To find this confidence, the starting consultant has to look back on his performance as an employee and see how he used consulting skills effectively to help his employer and customers. Once you're in business, this confidence grows with every successful engagement. One of the challenges in consulting is to pay attention to the results you're getting, and keep improving your methods to increase your value.

When I started helping clients with long-range planning, I considered my work complete once the client's management team had agreed on a five-year vision for their organization and the goals and objectives required to achieve the vision. I found that consensus on a vision is of tremendous value. It energizes the entire management team, because everybody commits to working toward the same future.

When I followed up, though, I found clients were having a hard time translating high-minded goals into day-to-day tasks. The plans weren't being implemented.

I modified my methods to include implementation planning. Now once we have the goals and objectives in place, we break them into tasks. We identify which tasks must be accomplished over the next twelve months. We set a target completion date for each task and agree who will take lead responsibility for seeing it gets accomplished. We agree on how we'll monitor progress. The implementation plan is a bridge from where the organization is today to where it wants to be in five years. It's what puts change into motion.

Most recently, one of my clients asked me to help his managers incorporate the twelve-month tasks into their individual work objectives, so that each had an accountability for contributing to the long-range plan on a day-to-day basis. We did that, and my methodology took another step forward.

These discoveries are some of the best rewards of consulting and are the real confidence builders when it comes to trusting your ability to be of value to your clients.

Confidence in Your Problem-Solving Skills   The difference between this and the kind of confidence I just talked about is subtle, but important. It's being cool under pressure, thinking clearly in a sea of ambiguity.

Earlier in this chapter I mentioned the anxiety that wells up when you take on a new client and accept accountability for helping address his problem. The kind of confidence you need here is a little inner voice reminding you that whatever the situation turns out to be, you'll find your way through it. This is what you're good at, why you're in the business. At the core is confidence that when you don't have the answers to a client's problem, you do know how to frame the questions and help the client identify the steps to find the answers; a belief that common sense will get you back to firm footing whenever you're over your head in the client's pond.

I reinforce my confidence in this area by recalling jams I've worked my way out of in the past. I also hang on to scraps of praise. I'll stick a client's note to the side of my computer and let it catch my eye. It makes me feel competent, and feeling competent helps me take risks. For another example of how this kind of confidence can be important to your business, read the profile of Verne Severson in chapter 6.

Confidence in Your Relationship Skills   Consulting requires confidence in your ability to be liked and trusted, to negotiate, to feel centered when you stand in front of a group of strangers.

For me, there are two issues. One is fighting my proclivity to hide out in my office. It's a lot of work to be gregarious, and there's always a certain risk you won't be liked or you'll screw up. Of course, the best energy I get from consulting is the energy I get from my clients. And you can't run a business, at least the kind I'm in, sitting at your computer. So I get out and work with people, and it often surprises me how good I feel about the experience.

The related issue for me is building my confidence in front of groups. I facilitate a lot of group problem-solving meetings. When I expect to work with a group, I try to meet the people in advance, so I don't find myself standing at the front of a roomful of strangers.

If I can't take the time to sit down with them individually before the group meets, I ask my client to describe each person, and to tell me something significant about each. I memorize the names. More than once I've been driving down the freeway to a meeting, reciting the names of the people and what they do. I'll have my file open on the passenger seat with the directions to the place on top, and beneath it I'll have my cheat sheet with the roster of names. Pretty soon I'm hollering them at the radio, trying to rhyme them, imbed them into my brain for the next two hours. When I get in front of the group, I can call on people by name, and I feel grounded.

Another technique that increases my confidence when I work with a group is finding out in advance what we need to accomplish in order for the participants to feel that their time has been well spent. If I know the answer, I can come prepared with two or three alternative routes we can take to reach our objective, depending on what turns the group discussion takes.

Ability to Simplify

Everything is more complicated than it used to be. Somewhere I saw a quote I wish I could track down that went something like, What we have today are fewer problems and more messes. A mess is a combination of problems that is very difficult to solve because the problems are all interconnected.

You will be more effective as a consultant if you can learn the art of helping a client break his mess down to its component problems, and then plot strategies for solving the problems.

In my experience, the ability involves two specific skills. One is an ability to absorb many facets of a situation, and then be able to net out the significant elements in a summary of the whole. When you interview the blind men who are feeling the elephant, your summary of the beast needs to put across the pertinent facts. What's pertinent depends on the elephant's significance to the blind men, your client. If their objective is to find out whether he's a threat to their village, it's more important to summarize his size, direction of travel, and mood than to differentiate his trunk from his tail. If their objective is to find a new source of shoe leather, the texture of his skin becomes a salient issue. Many people aren't able to winnow out the unimportant so that they can focus on the important.

The second skill that will serve you well is an ability to break down a complex process into achievable steps. A lot of dilemmas don't get solved because people don't take the time to identify and articulate them. Put down what people agree on. Frame the question. Put down alternative answers. Agree on criteria for choosing among the alternatives. Discuss what additional information you need to gather in order to apply the criteria. Agree on who will get it, by when, and how.

If Stephen Hawking can explain in a single paragraph of *A Brief History of Time* the Heisenberg Uncertainty Principle in a way that can be grasped by this English literature major, you can absorb the significant facts relating to the problems that compose your client's mess and restate them in terms simple enough that work can begin toward solving them.

Ability to Shift the Customer's Focus

When I worked at Control Data, a service was available for employees and their families to call for confidential help with personal problems. It was called EAR, which stood for Employee Advisory Resource, and I remember an interesting pair of charts from a management review meeting. Both charts listed the numerous kinds of problems EAR helped callers deal with: alcohol and drug abuse, financial difficulties, marital problems, and so on. Interestingly enough, the problem most frequently identified by callers was financial difficulty, but the problem most frequently diagnosed by counselors was alcohol and drug abuse. Chemical abuse turned out to be the source of their financial and marital stress.

Clients aren't always right about what kind of help they need, either. The chief executive who interprets slow sales as the result of a marketing problem calls in a marketing specialist. The marketing specialist takes a look around and discovers that the slow sales are the result of too high prices, which in turn are the result of a cost-of-production problem. At this point, the marketing consultant had better have the know-how to help solve a production problem, or she will either be out of a consulting job or wasting the client's money by addressing symptoms.

The challenge is to shift the client's focus from the symptom to the cause and not lose the client in the process. Maybe I encounter this more frequently than other consultants because a lot of management teams that can't agree on what's causing their problems can agree that the organization needs a plan, and I represent myself as a planning consultant.

The way I try to get the focus onto the real problems is to take the time up-front to learn from the client and his associates in their own words what the issues and symptoms are, draw them out by asking naive questions, and then restate what they've told me, again using their terms and language, but shifting the focus to underlying problems that could explain their concerns and may be at the root. If I'm off base, they'll tell me. Sometimes there's even a sigh of hallelujah in the room because I've been able to state what they've been feeling but not been able to articulate and agree upon. That gives us the freedom and momentum to lay out a plan of attack, and I'm ready for the second phase of the project, which is addressing the problem that the first phase has defined.

Desire to Please

A desire to please—no, a *need* to please, a *compulsion* to please—is the single most powerful drive affecting your ability to perform. It's what enables you to rise to the occasion when the occasion calls for superior effort. It can get you into trouble, too. But if you don't have it, don't become a consultant.

I've always had it, and it really came through to me how badly I had it one day when I was visiting my parents and reminiscing about my schooldays.

I'd never been able to figure out something that had happened with my biology teacher between my sophomore and junior years in high school. I had no interest in science and was a C student in tenth-grade biology. The teacher barely knew I existed, which suited me fine. It was my luck to get the same teacher for eleventh-grade biology. But had she ever changed! Something I said or did seemed to have made a big impression. She suddenly seemed to think I was smart. I started doing extra-credit work. She said it was excellent and suggested other things for me to do. The happier about me she became, the harder I worked. I did field projects and even brought in some slides from my parents' vacation showing weird sea urchins in a tidal pool. After researching them I made a little presentation. The teacher was ecstatic, and of course I aced the class.

When I recounted that strange time, my mother chuckled and said she remembered it too. Then she confessed that she'd met with that biology teacher at the beginning of my junior year and said, "All you have to do with Peter is give him some attention."

Though it had been ten years, I was really embarrassed to think I had been so transparent, responded so predictably. Anyhow, the desire to please may be a weakness, but I've put it to work. Pleasing my clients has been number one with me since the day I went into consulting.

If you have a need to please, it can be your strongest asset as a consultant, but it can also make you vulnerable.

I've discovered two please-the-customer traps over the years that get me in trouble as a result of my own reluctance to say no. One trap is my agreeing to follow a risky plan of attack that the customer has developed and strongly favors, when my instincts are telling me the approach has flaws. This problem is not uncommon when you're starting out with a new client. Most clients approach a new consulting relationship with a set idea of what they want the consultant to do, and since the two of you don't have a history yet, it's not always possible to make the client comfortable with the idea that your approach will work as well. If you can't talk the customer into an approach that *you're* comfortable with, it's probably better to let somebody else take the job.

Here's an example. I was called by the president of a very diversified and successful corporation to facilitate a planning session at their annual executive retreat at one of those fancy golf clubs where you have to buy special clothes in order to show up "casual." Before the retreat, I went out to sit down with the president in her office. It was one of those newer suburban corporate campuses where the execs look out at duck ponds and keep spotting scopes at their windows.

I asked her what she wanted to accomplish at the retreat, and she shoved a sheaf of papers across her desk, including her ideas for the agenda, along with copies of the company's long-range strategic plan and short-range operating plan. She obviously had her stuff together. She agreed that I should interview some of the company's senior staff to get the lay of the land.

I did the interviews the following week and then went back to my office and developed an agenda that I thought focused on some central concerns of the management team. I faxed it down to the client with a cover memo, and half an hour later my fax machine spit up a memo back from her outlining the agenda as she wanted it. I said "oops," and wondered if her fax canceled my fax or our faxes had crossed in fax hell, or what.

The upshot was, she wanted me to facilitate an agenda that involved walking through a review of the trends in each subsidiary's business, followed by a discussion of each subsidiary's plans for the future. I expressed qualms: the people I'd interviewed were more interested in hearing one another's views on a handful of shared concerns, and I didn't think we'd have time to make it through all those reviews. She was tactful but persistent. I said okay and made up my mind to make her outline work.

It didn't work. The trends were redundant, so not only didn't we get through all the subsidiary reviews, but we also never got past listing the overriding issues people really wanted to discuss. I could read their frustration in their faces. These were busy people and I was wasting their time. They were polite, but there was no getting around the fact that the session was a flop. Nobody was happy, including the president whose agenda I had accepted. I'd set the trap myself by not saying no. So ended my first and last consulting engagement with that company.

The other way in which my compulsion to please gets me in trouble is when I go the extra mile to accept work from a client that I know in my heart will be abusive of my role, my time, and my schedule. I just have a hard time saying no.

Striking a balance between the compulsion to say yes and the need for self-preservation takes experience. You learn that in any job. When you're on your own, it's a lot harder to summon a no; and when you're in the thick of a job and the client's satisfaction hangs in the balance, your compulsion to go the extra mile will serve you well. You'll leave behind a happy client, you'll feel good about getting it done, and you'll be more discriminating in your future commitments.

Acceptance of What Is

I spent two years trying to get a contract with a beverage manufacturer. A mutual friend introduced me to him, and this guy invited me back to his office three times to talk about planning. He'd say he had this or that thing he needed to get done, and how would I approach it? I'd go back to my office and spend a couple of days working through an approach and proposal, call him up, sit down, and walk him through each step I was proposing. He'd say, "I love it. Get back to you." But we never did a deal. Those are the times when you invoke the consultant's prayer

("Dear God, let this be deductible"), and cross him off your list, because it dawns on you eventually that no matter how many times you do your dog and pony show, he's not buying.

Diane Page says that in the market research business if you conduct a focus group and the respondents don't like the client's product concept, the client figures there must have been something faulty with the way you set up the focus group. (Shoot the messenger.) But when the focus group is a "success" (the respondents love the product concept), it's obviously because the concept's right on the money. Ironically, the focus groups that "don't go well" are often the most valuable ones to the client because they save the client from serious marketing mistakes. Diane can control the quality of the research but not the results or the clients' disappointments in how their concepts are received.

I've worked with a department head in a large corporation on several occasions who likes to plan because it gives him a sense that he and his staff are getting control over chaos. But I have discovered they don't implement their plans. The reason is because they aren't willing to say no to the multitude of diversions that come at them from other parts of the company and from the community—they won't bite the bullet to get control over their time and focus on the priorities stated in their plan.

I've worked with them on this problem, but they never quite solve it, and I finally came to see that solving it runs against their nature and the culture of their company. Their department is the place where chaos is sent for handling, and handling chaos well is a more important criterion in how they are viewed by management than achieving their program objectives.

In a consulting relationship, you help the client change what he can and accept what he can't. Understanding the politics of organizations increases your sensitivity to the client's reality, so you can help him dance with the one he's with. But there are times when you can't change the market appeal of a client's product, the fortitude of a manager, or family dysfunctions that disrupt the management of a family-held business. When those times come, you need to let go and move on. Don't see it as your failing. Build on the relationships where clients want to accomplish something important and you can add the missing ingredients.

Acknowledging what you can't control and that you have choices about the clients you serve helps you pick the right kinds of jobs, focus where you can make a difference, help people, and make you glad you're a consultant. One path into what I call the Victim School of Consulting is taking whatever comes in the door and thus being stuck in the mire with clients where the client is always right, no job is too big or too small, and, when called, you serve.

Ideas to Take Away

- In consulting, process is the product, and *how* is as important as *what*. Don't underestimate what you know how to do.
- A network of other free-lancers with complementary expertise can extend your reach in the marketplace and increase your value to clients.
- To succeed, you need confidence in your value, problem-solving skills, and relationship skills. You can strengthen all three as you build your business.
- Consulting requires an ability to break the client's mess down to its component problems and then plot strategies for solving them.
- Clients often mistake symptoms for problems. You must be able to shift the client's focus without losing him in the process.
- The desire to please may be the single most powerful factor affecting your performance. If you don't have it, don't become a consultant.
- Acknowledging what you can't control, and that you have choices about the clients you serve, helps you pick the right kinds of jobs and focus where you can make a difference.

As an employee, Fran Wheeler was a round peg in a square hole and had a hard time keeping jobs. But she knew she had a lot to offer, so she went out to sell it on her own. Consulting, it turns out, is Fran's métier. She's having a ball, making more money than ever, and beating away clients at the door. The lesson? If you believe in what you're good at, don't be afraid to take it into the market.

BELIEVING IN WHAT YOU'RE GOOD AT
Profile
FRANCES B. WHEELER
Circuit Board Layout Designer, Charlotte, NC

Fran Wheeler is one of those strong-willed, independent types who do outstanding work but don't fit into the culture of large organizations. She was laid off five times in her first two years in the work force. The next thirteen years were better, but not much. For the last five years, she's been having a ball at what she considers to be her first truly successful employment experience—working for herself.

Much of the early turmoil in Fran's career could be chalked up to the turbulence that beset technology firms in the seventies, and to the type of work she was doing—drafting and circuit board layout design—for which firms gear up and gear down to suit the ebb and flow of new projects. But Fran was independent, outspokenly candid, and unwilling to "play the game by the rules" as she puts it, meaning lie down and roll over for office politics.

Fran's academic background is in liberal arts. Her first jobs were with young technology companies in Silicon Valley, because that's where she lived. She liked to draw and they needed drafting. Early on, she was sized up this way by a supervisor she admired: "Doesn't know a thing about electronics, but smart." From drafting Fran fell into circuit board design at the suggestion of a supervisor and learned the art virtually as it was unfolding—in northern California and Boston's Route 128 technology corridor, where the most advanced work was being done.

So while Fran was being hired and unhired by companies with names like Microwave Associates, Wavecom, Illumination Industries, Hewlett-Packard, Digital Equipment Corporation, Litton, Hughes Micro-Electronics, and Data Terminal Systems, she was also picking up a specialty—and, before long, amazing her employers with her talent for meeting impossible design specs by packing exceedingly dense arrays of microcircuitry into seven or eight laminations of fiberglass with combined thickness of a toenail.

"I'm a frustrated artist," she says. Thinking of Fran as an artist goes a long way toward explaining both her difficulties conforming to the corporate mold and her passion for the work. And there clearly is artistry in the boards she's designed. When you turn one over in your hand you notice how the sea-green luminescence of fiberglass offsets entire regiments of microcircuitry lined up like tiny schematics for

65

medieval fortresses, and how these in turn are threaded and circum-navigated by traces of gold and copper that bend and run, swell and fall and disappear, each a hairline scarcely eight-thousandths of an inch wide. Hold a board to the light, and the golden traces reappear as the circuitry of intervening layers. "What it really is, is just like a big puzzle," she says. "That's why I like it."

Fran started her own business in 1989, and today she works at a computer in a spare bedroom in the back of her house in Charlotte, using specialized circuit board-layout software from a firm in Austra-lia.

Her boards go into electronic devices ranging from the hand-held data scanners used by Federal Express drivers to the cinematographic sound-recording equipment used by Steven Spielberg. Her boards run Ingersoll-Rand power generators at construction sites around the world, and Hewlett-Packard heart monitoring equipment in hospital intensive care units.

Going on her own wasn't important just because it suits her personality. It's also provided more job security and a lot better income, the two things people most fear losing by becoming independent.

To understand why that's the case for Fran, it helps to understand how printed circuit board layout is normally handled. There are three typical employment options for somebody in Fran's field. One option is to work through a job shop, which functions like a temporary employment service for lower-echelon technical workers and takes a cut off the top that may run from 10 to 15 percent. "Job shopping" has its advantages and disadvantages. On the plus side, it's a way to get work, offers some vacation and health insurance, and the employees on the inside of the company where you get assigned tend to be cooperative because they don't see you trying to take over their jobs.

On the minus side, the jobs are temporary and unpredictable, the commission goes to the job shop instead of to you, and the job shop may not understand your skills or the clients' needs well enough to market and place you effectively. Fran Wheeler worked through job shops in Boston and was lucky to associate with one that enjoyed a reputation for having top-quality workers.

An alternative is to become a direct employee of a technology company rather than working through an intermediary. In Fran's experience, this offers the potential benefits of a long-term relationship and accession through the ranks of management, but it also makes you a part of the political makeup of the organization.

The third employment option for someone in Fran's field is to work through a service bureau. Unlike job shoppers and employees, who do the client's work inside the client's shop, service bureaus operate as contractors with their own stable of designers and technicians who work offsite designing circuit boards to the client's specifications. This is a form of "outsourcing," and it is growing.

Fran is a one-woman service bureau, doing business as Wheeler Design. At the time we met, she had seventeen clients in North Carolina and South Carolina, and others in California and Boston. For Fran, the big change came when she moved from Austin to Charlotte, where her new husband, Chuck Kindle, was being relocated for IBM.

"There was a company in Charlotte that was the client of a firm I'd done work for in Austin. They knew my work, so when I went to see if I could help them out, they gave me some business." At that point, with a contract in her pocket, Fran looked around Charlotte and found a job shop to work through. After two years working for the same client under this arrangement, the client went through a management change, and Fran got that old sinking feeling that she might be looking at another layoff. "So I went to the president and made him an offer. I said, 'I'll do your work offsite, you just pay me by the job.' He said, 'Fine.' "

As it turns out, that was a critical maneuver for Fran. She was valuable to the client and knew it. "I understood their system and how to run it. I knew their boards." She set herself up as a service bureau, the essence of which involved investing $3,000 in a computer and the basic design software needed to do the work. "The first three boards I did for them repaid the investment—after two months in business."

It wasn't long before circuit board fabrication houses in the area got Fran's name. She was doing design work that a person could only learn the way she did, by working in Boston and Silicon Valley. Nobody else in the region was doing that kind of work. The fabrication houses began referring business her way, knowing it would lead to more work for them. At the same time, Fran was making the software she'd bought do design work that was well beyond its intended capacity. She showed her work to the software company and started telling them how to improve their product and keep up with advances in circuit board design. Before long, the software company was sending clients her way, too.

Fran is extremely reluctant to turn away work, but she has more than she can handle. Her marketing is entirely word of mouth, and her reputation reaches from coast to coast. A typical job has thirty-two hours of billable time, some larger, some smaller. She bills forty-five dollars an hour, which is nearly twice what she would be paid working as a direct employee. Though this does not sound high by consulting standards, she has virtually no marketing expense, and her monthly billings have been known to average $7,500 or better over extended periods even at this comparatively young stage of her business.

Asked how long it took until she was satisfied with the money she was making on her own, she says two years. When she first went solo, she billed at twenty-five dollars an hour. She set the rate by talking to engineers and designers where she worked. As it turned out, twenty-five dollars was too low, and as demand has outstripped her availability, she has raised her rates as one strategy for winnowing clients and making the effort worth her time.

Fran's niche consists of designing smaller boards that don't require teams of layout designers for smaller firms that don't have their own circuit board layout capability. "The competition is in the large projects, the $20,000 boards, where you need a $150,000 computer system and three shifts working the computer twenty-four hours a day to recover your investment." Fran didn't even know the niche she's working existed until companies started seeking her out for help. "Service bureaus charge a lot of money and don't do such a good job. They might shortchange the small jobs to keep the big clients happy. I compete on speed and quality. I can make a nice living on small jobs, and my clients can't afford to hire someone in-house."

Fran's philosophy is to treat every client with the same respect, and when she gets a call from one client asking her to put aside another client's work so she can get the caller's job through faster, "I just ask them if they'd like to be treated that way, and they say 'No,' and that's the end of the conversation. They wait their turn." Asked about the future of her business, she shakes her head. "This little niche is one hell of a niche to fill. It'll continue to grow. If I knew someone really good, I'd refer the clients I'm too busy to take."

An early problem Fran encountered was difficulty getting all the information she needs from a client in order to do her job. To solve this problem she put together a seventeen-page booklet called "PCB User Guide and Checkoff Sheets," which she gives to every new client. The booklet lays out success factors for the job up-front, including a description of the client's responsibilities. Fran published the booklet with her laser printer, and it is a model of clarity and simplicity. She grins when she shows it off. "When I worked in-house, I'd tell them what I needed and they'd argue with me. Now that I'm on my own, I just say, 'This is what I need, or you don't get a board,' and they deliver it."

Fran says she faces a choice between expanding or staying small, and then in the next breath she answers the question. "I don't want to market, I want to design. Once you expand, you have to be in the people and marketing business. I'm great at talking to electronics engineers, but I'm not the one to talk to vice presidents in charge of projects."

What she misses most about being on her own is the professional technical feedback she got when she worked on the inside, both from her peers and from others involved in different aspects of the project.

"I've been a project leader, and I like to get an idea of the whole picture. When I get a client's specs, I go through them and I tell the client where their specs could be improved to get the kind of board that will perform the way they want it to." Fran also talks to the people who fabricate the boards she designs, when that's practical ("a lot are being fabricated in Singapore now"). "I ask questions, like, 'Did you have any trouble putting the board together?' You know, maybe I'm doing something stupid that they're having to design around, and every time they get one of my boards, there's that stupid problem again. I want to know that. You get more of that feedback when you're inside the client's organization, and I miss it."

When the question of job security comes up, Fran says that once you see people with twenty-five years' seniority being laid off, you understand that security is a myth. "If you're counting on security, you're going to be disappointed." Satisfaction is Fran's issue, not security. And she gets it by solving puzzles—"producing something I can see, touch, and hold."

Fran has three guidelines for success: no one client is more important than another; turn out good work at a fair price; and check everything, including the client's input. She's learned that since her clients don't use the input they provide, they don't understand the value of it, and it's worth it to her to make sure it's right. She also makes suggestions if she thinks there's a better way to accomplish the client's objectives than what the specs call for. "You can't be afraid to argue with your client if you think they're doing themselves a disfavor."

With her husband taking early retirement, is she tempted to ease up, take some time off? Fran says no way. Five or six years ago she might have been. But these days she's having too much fun and making too much money. "Besides," she says, "after all those years of banging my head against the corporate structure, I've discovered I'm the best boss I ever had."

4   RELATIONSHIPS INTO CASH

Marketing to get the business you want

The Four Parts of the Marketing Cycle

Perception: Marketing is the awful business of prostrating yourself at the feet of friends and strangers. It is the sly agenda of every social occasion, the bugaboo of consulting. Marketing is Willy Loman. It is the funeral director's handshake. It is a self-possessed mug shot on a brochure of blah blah blah, and an obscene daily billing rate you hope your mother never sees. Marketing is a dark voice in the night: get off your butt, kick the dog, hit the street, turn up next month's rent check.

Reality: Marketing is getting in the groove with a handful of good clients. It is the process of building your reputation, seeding referrals, and turning transactions into relationships. It is the area where you have the most control over profitability, because marketing determines the quality of the jobs you get and how much time you invest in getting them. The most profitable marketing is not about churning your clients, it's about optimizing billable hours by reducing client turnover.

In consulting, marketing is a four-part cycle consisting of:

1. *Prospecting*
2. *Selling*
3. *Turning transactions into relationships*
4. *Servicing relationships and refreshing your client base.*

Prospecting

Admittedly, there's a bit of Willy Loman in the starting consultant. You knock on doors to win the initial contracts you need to get revenues flowing and have a chance to prove yourself. You get those contracts from tapping your existing network: professional friends and acquaintances.

This will probably be the hardest marketing you'll ever have to do because you don't have a base, you're not sure of your pricing, you haven't served enough clients to discover what sells, you're asking people who know you from your earlier life to think of you in a new way, introduce you to their business acquaintances, vouch for you, move your name across their networks. If you've built bridges into consulting from your job—a retainer or start-up contract, mentor, portables—this will be easier. If you have an established reputation, it will be easier. If you have special expertise, it will be easier. But it is never *easy*.

Where to Find Your First Prospects

Once you're established, you get calls from people who are shopping around for a consultant and have been given your name. The best thing about these calls is that the caller already knows he needs to hire a consultant, and making the sale is a matter of qualifying the prospect and establishing why you're the right choice. When you're just starting out, you have a tougher job: you have to find somebody who needs a consultant before you can persuade him that you're the consultant he needs.

You're going to knock on a lot of doors, but here are some ways you can increase your prospecting productivity.

Seven Ideas to Increase Your Prospecting Productivity

1. *Focus*
   - Be clear in your mind about what you are selling, who needs it, who you are competing with, and why you're the better choice.
   - Figure out what kinds of prospects have the most potential, and target them. Possibilities:

     People who will be predisposed to hire you because they know your work: former employers, former colleagues, former customers, former competitors.

     People whose businesses and industries are in transition (see chapter 2) and therefore are more likely to realize they have an immediate financial stake in making the kinds of changes you can help them make: enhance their products, downsize or retrain their work force, outsource a staff or manufacturing function, develop an export department, develop a marketing culture, and so on.

2. *Be creative*
- Take what you've learned in one industry and show how it can solve problems in another.

   David Bjork, the senior consultant at Hay Management Consultants: "Anytime you're dealing with an industry in change, they need to look outside their industry for solutions to the future. Banking has had to look outside for marketing. Insurance has had to look outside for cost accounting and organizational effectiveness. People who only know their own industry are mired in the patterns of the past."

3. *Do some homework on the prospect before you make the call*
- Read their annual report.
- Check the library for news articles about the company and its industry.

   David Bjork: "If you can demonstrate just a modicum of understanding of the industry and the client's situation, their anxiety goes way down and they're no longer trying to poke holes in your credibility."

4. *Put your name in circulation*
- Ask your friends if they know anyone who might need your help, and ask for an introduction.
- Make speeches, conduct seminars, write an opinion piece for the newspaper, get yourself written up. (See John Niles in chapter 9; profile of Eric Mitchell in chapter 10.)
- Contact the trade association of an industry that is likely to need your services and offer to conduct a pro bono workshop at their next annual meeting. (See Alice Lucan's tactics under "Seeding referrals," below.)

5. *Collaborate*
- Find an established consultant or firm that serves your target market with complementary services, somebody who will see your expertise as an added capability and a potential source of clients. Don't go into business together; send each other clients.

6. *Take an assignment that is not directly related to your focus, provided it . . .*
- Gives you exposure in your target industry at the level you want to work.
- Doesn't keep you from marketing.
- Buys you time by paying the rent.

- Gives you confidence and credibility because the client is a respected organization.
7. *Listen up*
   - Find out what the prospects you call on are struggling with and be prepared to adjust your focus to fit what people will buy.

Seeding Referrals

As your business develops, you need a low but constant flow of prospects to fill in the holes in your calendar and to glean for new relationships. The most effective prospecting is usually through referral, because referrals are a form of two-way testimony—a trusted mutual friend brings you together.

Networking can be a productive strategy for seeding referrals. The trick is to focus on the networks that will generate the kinds of prospects you want.

A high-potential prospect is one that fits your pricing and the skills you have to offer, and whose business is complex and successful enough so that once he learns how good you are, he'll see other opportunities to use you. When your client is on the skids, you hate to take his money. When your client is busy and prospering, there's a can-do attitude, and you feel good getting paid for being a part of the success. As Don Coyhis puts it, you take on the nature of that into which you are placed. Anyone who has been a consultant for a while soon discovers that becoming well known in the wrong kinds of networks is a formula for bottom fishing, as Eric Mitchell calls it, hooking clients whose needs don't fit your skills or whose budgets can't stomach your prices.

How Four Consultants Seed Their Networks for Prospects and Referrals

- *Diane Page. Clients:* Product managers in consumer packaged goods companies who need Diane's market research services. *Technique:* "There's not a lot of ways for my clients to go up the ladder, so they change companies. When a client moves to another company, I make the call and stay connected. And I try to meet the young MBAs coming into the company who are going to end up assigning the work when the boss moves on."
- *Eric Mitchell. Clients:* Corporate pricing professionals. *Techniques:* Publishes monthly newsletter; conducts direct-mail mar-

keting program; conducts annual conference on pricing; is creating an association of pricing professionals. "My marketing activities are profit centers."

- *Don Coyhis. Clients:* Companies and institutions interested in changing their organizational culture. *Techniques:* Delivers keynote speeches, seminars, and training sessions on topics such as managing change, multiculturalism, leadership, and the teachings of the Native American Medicine Wheel.

- *Alice Lucan. Clients:* Smaller- to medium-size newspaper publishers needing expertise in First Amendment law. *Techniques:* Developed a seminar called "Managing Your Newsroom Legal Problems" and delivered it without charge to newspaper editors through state press associations. Stays active in ABA committees that are related to the news media bar, keeping herself current, reinforcing her expertise, and providing contracts.

Client word of mouth is the most powerful marketing tool. If your clients are enthusiastic about your work, they'll spread the word through their own networks, and if they're well connected, that gives you tremendous marketing leverage.

One of my former clients, who has become a good friend, is a St. Paul banker named Bill Sands. Bill is extremely well connected in the community. Among other things, he is a member of YPO, an association of young corporate presidents. He is active in the bankers association. At one time or another he has chaired the boards of a long list of prominent community organizations. He has a special ad hoc group of bankers he meets with quarterly—a half dozen people who are presidents of banks similar in size to his own. Bill is the kind of guy who enjoys introducing good people to one another, and over the years since that cold call and early work with Bill and his team, I have gotten untold consulting engagements with people who have called me on Bill's recommendation.

Selling

Selling is how you land a prospect once you've snagged one. The selling process has two principal objectives. The first is qualifying the prospect to see if you want the job. This includes discovering her key buying factors and establishing her expectations. The second objective is selling the prospect what she wants to buy. This includes finding out how she defines success, and negotiating the steps to deliver it.

Following is how I approach these objectives. When I meet with a prospect, my first question is, Why does she need a consultant? As she describes her situation, I try to get some insights into her organization, how firmly she has in mind what the problem is, the role of the consultant, the product she wants. I try to learn what factors led her to call me now instead of last month or next quarter, what will make her decide to engage me, who will be part of the decision process, what they're looking for, and what concerns they might have about bringing in a consultant.

As we talk, I sketch out ideas for how we could organize the project, what things might come up, and how we would handle them. I might talk in general terms about other client relationships, which helps indirectly to build pricing expectations. I try to fight the temptation to quote prices in the marketing meeting, because much of what I learn in the meeting should affect how I price the job (see "Five factors that should influence your fees" in chapter 5). I might toss out in broad terms what similar jobs have cost so I can gauge her reaction, asking whether these figures are in line with her budget for the project.

"Selling the prospect what she wants to buy" means finding out what she's looking for, and explaining how I can provide it. I try to do this by asking questions such as: What should we be sure to accomplish in the course of this project? When we're done, what would make you think this project was time and money well spent? What are the three most important decisions that this project should help you make? Whatever the measures of success are going to be, if I know them on the way in the door, I have the choice of accepting them or redefining them so that what the client expects is what I know I can deliver.

Negotiating the steps to deliver success involves a give-and-take on the key elements that will go into my written proposal: the objectives, tasks, product, billing arrangement. I try to be clear about what things I will do, and what I would expect the client's team to do. It's as important to me for the client to commit to the steps her organization will take as part of the relationship, as it is for her to know what I will do.

I follow up the prospect meeting with a written proposal, usually a letter that spells out each of the elements listed above plus a price. If some questions remain, I may fax a draft to the prospect and discuss the questionable areas, giving us both a chance to negotiate refinements before the proposal is official. In the end, this give-and-take process tells us each a lot about how we will work together, enables me to target my bid, and puts the transaction on the kind of footing it will need in order to grow into a relationship.

Bidding the Job Before You Know How the Customer Defines Success

Nothing is more important in the selling process than finding out the customer's definition of success. To illustrate why, let me tell you how I learned this lesson.

The client was a charity fund-raising organization. A board committee was seeking bids from long-range-planning facilitators. There were two bidders: me and the other guy. He was from a buttoned-down East Coast accounting firm that did a lot of planning work with large corporations. I'd never facilitated a long-range plan and didn't see that I had a chance. But the executive director of the organization was the one who had asked me to compete for the contract. I had done work with his staff in the past in other subject areas and wanted to cultivate the relationship. A friend helped me structure my bid, I pitched it to the selection committee, and was surprised to get the job.

When I sat down with the executive director to lay out a work plan, it became clear that his definition of success involved focusing as much on community consensus building as on planning. It turns out the organization had had a bad experience with planning that didn't involve all of their constituencies, and they were intent on not repeating the mistake.

This was early in my consulting career, when I thought consultants were supposed to be experts and not ask the prospect how to approach an assignment. As a result, I'd bid the job without knowing enough about what was required to make it succeed. I actually had a call one day from the consultant who had facilitated the earlier planning process. He just wanted me to know that local politics were so ferocious I couldn't possibly come out with my skin intact.

I didn't report this phone conversation to the client, but the client and I did talk at length about strategies to involve community agencies, business, organized labor, local government, and others in developing the plan, and then I refigured the costs of facilitating the process. There was no way I could do the job for less than nearly *double* what I'd bid.

I called on the chairman of the planning committee, a scion of St. Paul, and sat across his desk in an upholstered wing chair where I confessed my mistake. I expected to be dropped through a trap door into the Purgatory for Whining Consultants (*wished* to be dropped). But no. Apparently the chairman had talked with the executive director, because he agreed with my assessment of what must be done to succeed. He didn't look happy, but he didn't pull a lever in the kneehole of his desk, either. Instead, he made some calls, and we rewrote the contract.

I sweated out the next sixteen months doing everything conceivable to make the project a success. The relationships I cemented during that period have brought me a lot of business in the years since. The job also taught me a lot about consulting, including these lessons: (1) it's better to know how the client defines success *before* you quote the price, and you can't know without asking; (2) it makes no sense to sell on the basis of price when the client is buying on the basis of value; (3) a good client is one who knows that if you can't win, he can't either.

Turning Transactions into Relationships

Power of a Strong Relationship

A single strong relationship can change the course of your business.

Pattie Garrahy left a big job as media director at Fabergé to focus on raising a family. Once home, she was approached by former associates to take media consulting projects, and this work evolved into a growing media-planning practice (see profile in chapter 7).

One day a former client named Betsy Richardson hired Pattie to develop a media strategy for her employer, a company called Lifeline. Pattie presented the new strategy, figuring it would be carried out by Lifeline's ad agency. But Betsy thought Pattie would do a better job and asked her to bid the execution.

Media planning is billed by the hour; execution—buying the ad space—is a business of commissions. Financially, the step from one realm into the other is enormous. With Betsy's encouragement, Pattie made up a name for herself, PGR Media, a mission statement, some presentation boards, and went into the company's executive offices and pitched their account. "Two days later I had the business—several million dollars."

She hit an early snag in executing the plan. "Here I was, ordering millions of dollars of media insertions and didn't have the track record to secure credit. *Better Homes and Gardens* would say, 'Who are you?'

They knew who I was from my days at Fabergé. I'd say, 'Look, I've been in the business fifteen years.' They'd say, 'Sorry, Pattie, but it wasn't your name on the checks. There's nothing we can do.' "

There was one solution: persuade Lifeline to pay the media bill in advance, so Pattie could submit a check with her insertion order. Lifeline agreed, problem solved. "So Lifeline—really Betsy Richardson, who believes in me so much—has not only opened doors for me into the commission-based business of media execution, they're helping me to establish a credit history. That's the power of strong relationships."

Relationships were probably the most powerful factor in the success of the consultants I interviewed. The impacts aren't always as dramatic as they have been for Pattie Garrahy, but where relationships breed loyalty and continuity, both parties benefit, and the consultant finds she has a critical base from which to build the business.

Money in Your Pocket

A strong relationship is money in your pocket.

Think of the first job you do for a client as a *transaction*. You're selling, she's buying. You focus heavily on the moment, keeping an eye on each other because you've never worked together. You deliver a service, send the bill, and the transaction is complete.

A transaction becomes a *relationship* when it grows into a series of renewable assignments. You turn a transaction into a relationship by showing the client you can continue to add value to her business. Servicing is selling. Each assignment is another test of the relationship and adds to its strength. The client comes to see you as an ally rather than a solution to a one-time problem. Months later, what brought you in the door the first time may fade in her memory, and if you hit a bump or two, your past successes together carry you over them because, unlike the first transaction, a relationship has a history that enables you both to reach beyond the moment.

The business adage that it costs more to get a client than to keep one applies in spades to consulting. Every client you lose when the job's completed leaves a hole in your schedule that can only be filled by investing the time to turn up and win over another prospect. Every client you renew frees his share of marketing hours for you to sell as consulting. That's the money in your pocket.

Relationships Are Cultivated, Not Sold

By this I mean simply that you don't turn a prospect into a relationship in the selling stage. You turn a prospect into a client, and it is only through the proper cultivation of that client that the ongoing relationship emerges.

Nevertheless, you have to have relationships in mind during the prospecting and selling stages, because when you look at prospective clients as relationship material, you realize it pays to be selective.

If you make relationships your marketing goal, you will find that the size of your first contract with a new client is not as important as the opportunity to establish proper pricing expectations, show what you can do, and discover ways in which you can add value to the client's business. In fact, a smaller initial contract may work to your advantage by providing the insights you need into the client's business to identify where you can make the best contribution over time, whereas a big-ticket contract that's a bit off target is likely to get mixed results and sour the client on future work.

Serving Is Marketing

Once you've turned a prospect into a client, you need to achieve three objectives: demonstrate your value, discover opportunities to turn the transaction into a relationship, and turn the relationship into cash.

Consulting relationships are both personal and professional. John Niles (see chapter 9) says wisely, "To succeed as a consultant, you've got to have relationships with lots of people, and in the end, you've got to turn those relationships into cash. I've met people who are not in business for themselves, because in the end they couldn't stand that idea."

Consulting relationships grow for two simple reasons: one, the consultant and the client find they can meet each other's business needs, and two, they enjoy working together. Both ingredients must be present for success. Consulting isn't about turning *friendships* into cash. It may be about turning some friendships into business relationships, in those few cases where you have something to offer professionally that a friend needs professionally. It is about turning business transactions into relationships, which include some of the elements of friendship—taking pleasure in working together—and about turning those relationships into cash.

The notion of turning a relationship into cash isn't as mercenary as it sounds. What it means is this. Every relationship has its own patterns of expectations and behaviors. By not paying as much attention to your own needs as the client's, you can find yourself in relationships that are very successful from the client's perspective, and even personally satisfying to you, but that don't yield their financial worth in terms of hours spent or revenues you could have earned serving someone else.

A successful business relationship is profitable. To be profitable, it must be founded on a pattern of expectations and behaviors that bring cash to your bottom line. These include: creating expectations of the relationship in the client's mind that jibe with your own; pricing on the basis of your value to the client rather than your costs (see chapter 5); establishing a habit of defining new opportunities in the course of performing current assignments; structuring your billing to fit the client's method of paying (see chapter 5).

Servicing Relationships and Refreshing Your Client Base

The Client Relationship Seeks Its Own Level

A client relationship goes through phases, determined both by the client's needs and his perception of your value. Your role is to make it easier for the client to do business, and you can nurture the relationship in three ways: by continuing to perform well, by being easy to have around, and by working to be ever present in the client's mind.

One relationship will be best for the client when it is very low key, another will be timed to the cycles of a client's business, a third may run hot and heavy while a client copes with an extended period of change and growth. You can't force a relationship to fit your calendar or revenue targets; you have to let it gravitate to its own level and learn to work around it. Most will fade away eventually—clients change companies, get golden parachutes, lose reelection, fall in love with a fresh face.

The most effective strategy to sustain your value to the client is to nurture whatever the something is—insecurity, pride, hunger for praise—that makes you go the extra mile to satisfy again and again, rather than rest on the laurels of your past performance. Here are some strategies to keep yourself in the client's mind: follow developments in the client's field and let him know you're thinking of the things he would think of if he only had the time; be available on short notice when the client's in a jam and it didn't occur to him until the eleventh hour that maybe you could help; get along with the client's team and help them be winners in every project you do.

In short, be the kind of consultant you'd like to have.

Refreshing Your Client Base

This is where the marketing cycle turns and repeats itself. You maintain a low-level flow of prospects through the techniques described earlier, selectively turning them into clients and then into relationships. Turnover depends on the kind of consulting you do and the cyclical nature of your clients' businesses. In my business, old relationships that have fallen dormant sometimes renew themselves because plans become outdated. I may go through two or three consulting transactions before I connect with a client that blossoms into a new relationship. And I may not need to add a new relationship any more often than once every couple of years.

Relationships vs. RFPs

I sell best when I'm eyeball to eyeball with the prospect. I don't like competitive bid processes. With a request for proposals (RFPs), the prospect puts all us vendors at arm's length, defines his problem, and asks us each to take our best shot at winning a contract to solve it. I'd like the prospect to have something invested in me if I'm going to invest something in him. Better to work *with* the prospect in defining both the problem and the solution.

Here is how three other consultants feel about RFPs.

Len Smart: "It's been my experience that when an RFP goes out, there's usually a mental short list, if not a decision in place about who's going to get the job. And they go through the formality of an RFP because of policies requiring competitive bidding. You can waste unbelievable amounts of time in responding to RFPs. The people who do respond are larger organizations that can carry that risk."

David Bjork: "In a small consulting firm, you rely heavily upon a handful of satisfied clients who say 'This guy is terrific,' and they keep thinking of you the next time they need some work done. Doing a lot of marketing and chasing RFPs can be a waste of time. It's very competitive, you have to prove yourself every time, and your chances of winning the contract if you've never worked with them before are slim."

Kathy Tunheim: "We do RFPs from time to time and they're an important part of the business, as much as anything because they help you hone your own skills: are we being articulate about what we're good at? RFPs are good discipline builders for all of us, but the vast majority of our work comes from relationships."

Why Your Phone Will Ring

Jack Brizius and Sue Foster (see profile in chapter 8) told me it took them five years in the consulting business before they learned to trust the fact that at least twenty-five percent of their business will come in over the transom from unpredictable sources.

Going into consulting is a little like learning to fly. If you liken marketing to wing flapping, you could say it takes a good bit of energy to get launched, less to cruise. The more experienced you are, the less hard you have to flap. You make each flap—sales call—count, and you discover where the thermals are, those updrafts that will keep you aloft without marketing. Doing a good job for a client who is well networked is like a flier knowing where to find thermals. The phone will ring. But you can't glide forever. Jack and Sue consult to governors. They spend considerable effort keeping themselves visible. Contacts are perishable. In Jack and Sue's business, one election can make an enormous difference in the size of their network.

Three Things Cause Your Phone to Ring

1. *Being known.*
2. *Having a reputation for doing good work.*
3. *Offering something that people need.*

All three of these lie within your control. The first two take time to build: you probably need to serve a critical mass of clients before you have enough people bandying your name in the right circles.

In conducting the interviews for this book, I asked people how long they were in consulting before they were satisfied with the money they made. Three to five years was the typical response. In part that reflects how long it took for them to get their rates up to an adequate level and become better marketers, but in part it also reflects how long it takes to build a reputation.

The rate at which your reputation builds depends a little on whether your clients are the kind who are well networked themselves, like my friend Bill Sands. It also depends upon how you define your market.

When I went into consulting I left a sales job with Control Data that had me traveling a great deal. I decided to concentrate my consulting in the Twin Cities. I soon discovered that another benefit to a geographic focus, beyond reduced travel, is the simple fact that word of mouth spreads faster through a metropolitan area, where your clients bump into each other daily, than if your clients were scattered in various cities across the country. Jack Brizius puts it this way: If you can stay on your clients' radar screens, you can trust your phone to ring.

Why the Jobs You Don't Get Are the Ones You Don't Want

I confess I harbor a grudge toward a prospect I worked hard to land three years ago. Everything about the situation seemed right for a planning contract, leading to a long-term relationship. He came in by referral, what he needed was an excellent fit with my skills, getting a plan done was one of his personal accountabilities, he had a budget for it, and he was behind times getting at it. Where had I been, he asked, because my approach is what he'd been looking for.

I wrote up a careful proposal and followed it up in a week or so with a phone call. He didn't get back to me. A couple of weeks later I tried again. Nothing. Something went wrong somewhere, and I wrote it off. Six weeks later he called. Loved my proposal, sorry not to have responded, had wanted to show it to his board, which had only just met. He said everything looked great, except would I revise one part of the proposal.

No problem. I made the changes, sent it back, waited to hear. Nothing. After two weeks, I left a call for him. Nothing. I wrote him off a second time.

Two months later the guy called, apologetic as hell, and said he'd like to take the proposal to his full membership before giving it a final blessing, just a formality. But would I make a small change. Of course. We talked through what he wanted, I rewrote the proposal, sent it along, and that was that. Called him after a few weeks, but he never got back to me. Bumped into him one evening at the orchestra a couple of years later, and he greeted me like an old friend.

You figure it out.

Of course there is a reason we didn't do business, I just don't have a clue what it is. But if he couldn't bring himself to tell me, he was lousy relationship material, the kind of client who'll let you wander into the jaws of disaster thinking all the while how clever you are to be doing such a great job.

Some of the contracts I haven't won over the years were lost on the basis of price. Some because my pitch fell short. Some because the prospect was wedded to an idea of what the consultant should do that I didn't feel comfortable doing. And so on. Forcing those jobs to fit, or prostrating yourself to win them, is one way to make yourself crazy. The chemistry is wrong. Let them go. They're jobs you don't want.

Ideas to Take Away

- In consulting, marketing is a four-part cycle of (1) prospecting, (2) selling, (3) turning transactions into relationships, and (4) servicing relationships and renewing your client base.
- The best prospects are those that come by referral, and referrals come from doing good work and seeding your networks.
- A high-potential prospect is one that fits your pricing structure and skills, and whose business is complex and successful.
- Effective selling includes finding out how the prospect defines success and negotiating the steps to deliver it.
- A relationship is money in your pocket.
- Your phone will ring if you are known, have a good reputation, and offer something people need.
- The jobs you don't get are the ones you don't want.

For many people who are leery of the consulting life, the bête noire—dark beast—seems to be the fear they'd have to live their life on the prowl for business, exploiting friendships, and promoting themselves against the grain of their natural reserve. If that's your fear, read about Len Smart, profiled below. Len is as mild mannered as Clark Kent, and twice as successful. His secret? A remarkable marketing network of other businesses that are constantly turning up clients that need Len's skills.

THE CONSULTANT WHOSE CLIENTS DO HIS MARKETING
Profile
LEONARD W. SMART
Data Communications Consultant, Vancouver, BC

Two aspects of Len Smart's consulting practice are striking. First is that over the years a training firm has booked fully one-third to one-half of Len's calendar every year, paying his going consulting rate to teach seminars on his specialty across Canada and the United States. The training firm and its broker have marketed the seminars and handled all arrangements, giving Len a schedule of commitments, usually months in advance. If you think that sounds good, listen to this second part: another third of Len's business calendar has been filled by three or four consulting firms that call him in on jobs where their clients need his expertise. The consulting firms do his marketing, he does the consulting.

Although he wouldn't say so himself, in a business where marketing is the dark beast of many peoples' nightmares, Len is the cat that swallowed it.

Len does business as L. W. Smart & Associates Ltd., working out of an office in the lower level of a two-story rambler he shares with his wife, Thelma, in Burnaby, a suburb of Vancouver. The Monday morning we had agreed to meet, I threaded my rental car through the rush hour traffic, carefully following a map Len had faxed me, and eventually found my way to the end of a quiet cul-de-sac where the houses are set back on trim lawns and screened by hedges and shrubs.

The setting felt more like a refuge than a hub of commerce and technology. Len showed me his office, which looks out onto a private backyard whose fringes are lush with growth. The office is packed—reference volumes, computers, phones, fax, files. Len apologized for the sheer density of it all and, by way of explanation, opened a door down the hall where a workman was hanging Sheetrock in a room twice the size that Len had laid out and wired to better suit the demands of his business. We retreated upstairs to the den.

Len is an attractive, fit man in his forties with brown hair, a cardigan and open collar, and that peculiarly Canadian combination of American approachability and British reserve. He poured us coffee, motioned to a sofa, then took an easy chair and propped his feet on a leather ottoman.

His expertise lies at the intersection of computers and telecommunications. By understanding both technologies, he explains, he is useful as an associate to telecommunications consultants who lack computer expertise, and to computer consultants who lack telecommunications background. Listening to him, it is not difficult to imagine that most big businesses and government agencies must sooner or later find their way through this intersection.

Len knew he wanted to become a consultant since he graduated from university in 1968 with an undergraduate degree in electrical engineering. His first taste of it came five years later when he left a staff engineering job to join a consortium of consultants that had formed to help plan a major gas pipeline. The project lasted three years, and when it concluded, Len hooked up with a former associate who had set up a telecommunications consulting practice named Cantel Engineering Associates, Ltd. Cantel's principal client was a Saudi oil company. Len incorporated himself to take advantage of Canadian tax laws and worked for Cantel as a contractor. But in 1979 the Saudi oil company cut back its contract and Cantel fell on hard times.

"I woke up one March morning and found myself sitting on the sidewalk. My wife didn't work outside the home, we had kids, and we needed a healthy cash flow to keep everything going." But after his second taste of the consulting business, Len knew it was what he wanted.

He wrote a résumé and a capability list and beat the pavement. Through his professional contacts he landed a contract helping the telephone company to develop an internal computer network as part of its management information system. What began as a three-month commitment ended up lasting three years. "The phone company's business was profoundly important to me. It kept the mortgage paid and gave me the base to build my business."

Just the same, he says, being a solo practitioner working for a big company poses its own set of problems. "When you're a one-man shop, large organizations want to eat you up, which is a dangerous situation to get into, because you're back to the start-up mode again when the project ends. For the first six months or year, I was pleased to be consumed. And then the next couple of years involved a graceful kind of extrication of my 100 percent commitment to that client, backing it down to four days a week, then three, until in 1982 a recession hit and ended the contract.

"It was very clear that I didn't want to have one client represent a hundred percent of my revenue because it makes you too dependent.

That's a lesson we'd learned when Cantel lost the bulk of its Saudi contract. The other thing is that once you're dependent, you have as much at stake in organizational politics as any employee. But if you have half a dozen clients, then any one of those can come or go and its not going to ruin your day. The best client is one that's expendable."

He has focused his consulting practice in western British Columbia to minimize travel and build a more tightly knit marketing network. His consulting projects typically involve the design of computer networks for companies and large agencies, helping them manage their affairs by enabling their computers to share software and data. Typical clients include Alcan (the aluminum refiner), the Canadian Atmospheric Environment Services (the weather bureau), and Vancouver General Hospital.

A large share of his work comes through close relationships that he's developed with a handful of larger firms that do most of the marketing. One such firm is HN Engineering, Inc., a telecommunications consulting group with an extensive marketing network and a staff of about fifteen consultants. Len's computer expertise is a specialty that complements HN's telecommunications knowledge.

Another of his affiliations is with Sierra Systems Consultants, Inc., Vancouver's largest information systems consulting firm, doing information-system integration, custom software development, and computer consulting. "I work with them on computer-communications issues and help them deliver the total package that their clients need."

Another such affiliation is with Intelecon Research and Consultancy, Inc., who's forte is economic feasibility studies for organizations like the World Bank, helping to develop the business case for large, offshore telecommunications systems. At the time of our interview, Len was working with Intelecon on feasibility planning for a provincewide data network to support public education.

Len says he very much values these relationships because they bring him exposure to large clients that would require too much marketing overhead to reach on his own. Asked how he found these groups, Len says, "Networking." These groups are major players in his field, and he made sure they became a part of the professional network he developed and continues to cultivate.

His relationship with these firms is informal and is based on a fee-sharing arrangement in which Len forgoes a portion of his fee in exchange for the affiliate's handling of marketing and project administration—paying, in effect, a finder's fee. A typical fee split directs 75 percent of Len's billing rate to his own business and 25 percent to the affiliate's. Sometimes he negotiates 80 percent, and other times 66 percent. The rule of thumb is that the greater his involvement in nonbillable project support like proposal writing, the greater his share of the take. The fee also varies to reflect the kind of work Len is doing.

"Different markets are worth different amounts of money. Telecommunications consulting is a leaner business in terms of hourly revenue than information systems." He sees the fee split as simply reflecting the cost of marketing. "I take no marketing risk and focus on what I do best. I find it a very satisfactory relationship."

A logical question is whether these affiliations lead to marketing or confidentiality conflicts. Len pondered the question briefly. "None of these groups really compete with one another," he said. "But it's important to be completely open—follow a 'no surprises down the road' strategy. When I work with Sierra, HN doesn't see a threat, and so on. Sierra and I banged into each other one day when we were both out marketing to the same prospect. They were marketing me and so was I. That's really a problem, so we agreed on a strategy to prevent that. Now, before they'll pass out information that involves my contribution, they let me know."

What happens when he's working through an affiliate, they bid the project on fixed price, and the project goes over budget? "There has to be a lot of trust in both directions. If a project goes over budget and can't be renegotiated with the client, you can't expect your associate to pay you beyond what you had agreed to in the bid. You have to be a partner in that risk. You may have to swallow some hours, but you do it because you've made a commitment, and you can look upon the added expense as an investment in maintaining a long-term relationship."

The other half of Len's business since 1983 involves four-day training seminars that he conducts for people in business and government who want to learn about telecommunications. The seminars are scheduled across Canada and the United States, most frequently in Toronto and Washington, D.C.

"There's a training group here I am affiliated with called Infotel Systems Corp. They work with brokers who promote and schedule seminars. The brokers do all the organizational things—mailing materials, establishing the agenda, taking the marketing risk. The broker markets the seminar, and if enough people sign up, it's a go. Infotel owns the courseware. They do the research and the technical assembly of the material, maintain that material, and provide an instructor to deliver it. That's me in the area of data communications. There are three or four of us who work as instructors for Infotel on a straight fee-for-service basis."

Training has been very beneficial as a load leveler, moderating the peaks and valleys that typify consulting, because it gives Len a schedule of what he'll be doing weeks and months in advance, and he can count on it. Training and consulting also work to enrich each other. "Consulting provides experiences to illustrate the teaching. Good war stories are what makes the difference between reading a textbook and going to a seminar." On the other hand, traveling across the country to do training reinforces Len's images as an expert in Vancouver.

We talked about lessons Len has learned from his years in consulting. One is that consulting can't be sold like a commodity. "It's not like hawking ice cream from the back of a cart. You don't find people committing to you for services that may have a big effect on the organization unless they trust you deeply."

Marketing consulting services is a subtle issue of maintaining networks and relationships, so that when a project comes along, the footings are already in place. "A strong network is, in effect, an equity you carry that will pay back whatever you invest to maintain it. Your relationships are your goodwill. Together, they're the difference between having something to offer and turning that something into an ongoing business."

5   **KNOWING YOUR OWN WORTH**

How to name your price

If You Want to Get a Check, You Have to Send a Bill

One day my secretary stood in the door to my office and lobbed some envelopes across the room into my in-box as if she were making a long shot into the trash with a pile of junk mail. "How come nobody ever sends *me* a check?" She spoke in that annoying tone she used that let you know she was just as deserving of a rich and trashy life as the people in her *People* magazines. But I had her on that one. I asked, "Do you ever send a bill?" She gave me a sullen look and went back to her desk and figured for a while, wondering whom she could bill.

Nobody will send you a check if they're not expecting your bill. And they won't be expecting your bill if you haven't done something to bill them for *and* quoted a price, in advance, to which they've agreed. No price, no service, no bill.

Pricing is hard for a lot of people because, unlike the other parts of consulting, which are various ways of saying "here's what I will do for you," pricing is saying "here's what you must do for me." Quoting a price is one of the first steps in every consulting process, and it is as important to consulting as marketing and serving the client. Without it, you can't turn on the meter, do the work, call for your money, and move on to the next show.

Much of consulting involves laying the pieces into place that bring you to the billing moment.

- Your selling proposition, which establishes why the client needs you rather than somebody else.
- The client agreement, which summarizes the terms of the assignment, including the price.

- Your consulting method, which is what you do in the course of the assignment to solve the client's problem.
- Your product, which is what you deliver to the client that adds value to his business and fulfills completion of the assignment.
- Your bill, which is your official statement of completion. It's how you say, "I've done the job, this is what you agreed to pay, it is now due."

Without the first one, you won't get the assignment. Without the next three, you won't be in a position to send a bill. And without the bill, you won't get a check.

Pricing Qualifies the Client

One role of pricing is to keep you focused on the business you want by helping you deflect business you don't want and smoke out indecisive prospects.

Being in a service business, you adopt the attitude that your foremost responsibility is to satisfy your customers. The two operative words here are *satisfy*, which implies a responsibility to deliver on your part, and *customers*, which implies a financial commitment on their part. You don't want to break your neck for somebody who isn't going to hold up his end of the bargain. There are plenty of people who will be happy merely to shop your brain for ideas with no real commitment to buy, or who are so vague as to what they need that you find you've got to sit down and work with them just to figure out what the problem is that made them call you, so you can focus a proposal on solving it.

One of the worst places to find yourself is adrift in a new relationship without having turned on the meter before you got in the boat. It happens. You look up one day and discover you've spent the better part of a week on a prospect's behalf without having defined up front the point at which your time started to become billable, much less at what rate or when you will expect a progress payment.

Knowing what price to quote for your time, and when to quote it, enables you to qualify your prospects, winnow those that aren't good client material, and draw a clear line between marketing and consulting.

Consulting Is Not a Commodity

Businesses have three options for competing to win customers: (1) *low price,* which is how commodities compete because there is no other differentiating characteristic; (2) *superior performance,* like higher quality, faster service, more effective methods, or some other attribute that is of greater value to the client than what competitors offer; and (3) *market focus,* in which you understand and address the particular needs of clients occupying a market niche.

There are vast differences from one consultant to another. Don't assume you need to compete on the basis of price. You will be far more successful competing on the basis of your ability to add value to your clients' businesses.

When Skip Pile (see profile in chapter 14) bids a contract to manage a corporation's ad agency selection process, he brings two competitive distinctions. One is his focus on this new niche in consulting—Pile and Company is prominent among only four or five companies in the country that provide this service. The other distinction is that he spent fifteen years on the inside of Boston's biggest ad agency and knows whereof he speaks when it comes to getting agencies to do handstands for clients.

Brizius and Foster have broad public policy expertise, but they get their consulting business by focusing their expertise on, and knowing how to work with, the special needs of a narrow but powerful market niche: governors.

One day I lost out to a competitor on a strategic planning contract. The prospect was a public housing authority, and the planning process had to tackle some tough choices, defuse politics, and build consensus among many interest groups. When the prospect told me I'd lost the job, he said he preferred the approach I had outlined to the one my competitor presented, but my competitor had bid the job at less than $4,000, whereas I had priced it over $16,000. I was selling on the basis of value, but the prospect was buying on low cost.

You must find some basis other than low cost on which to compete, because there will always be somebody ready to do a job cheaper than you. A client whose first concern is to get the cheapest consultant he can find to do the job is a client you probably don't want.

For examples of how several other consultants add value to their client's businesses, see "Clients' equity" in chapter 10.

Profits Are the Last Dollars Earned

When you take a consulting assignment, every hour you bill pays not only for that hour itself, but also pays a share of your overhead: marketing, rent, support services, office expenses, and so on. Profit, by definition, is what's left over after expenses. If one hour of your time and that hour's share of your expenses cost you fifty-nine dollars and you sell it for sixty dollars, the last dollar is your profit. If you sell it for sixty-five dollars, you have increased your price only 8 percent, but your profit has risen sixfold, from one dollar to six dollars. Small concern to your customer, but a mighty big one to you.

Consider the flip side. When you discount your price, the first dollars you give up are the ones that would have gone in your pocket. Next come the dollars that pay the rent and cover other expenses. If it costs you fifty-nine dollars an hour to stay even and you discount your fee to forty dollars an hour to give a new client a break, you aren't simply foregoing profit, you are *subsidizing* your client at the rate of nineteen dollars an hour.

There are times when discounting can make sense—when you're starting out, doing a favor for a community organization, or trying to break into a new market or preempt a competitor. Reminding yourself every time you bid a job that profits are the last dollars earned will make it easier to quote a profitable price and result in a healthier margin at the end of the year.

To figure out how much your time costs you and the effects of different billing rates, run financial projections like those in chapter 12. They're easy to construct and will illustrate how slight variations in your costs and revenues affect the number of months it takes for you to break even and the profit you'll make.

Five Factors That Should Influence Your Fees

When I interviewed Eric Mitchell, president of the Pricing Advisor, Inc. (see profile in chapter 10), I asked for some insights into pricing consulting services, and he offered the following criteria. I have interspersed with Eric's comments insights from my own experience and from my other interviews.

1. Costs and profits You don't sell all your hours. The first rule of pricing is that the hours you do sell must pay for those you don't sell. This is cost-based pricing.

Eric Mitchell says, "There are twenty-one working days in a month, and if you're lucky, you'll consult ten of them, and then you're working pretty hard. You have to figure out what's a fair charge for your whole time, which includes your customer covering your marketing time, your administrative time, and so forth. So you work up the figure from the cost side, and divide by the hours you think you can sell."

Skip Pile teaches pricing in the advertising field and offered the following formula. "Pick a figure you want to make, divide it by 1,500 hours, add a 'load factor' of 100 percent, which covers indirect costs (secretarial support, rent, heat, light, postage, etc.), and then divide that subtotal by .75, which adds a profit equivalent to 25 percent of the total. If your target for net pretax income is $75,000, this formula suggests you need to bill at an hourly rate of $133 per hour." (See table on page 95.) Where does the figure 1,500 hours come from? It's 72 percent of 2,080 hours (which is 260 eight-hour days, or fifty-two five-day work weeks). Why 72 percent? It represents what the PR industry considers to be a minimum target for billable hours. Under this formula, 28 percent of your time (582 hours; 73 days; 14.5 weeks) is left free for nonbillable activity: marketing, administration, sick leave, vacation, and holidays. The profit figure represents retained earnings that can be invested to develop new products, buy equipment, and so forth.

Skip's formula is probably a little more sophisticated than most consultants use for figuring cost-based pricing, but it's a useful model that can be adapted to any consulting setting.

Other consultants have similar formulas. For example, David Bjork, the senior consultant at Hay Management Consultants, told me that Hay charges $80 to $350 per hour, and that most of Hay's people bill out at $100 to $200 per hour. "For a big firm with lots of overhead the hourly billing rate equals three times what the consultant earns. One-third is direct compensation, one-third is local office overhead, one-third is corporate overhead and margin. The firm breaks even when all professionals are 65 percent billed out. In a *small* consulting firm the hourly rate is *double* the consultant's earnings. Half of the fee is direct compensation, a quarter goes to pay overhead, and a quarter goes toward margin, provided the consultant bills enough hours.

When it comes to figuring a daily rate for one of the consultants at the Stevens Group, Susan Stevens takes the consultant's total compensation times three to account for marketing and overhead, and divides the total by 75 percent of the work days in a year (leaving 25 percent for unbillable time). "If somebody comes to me and says, 'I need to make $60,000 a year,' I say, 'Can you bill $180,000? If you can, then fine.' But

PILE AND COMPANY PRICING FORMULA

Direct Costs	$\dfrac{\$75,000 \quad \text{(consultant's target income)}}{1{,}500 \quad \text{(billable hours)}}$	= $ 50
Indirect Costs	+ 100% (secretarial, rent, etc.)	= $ 50
Costs Plus 25% Profit	+ $\dfrac{\$100}{.75}$ (to fund growth, etc.)	$100 = $133
Billing Rate	=	$133/hr

we don't commit to an income until someone has been with us a year, because it takes that long for them to learn the business. And we don't keep consultants that can't bill their time—that's not good business."

I offer these formulas to give you different ways of thinking through the hourly-rate dilemma. The main lesson is that your rate should be in the range of double to triple your target pretax income, and then adjusted up or down based on the factors outlined below.

2. *Similar services or competition*   Beyond looking at your own costs, Eric Mitchell says to look at pricing from the customer's point of view.

"They're going to have some idea of what's a fair range for the expertise they're buying. No matter how well- or ill-informed they are, people have a perception based on similar services that they've bought. So you need to go out and ask people, 'How much do you pay someone for analogous services?' Some people get timid about asking what a competitor gets paid, so it's helpful to find a substitute and ask what's a reasonable rate for that. It could be for legal services, or accounting, or a training consultant, or some other area that's like yours. If you can, find out how much they pay people who do exactly the same thing you do." Eric adds that it is more realistic to find out what customers might perceive to be a fair *range* rather than to search for a specific number.

Feedback is important, too. You may be losing business because of overpricing and not know it. People seldom give honest feedback; it's just easier to find another explanation than to say, "We thought you were overpriced." What does Eric Mitchell suggest? "You look for disturbances, and you have to look at the frequency with which your proposals are getting rejected. If you keep quoting $2,000 and people keep saying 'We'll get back to you,' it's a good indication there's a pricing problem.

"On the other hand, if people are continually saying yes, then you have to begin to feel you're undercharging. Words that I hate to hear after I give a quote: 'Gee, that's really a very fair price.' It means they expected to pay more, and I've just given away profits. But you can never hit the bull's eye. The value lies in being sensitive, listening to the feedback, being flexible. The biggest pricing sin is just to go with a number and not think about changing it to fit the circumstances. People will say, 'I'm a thousand-dollar-a-day consultant.' Even with the same customer they served four years ago, when the customer comes back they say, 'Well, it's still a thousand dollars.' Meanwhile, the customer's long forgotten what you charged, just that they were satisfied at the time."

Should you try to negotiate at a reduced price if your initial bid is rejected? The answer depends. How badly do you want the job? Is price the reason it was rejected? What precedent would you be establishing? If you can get candid feedback and the client is still open, you may want to give negotiation a try. But don't offer price concessions until you know that price was the stumbling block. Possible strategy: get the prospect to establish a base from which you negotiate upward toward your bid. Start by asking what she's budgeted for the job or what she considers to be a fair range. In the negotiation, be sure to relate your price to the value of your contribution. If it helps to make your case, talk about what others have paid for similar services.

Another negotiating strategy is to seek concessions from the prospect in exchange for your accepting a lower fee. For example, ask for a larger share of the project fee to be paid up front; get the client to provide in-kind support like space, equipment, or clerical and research services that you had figured in your costs.

A note on mandated fee limits: some clients such as state and federal government agencies put a limit on daily consulting fees. The reason is fairly obvious. A fee of $800 or $1,600 a day might be reasonable considering the overhead it has to cover and the value delivered, but on its surface it can look downright greedy, especially to a taxpayer reading about it in the newspaper. If your target market consists of public agencies or nonprofit institutions, especially where consulting fees will be paid from taxpayer funds, investigate whether fee limits exist, and whether conventions have been established such as pricing consulting services by the job rather than by the hour to make it feasible to serve a market with restrictive fee limits.

3. Value to the customer   In addition to investigating what price range the customer will consider appropriate, Eric advises against setting a fixed rate for all customers. Rather, adjust your price on the basis of value. "I'll be darned if I'll have a standard fee. If I'm doing a pricing seminar for a client, I have a much different rate for a company that's going to bring in a hundred people than for one bringing in ten people. The company that's going to bring in a hundred is getting much more value, and I charge them more."

What about other consulting situations where relative value is harder to gauge? "Get surrogates for the value of your work," Eric suggests. "Before you spout off with a standard rate, ask some questions. Who's going to be involved? What level are they? What do they want to get out of it? How urgent is it? How important? How soon do you need it? If the client tells you not until the middle of February, don't overdo the price. If they tell you next week, you've got a different rate."

4. Type of customer   Customers who have ample ability to pay (because, for example, they have a dedicated budget for the project, or they're large and profitable and have a tradition of using consultants), and whose needs fit your expertise, will support higher prices.

"Nine out of ten people I've met don't think about whether the customer fits them before they open their mouth to quote a price," Eric says. "Too often they see a situation where, because the customer doesn't fit, he won't support full price. So the consultant agrees to do it on the cheap, or even for free, by rationalizing that this will lead to future business, and then the future business never comes, or if it does, it's more bottom fishing."

The type of customer can affect not only how much you charge, but also how you structure your pricing. If you can see the relationship between your services and the customer's bottom line, you can consider linking your compensation to your impact. You might consider commission-based pricing, payment in the form of equity (stock ownership), or profit sharing as options. A cash-poor start-up with strong profit potential might be in a better position to offer stock for services than cash. A company whose objective in hiring you is to implement cost-reduction strategies might be willing to pay you a percentage of the costs you help them save.

Bryan Robertson, who helps American branded fashion goods manufacturers get established in Europe, charges a monthly retainer in the initial stages of the client relationship, pricing his services at a fraction of what the client would pay to set up a European office of its own. As he succeeds in growing the client's European sales, his fee converts from retainer to commission. This pricing structure fits his clients' ability to pay and provides Bryan an attractive incentive to help his clients succeed.

5. Your objectives   "Before you quote a price," Eric Mitchell advises, "ask yourself where this consultation fits in with building your business. Is it strategically important, like adding to a credible base, or will it be a diversion and interfere with other things that you're trying to accomplish? If it's strategically important, you might charge a little less to be sure to get the contract. If it's something that's going to be a diversion, you might charge a premium so at least you feel good about the money."

Discounting to Build

As I note above, there are times when you may be tempted to discount your price. One is to capture a contract that is strategically important, as Eric points out. The contract may provide entrees or a way to get paid for getting smarter in a new market that you've been trying to penetrate. This is discounting to build your business, and it can work for you.

Accepting low fees simply because a prospect cannot justify paying your market rate not only leads to bottom fishing, it is also very hard on your pricing confidence. This is worth emphasizing. The best way to feel confident of your rates is to have clients who pay them. The quickest way to erode your rates is to feel unworthy of them, and to perpetuate the problem by undercharging.

Susan Stevens summarizes the discounting question this way: "The test for me has always been twofold. One, does the client really need the discount? Two, can I leverage this into something that will be in my best interests in the long run? In the beginning you don't give it away, but you have to do more for less in order to cast the net out widely enough so that you get the revenue flowing, build your contacts and visibility, and earn the option of becoming more selective."

You may want to discount or forgo your fee to support worthy causes. This can be very satisfying. But if you are asked to do it often, you'll need a graceful way to say no. *Tip:* Establish a budget for contributed time, much as a company sets a budget for charitable contributions. When you get a request you can't handle, explain that it exceeds your budget.

Eric points out that the forces affecting how you price a job are often in competition with one another. How to reach resolution? "After I've thought through the different criteria, and before I answer the pricing question, I sit down and establish my indifference point. That's a price at which I would be equally happy or unhappy whether the customer says yes or no. 'If they'll pay me five grand to do that, I'll take it, but if they won't, I've got other things to do.' The indifference point is different for different clients. To set a price is to trade off competing pressures. The indifference point is the final check."

How to Quote Each Job Without Regrets

The earlier in a relationship you quote a price, the better you can use price to qualify the prospect, but the less you know about the job you're pricing. Here are some tips to help you balance your timing and accuracy:

- *Resist quoting under pressure.* Say, "I'll have to get back to you," and then take time to develop a bid that fits the opportunity.
- *Know what to ask about a job in order to establish a price.* Keep a list of Eric Mitchell's five pricing criteria by the phone, and when a prospect calls, ask the salient questions.
- *Don't invest a lot of time to price a small job.* Instead, have price ranges in mind for the different kinds of work that you do.
- *If you quote a range, make sure the bottom end is a price you can live with,* because it is the number the client will remember.
- *Find a way to get paid to bid complex jobs*—those where you need to know a lot more about the prospect's situation before you can define your role and put a price on it.

I will sit down with a prospect once or twice to find out what they need and explain how I can help them. I may write a proposal for the entire job, outlining a general plan of attack and likely price range. But my proposal will break the project into phases that begin by my investigating the client's situation in more depth, enabling me to develop a more focused consulting approach and a firm price. And I price that first phase of work, giving the client the option of whether or not to proceed with the balance of the project once it has been defined and bid.

How to Structure Your Pricing and Billing

The two most common ways to price consulting are by the hour or day, called time-and-materials, and by the job, called fixed-price. Some consultants work under retainers, others work on commission. Eric Mitchell says the first rule is to charge however the customer is set up to pay.

Time-and-Materials Consulting

Under this method of pricing, you quote an hourly or daily rate plus expenses.

Advantages

- In theory, you get paid for as much time as you put into the project. This is especially useful when taking on a new client or working in unfamiliar territory where it is hard to estimate how much time the project will take.

Disadvantages

- Most clients will want an estimate of the total cost that they can budget against; some even ask for a guaranteed cost ceiling. Asking for a guarantee always strikes me as running against the notion of time and materials. Asking for an estimate seems fair enough, but no matter how you hedge your estimate, the figure you quote will set the client's expectation, and if you end up spending more time than you'd expected and charging more money than you'd estimated, the client invariably will see the extra cost as an overrun.
- Therefore time-and-materials pricing tends to limit your upside potential: If the job costs more than your estimate, you tend to swallow the excess or risk tarnishing your goodwill with the client. If, on the other hand, you are very efficient and complete the job in ten hours fewer than you'd estimated, you don't get a financial benefit because you agreed to charge on the basis of your time.

I try to manage this problem by quoting time-and-materials for the initial stages of a new client relationship, the time involved in becoming familiar with the client, and defining more specifically what the project will entail. I try to bid the second phase, the meat of the project, on a fixed-price basis, building in some room to maneuver, and laying out in detail the assumptions that underlie my bid: notably, what I will do (how many meetings we will have, how many people we will interview, etc.) and what the client will do (gathering background materials, analyzing current operations, etc.). I then add a sentence to the pricing paragraph of my proposal in which I indicate that if circumstances arise requiring us to deviate from these assumptions, I will alert the client and, with the client's approval, bill additional hours on a time-and-materials basis at the following rate.

Fixed-Price Consulting

A fixed-price bid is just what it sounds like. You define the product, what you will be responsible for doing, what the client will be responsible for doing, and the total price.

Some fixed-price bids include out-of-pocket expenses; others are "plus expenses." Some quotes leave wiggle room for the consultant by including a summary of underlying assumptions (e.g., that the client's data is timely and accurate, obviating the need for additional research), and how the price will vary if the assumptions prove faulty.

Advantages

- In a situation where the job is predictable and you control the variables, you may become so efficient over time that you can complete the job in two-thirds the time it would take somebody else.
- By pricing the job on the basis of its value to the client rather than the cost you incur in delivering it, fixed-price consulting has the potential of generating much higher profit margins than time-and-materials consulting.

Disadvantage

- You are committed to deliver the product and satisfy the client at the quoted price. If you encounter costly surprises along the way, you stand to lose money on the job, unless you have built into your proposal a clear understanding about what constitutes a negotiable change order.

Consulting on Retainers

A retainer is a regular monthly fee that a client pays for ongoing work by the consultant. The amount of the retainer is determined by two variables: (1) the average number of hours or days per month that the consultant will work for the client, and (2) a lump-sum price the client will pay for those hours. The payment remains steady from month to month on the assumption that although the work load varies, it will average out to something approximating the agreed commitment. Retainers are usually renegotiated from time to time to adjust for rate and time changes.

A retainer is much less common than time-and-materials and fixed-price consulting and reflects a high degree of trust that neither party will abuse the commitment. The client can abuse the commitment by asking more of the consultant on a regular basis than the client is paying for, and the consultant can abuse it by taking the client for granted, underserving the client, or not staying alert to the client's satisfaction over time.

Advantages

- The best thing about a retainer is that it transforms unpredictable project-based revenue into an ongoing revenue stream you can count on every month to pay the rent.

Disadvantages

- As with young love, it's easier to delight a new client than to keep delighting one who knows you well. You must work to keep the relationship fresh, let the client know you value the work, stay alert and anticipate the client's needs.
- A disadvantage for the client is that a retainer begins to make a consultant look like more like a fixed than variable cost. For this reason, on the few occasions where I develop a pattern of consistent monthly invoices, I seldom call it a retainer.

Sometimes what begins as a fixed-price or time-and-materials relationship evolves into a retainer relationship as the client and consultant discover new ways of working together. (For more on this topic, see chapter 10, "Sustainable revenue streams.")

Commission-Based Consulting

Commission structures are usually a pricing convention of selected industries, for example merger-and-acquisition consulting, portfolio management, media buying, interior design. If you are consulting in an industry where commissions are the convention, your pricing methods may follow the convention or they may deviate, depending on your competitive strategy.

Change Orders and Cost Overruns: Who Swallows?

It's up to you to spell out in the client agreement the circumstances under which your estimate or fixed price will need to be renegotiated, and then, if such circumstances arise, to bring them to the client's attention at the time. If you follow this procedure, you have reasonable odds of recovering your added costs and maintaining an equable client relationship.

Overruns that occur as a result of events you should have foreseen are costs you must swallow in order to maintain harmony in the relationship, unless the bid contains provisions for recovering them. As a general rule, you will come out whole over the life of an extended relationship because the jobs that claim a hunk of your hide will be offset eventually by those that come out better than your deserved.

Billing

Structure your billing to fit how the customer is set up to pay, and don't let your bills contain surprises.

For a period early in my consulting career I was on the payroll of the United States Senate, because that was how my senator-client was set up to pay. One corporate client sends me a monthly purchase order "for consulting services." The purchase orders are in round figures. At first I invoiced odd amounts—whatever the hours and expenses totaled for the month. He called and said I was screwing up his accounts and would I please bill the face amount of the purchase order. So I bill the round figure and keep my own running total of hours and expenses, and every six or twelve months, we adjust one of his purchase orders to bring our accounts into line.

Another client sometimes asks me to double invoice him toward the end of his fiscal year because he has money left in his consulting budget that may not be available in the new year. I work off the credit balance over the next few months until it's time to start billing again.

A bank holding company client had me work serially with the management team in each of the company's banks to help them develop long-range plans, and then help them develop annual updates and work plans. Each assignment was separately bid and invoiced to the subsidiary bank, because that's how they were set up to do business.

I have a relationship with the president of a hospital, helping implement a five-year plan we developed. There is no regular pattern of payment. I simply accrue my time and expenses, and when the total looks big enough to bill, I submit an invoice and he pays it.

The policy of no surprises is common sense. A bill that meets the client's expectations gets paid without question. A bill that surprises gets questioned, and you aren't there to defend it. Clients don't like to confront consultants over money; uneasiness caused by your billing may cool the client's ardor. You may sense the relationship is softening, but never know why. If your charges will deviate from what your client expects, discuss them before you bill.

What about late payments and bad debts? If a bill is forty-five or sixty days old, ask your client to check with his bookkeeper about its status. Give your client a way to save face, even if you suspect the bill has been moldering on his desk.

Late payments are more of a problem the first time you invoice a client, because accounts-payable departments often require a signed contract or purchase order on file before a check can be issued, and most managers hate to do that paperwork. When your client sends your first bill down the hall for payment, it comes back with a note saying "no PO on file." You can help avoid that kind of delay. When you get a new client, ask whether a contract or purchase order will be required in order to process your invoices, and offer to help get the wheels turning.

I have had late payments, but never an unpaid bill. If you're having problems getting paid, you may need to do a better job of qualifying your clients or of putting in place the essential pieces that create the billing moment, summarized at the beginning of this chapter.

Ideas to Take Away

- Knowing what price to quote can help you get the business you want and deflect the business you don't want. Knowing when to quote a price can help you know when to turn on the meter, which draws the line between marketing and consulting.
- Consulting is not a commodity. Don't compete on the basis of price, but on your ability to add value.
- Every time you bid a job, remember that profits are the last dollars earned.
- Five factors should influence your fees: (1) cost and profit, (2) competition, (3) value to the customer, (4) ability of the customer to pay, (5) the job's fit with your objectives.
- Trust your indifference point as a guide for balancing these factors.
- Use discounting as a tool to build your business or as a way of contributing to the community, but not for bottom fishing.
- To quote each job without regrets, develop habits that enable you to stay in control of pricing.
- Structure your pricing and billing to fit how the customer is set up to pay.

Value can be defined as the *benefit* you get for the *price* you pay. "Good value" implies you get a lot of benefit for the price. Diane Page ought to know. She's a market research consultant. She makes her living helping companies find out what benefits consumers want from their products and services, and when they feel they're getting good value. Her competitive strategy? Positioning herself as the good value brand in her field.

POSITIONING HERSELF AS THE "GOOD VALUE" BRAND
Profile
DIANE SIMS PAGE
Market Research and New Product Development Consultant,
Minneapolis, MN

Diane Page is a contradiction. Everything about her says "best of class." She has the slim figure of a runner and clothes you'll see in this fall's SoHo fashion catalogues. Her Mercedes station wagon is an icon of momhood-meets-professional success. She does business on foil-embossed stationery set in simple block letters, created specially for Diane by Sheila Chin, the prominent commercial designer. She has her office on the twenty-fifth floor of a class A Minneapolis office tower. Consulting keeps her busy fifty hours a week, and her client list reads like a *Forbes* roster of premier American brands. In all respects, Diane is top of the line—except when it comes to price. In that department, she steers a decidedly conservative course, placing herself squarely in the middle of her market.

Diane has been in business for herself for sixteen years. She sells two kinds of consulting services: qualitative market research, which centers around moderating focus groups, and new product development, which centers around facilitating brainstorming and creative strategy. I interviewed her in her office, which is crowded with artifacts. Pictures of Diane with her husband, Alan (football star, Minnesota supreme court justice, benefactor), and their four kids biking, jogging, making a pig pile. Client files. Shelves of consumer products that Diane has helped invent or had a hand in researching.

When the question turns to pricing, Diane shakes her head. "All consultants struggle with it. You need an hourly rate established in your mind, and you need to be flexible about money so you can take advantage of opportunities. When I started, the market price for a focus group was $500. Then it went to $1,000. Then $2,000. Now they run $2,500 to $5,000. I price myself in the middle. I'm the 'good value' brand. I get a lot of pressure from my colleagues, who say, 'Raise your prices! Work less! Make more!' But I want my clients to come back."

It is possible that Diane's success as a marketing savant and her conservative approach to pricing both stem from the same source, a keen sensitivity to other people's attitudes and choices. A lot of what she does is aimed at keeping the client comfortable. She says one rule of thumb is "no surprises." She's always careful to provide a detailed quote: what she's going to do, what the product will be, what it will cost. If the job is big, she likes to break it into phases so she can describe what each phase will entail and talk about its costs and benefits to the client—giving the client the option of proceeding to the next phase or not—rather than showing a grand total that might scare him off or be difficult to evaluate in terms of costs and benefits. On the rare occasion when she runs over her estimate, she's more likely to eat the overage than deliver the bad news to a client with whom the long-term relationship is her first priority.

Diane's the rare consultant who can't tell you the first client she landed. My first sales call is burned into my memory—what I said, what he said, how I felt, the table we sat at. Diane searches her mind. What comes up is something much more personal. "I can tell you everything about the hour and the second when Justin was born, which was during the same period. But who knows who that first client was?"

This is amazing to me until Diane helps me understand that getting time to be a mother was why she left her ad agency job. "I had two babies at home under eighteen months and needed the flexibility." Being a new mom replaced a career as her center of focus. Consulting was a way to make money on the side doing what she knew how to do. Her work was very project focused, so she could fit it into her life where there was room.

I asked how she felt at the time, leaving the security of a job. "Apprehensive. But willing to take a cut in pay to make time for my kids, get the flexibility." The key, she says, was to "stick with an equity." In her case, the equity was her knowledge of market research and the fact that she was already networked into the field. That base and the ability to take work one project at a time made for an easier transition than if she were trying to change professions or markets at the same time she was firing her employer and changing her schedule and place of work.

A typical day has Diane at her office by eight-thirty. Her market research projects generally last about a month each, and she typically has three to six projects in various stages of completion. Among other things, her day involves hearing from clients about their research needs and developing proposals and cost estimates—which, if the research will be done out of town means she has to get bids from suppliers who will provide the focus group space, cater refreshments, recruit the respondents, and so on.

Her day also involves writing the screening questionnaire that recruiters will use to make sure the people they invite to the focus group fit the profile of her client's target market. And her day involves developing discussion guides that control the focus group, and in the process, conferring with her clients to make sure she's probing the right kinds of issues, characterizing their product concepts accurately, setting up the concepts in the right sequence.

She spends a little time paying bills and doing administrative tasks. And she spends a fair amount of time culling transcripts of her focus groups and writing up summary reports. She gets away from the office by five-thirty.

The focus group moderating gets done in the evening, usually twice a week, and about half of her focus groups are out of town. When she's really busy, writing client reports ends up waiting till the weekend. The price, Diane is quick to point out, is stress: the hours, the travel, the deadlines, keeping the customer happy. "You come up for air now and then to look around and wonder. Is there a life outside of consulting?"

Diane had an office at home for the first five years. As her kids grew up, the mothering part of Diane's life took less time and consulting took more. She moved her office out of her home to make a cleaner separation between work and family.

"At home I was never not working. If there's five minutes open, you're doing the dishes or laundry. You never get a coffee break. Also when you're at home, there's an attitude among clients. You have less status. You're less professional." Here again, perhaps, is another clue to the source of Diane's attitudes about pricing and her success with clients. For all her flair, she has a pronounced practical streak, and you can't help but think how a stint at motherhood will have that effect on a person, and that a practical streak would clearly be an asset in the sensibilities she brings to clients who need to know how consumers are going to respond to a line of designer condoms or a new concept in prepackaged, shelf-stable meat entrees.

I ask Diane what, in her clients' eyes, she brings to a job that they value most. "Confidence. I know how to get the job done. And skills—I'm a good focus group moderator, I know how to get the information they're looking for. I can put it into a report that they can use to make decisions. I guess they see me as pragmatic."

In her own eyes, what does she bring to the client that adds value? "I stay current. I'm on top of trends. I know the best research facilities in all the major markets. I keep up on all the facets of getting the job done."

Her secrets for success? One thing that's worked very well for her is something she calls her dual positioning. "There are a lot of market research consultants out there. New product development consulting was down because of the recession, the Gulf War, and a general consumer backlash to new products—consumers want fewer choices. I've taken one set of strengths and positioned myself in two businesses: focus group moderator and facilitator for new product strategy. So when the economy hits the skids and nobody's spending money on new product development, they're spending more than usual on market research because it's more important to be on target. I didn't have any decrease in billings last year. Making your skills earn for you in more than one way is a strategy for making your business recession resistant."

Another success factor: "Listening. Staying on top of trends and being able to read people's attitudes. Getting behind the words to figure out what they're really saying. Netting it out. Applying it to the customer's situation."

Diane gets her sense of job security when clients come back for another project. "Insecurity is when the phone doesn't ring. It happens to all of us. My advice is to keep the overhead low, so when the check comes in, as much as possible is yours." She keeps her own overhead low by using free-lancers instead of hiring staff. She pays an hourly rate for people to recruit focus group respondents, transcribe tapes, word process, handle her filing. This is facilitated by her renting space from a larger market research organization. "I get classy space, I'm in a research environment, and I have access to support services. It's a way to be professional and have convenience without the overhead of your own lease."

What gives her kicks and keeps her going in consulting? "Interaction with people. I'm good at providing helpful marketing insights, and that makes me feel good." She pauses. "Plus, consulting is a good fit for me. I have good leadership skills. That enables me to direct and coordinate a project. A lot of clients are looking for leadership." Then she hesitates again and smiles at me. "Plus—and I don't know how to say this exactly"—then there's a self-conscious laugh and I feel a confession coming—"the money's so good. You do a good job for a client, have a successful relationship, and then you get to send the invoice. I love that moment."

6

BEING THERE

Knowing your role in the client's world

People who invite consultants into their organizations have their own reasons for doing so and have a preconception of how the consultant should fit in. To build a successful relationship, you need to understand your role and contribution.

Two short stories will help make the point. First this one. The president of a bank called me one day. I'd helped this management team develop a long-range plan, and he'd subsequently recommended me to the president of a sister bank owned by the same holding company. I went on to help the second bank, and now he was calling to talk about my working with a third bank in the same family. I was delighted.

"One thing," the banker said. "Don't learn too much about banking."

I laughed and said there wasn't much danger, but his comment brought to mind a conversation I'd had with his management team in one of our planning meetings. They'd been talking about the need for the bank to develop new products and services. As they kicked around ideas, it became clear that they had no method for evaluating feasibility. I asked how they evaluated profitability of their current products. After a pause somebody said, "We don't."

I was caught short. This very successful bank—like most banks, as it turns out—chose to offer more or less the same products and services that other banks offer, and set their fees more or less on the basis of their competitors' fees and their target margin for interest rate spreads.

The upshot from our discussion was that if they were going to compete and grow in a deregulated industry, they'd better learn how to become entrepreneurial in ways that had never been required of them in the past.

My naive question had helped them think about their business in new ways and point the discussion at a gap in their management tool kit.

Now here's the second story. I'm standing before the board of directors of a different bank, a small-town bank. The dozen men sitting around the long table in a windowless meeting room at a Holiday Inn are mostly retired businessmen who'd joined together eighteen years earlier to found the bank. One was a car dealer, one had a bowling alley, one was an attorney, and so on, all in the same town. With the financial services business changing so much, the bank's president had convinced them their bank ought to have a long-range plan, and he's hired me to facilitate a one-day planning event.

The way the president introduces me makes me sound as if I'm some kind of expert who's driven out from the city to tell these hayseeds how to run their business. All heads turn to me. I feel a rush of anxiety. I sure don't want to come across like some uptown know-it-all. Standing up, I hear myself saying in an aw-shucks tone that while I know how to do planning, I'm no banker, and I'm looking to them to be the experts. I study their faces but can't get a clue as to what they're thinking.

At the break, the president pulls me aside to say I've nearly blown the job. He tells me how hard he's worked to persuade these men to take a day off for planning, and the last thing they want is to spend a day with some guy who says he knows even less about banking than they do. Their idea of a consultant is an expert, or why does he cost so much?

The day progresses. I draw out these directors on trends in their community, where their competitors are headed, what the bank's strengths and resources are, where they want the bank to be five years down the road, what it will take to get there. By midafternoon I finally feel pretty sure the day's going to be a success: the meeting room walls are papered in flip chart pages filled with notes. By four o'clock, we've developed a plan. Everybody's full of ideas. Nobody leaves early. They talk about making progress checks a priority for future meetings. When I pack up to leave, my client puts his hand on my shoulder and says he's never seen his directors so excited.

So what's the lesson? You can undermine an engagement in a hurry simply by not understanding what you represent to your audience. Some clients need you to help build consensus, others need you to help implement unpopular changes. Some need you to become an active partner to the management team, while others prefer you to operate in the background. Some need you to be an expert, and others need you not to be. Though every engagement will be different, here is my take on the roles that clients most often look to their consultants to fill, and some thoughts about how you can fill them without getting out of your depth.

A Shoulder for the Accountability Burden

The moment you say yes to a consulting assignment, something happens. You can feel it. A mantle of accountability transfers from the client to you. The client experiences the uplift that comes with unburdening, accompanied by a twinge of anxiety that comes with giving up control—he's wondering whether you can perform. You feel the fleeting exhilaration that comes from making a sale, accompanied by the anxiety of knowing you've just put yourself on the hook to deliver. Again. And you're wondering what you'll uncover when you begin digging into this one.

Accepting accountability is part of what you're being paid for. When a corporation hires a Wall Street consulting firm to conduct due diligence prior to a $100-million acquisition, the consulting firm charges a percent of the deal—hundreds of thousands of dollars. This fee doesn't reflect the actual hours involved in doing the job but the value of the consulting firm's accepting accountability for the accuracy of their work.

In Verne Severson's business (see the profile at the end of this chapter), when he accepts a job to design and produce a working prototype of a new electronic device, he has accepted accountability for the success of the device, sometimes even without knowing in advance how the design will be accomplished.

Verne uses a couple of techniques to help him deliver on that accountability. One is to insist that the price of the project include his developing customized test software to help him verify the correctness of his designs. The second is to insist that the project not end with the delivery of a working prototype but carry through to a second generation prototype. Verne says the first prototype invariably will be found lacking, and only by his working with it alongside the customer can the final design refinements be identified to fully meet the customer's needs. Knowing these steps are included in the project enables Verne to accept the accountability burden and feel confident in his ability to deliver.

Shedding responsibility is progress in the eyes of the client. When a client engages me to facilitate planning, getting the job done on time and on budget is my sole focus with that client. The client clears his desk of an annoying pile of papers relating to planning by giving them to me. The papers are usually minutes and background pieces from old planning committees, which are not particularly helpful. They document a lot of unresolved conversations about things that need to be done, and now that they're in my hands and off the client's desk, the client feels a sense of movement, progress, even if they've only moved to a corner of my office floor. We forge ahead.

Success requires limiting your accountability to what you can control. Some consultants actually conduct the client's work—for example the due diligence process for an acquisition—and in that sense their acceptance of the accountability burden is comprehensive. I don't work that way. I accept responsibility for designing a successful planning process and meeting a deadline with a quality product, but I make it clear that the work of planning will be performed by the client's team. In effect, I have accepted accountability for leadership, but I have not promised to replace the client's troops, and if his troops let me down, the project will falter. This works because it limits my accountability to things I can control, even in an unknown situation, and it still unburdens the client.

Prospects who lack the staff capacity or commitment to hold up their part of the work plan are the consultant's equivalent of quicksand. Part of your job in qualifying prospects during the marketing process is to find out if they have the capacity to be effective clients. How you qualify the prospect depends on what business you're in. Fran Wheeler, who's in the circuit board design business, wrote a booklet she gives to her clients outlining the information and tasks they're responsible for if she's to accept accountability for producing a circuit board design to meet their needs.

As a consultant, you're not the management or board of the client's organization, and you can't accept responsibilities that rightly rest with management and directors. Example: you get hired by a hospital to help them decide whether they should merge with another hospital across town. You can help them explore all sides of the issue and reach an informed decision, but you cannot make that decision for them, even if you had the background to make it. It's not your role, you don't have the authority, it would be presumptuous, and you probably aren't qualified to make it.

For me, the minute I find myself feeling responsible for the client's problem, consulting stops being fun and I get immobilized by panic.

Before I knew better, I worked for some organizations that weren't used to using consultants and thought they could hand their problems over to me, pay a fee, and get a solution in return. That's like hiring a therapist and asking her to give you a call once she's gotten rid of your hang-ups.

Speed and Access Manifest

When clients are ready to "work the problem," they want you to be available to do your part. If you're being brought in as a specialist at one phase of a project—say you're doing qualitative market research on a new product concept—there's a point in the development process when the client needs your work or the entire project stalls. If you're a general management advisor to a corporate executive and that executive needs your advice, he wants the answer as fast as he thinks of the question.

The tyranny of the fax machine is that we consultants can't get any distance from our clients. We and our clients are one. It's been said that good writing is an intimate act, as if the writer were whispering into the ear of the reader. Many consulting relationships require intimacy of accessibility: when the client thinks of you, you're there. I've discovered that the rare prospect who's not in a hurry seldom turns into a client, and when he does, seldom amounts to serious business because there was nothing substantial at stake driving the relationship: he doesn't need you *now*.

These days there's no end to the technologies we can use to make ourselves accessible: phone, fax, voice mail, pager, cellular service, modem. Make use of the tools that suit your situation, but build-in some controls. The more immediate and personal the number (pager, cellular), the more selectively you should share it.

When you're feeling overwhelmed because everybody needs you now, follow the adage that "less sooner is better than more later." Give the client something to hold: confirmation of what you're going to do together, a game plan and schedule, a meeting date. Let him know he's on your priority list and you're paying attention.

You should also look for techniques to shorten the time it takes to produce results. Nearly every successful organization is trying to get more efficient in every aspect of its business to drive down costs and raise productivity: R and D, manufacturing, new product introduction, distribution, responding to customers, adapting the organization to change—you name it. Some companies are calling this push for efficiency "time compression." If you can help your clients meet an objective significantly faster than usual, you're going to get their attention.

I was asked by a corporate client to conduct a retreat for managers and ad agency representatives flown in from around the world. The product was to be a global roll-out plan for a new communications strategy by which the company will develop a consistent image in all its markets around the world. The program affects branding, advertising, packaging, PR, signs, product literature—every part of the business. Offices in fifty-seven countries needed to translate, adapt, and implement the program in unison. The retreat provided only five days in which to iron out the logistics.

For the first three days, I facilitated presentation and discussion of issues, concerns, strategies, and tactics. Every evening I summarized the day's material with my laptop and made overheads so we could build on our progress the following day. On the fourth day, while participants attended offsite meetings, I organized their material into a draft roll-out plan. For two hours on the morning of day five we reviewed and revised the draft plan. Then I excused myself and made revisions while the group heard special presentations.

While we at lunch, the plan was printed and bound. When we adjourned at 2:00 P.M., everyone headed for the airport with the completed plan in hand, along with a timetable and a set of visuals they could use to communicate the plan to their colleagues at home.

The idea of producing the actual printed plan and support visuals by the end of the retreat was new for all of us. My client and I dreamed it up. It was worth a lot to him because it meant his people would take their marching orders with them when they left, while they still had a sense of urgency. Filling this role for a week is like being that guy who used to speedtalk on television for Federal Express. It's intense. You squeeze out the rest stops to reach the conclusion faster. It knocks you out for two or three days afterward while you reclaim the rest stops on your own time.

There are two principles at work here: (1) you can spend *yourself* to compress time and add value to your client's business, and recover after the job is done; (2) to come out whole, you need to budget the recovery time, and price on the basis of value rather than the hours spent.

Co-conspirator

Clients put a premium on your ability to work with their management team. In the first place, if you can't work with their team, the project will go nowhere, unless you've got a specialty that can be performed by one person alone in the dark. Second, whether you're a specialist or a generalist, your business is to help the client improve his business, and that means helping his management team do something new or different than business as usual.

Being a consultant means becoming a partner with your client in her situation. You know that every client's situation is going to be different, but how do you scope it out before you agree to become part of it?

My rule of thumb, as I have already described, is to try finding out up front how the client defines success, and then agreeing on how we're going to work together to achieve it. Next, if I can, I find out how other key people involved in the project will define success. I meet with them individually to learn about their jobs and how they see the project we're about to undertake. I look for some basis of rapport. If I can get someone to confide a hope or frustration, we've shared a small secret, and that's a signal of trust. Trust is the germ of a relationship. I call on each of those seedling relationships when I'm working with the group. And every secret or discrepancy in how people define success gives me a glimpse into the client's situation by revealing the competing forces at work in the organization.

When a company calls in Verne Severson to meet with their marketing staff to talk about a new product idea, one of Verne's greatest strengths as an electronics engineer is to see the concept through the customer's eyes and bridge the gulf between marketing (what the customer needs) and engineering (what's technically feasible). Verne doesn't come in as a contract "techie" to sit in the back of the room and comment on the limits of current technology. He makes himself a member of the customer's team by helping brainstorm, shape ideas, and define the opportunity. The distinction may be subtle, but it is significant in the eyes of his customers.

In my own business, I have found that if I can win the trust of each member of the client's team and build on those relationships during the course of the project, each one of them will want me to succeed in the project, and that becomes a subtle, powerful force in my favor when a consulting project runs into rough waters. The fact that I have no power in the organization is one reason this works, and probably why the CEO called me to begin with. If I am seen to be a personal friend of the boss, my perceived neutrality evaporates and I'm working at a serious disadvantage because I can't be sure I know what anybody else on the team is really thinking.

I think most consulting clients are looking for someone from the outside who knows what it's like on the inside. They want someone with objectivity and freedom from local office politics who can ask questions and make observations that insiders may think but cannot comfortably utter. At the same time, clients want a consultant who knows instinctively what the client's situation is likely to be, what kinds of ideas will go over and what won't.

Here are three examples of what I'm talking about.

1. An Insider's Ability to Think Like the Client

Kathy Tunheim was vice president of PR for Honeywell when she and five of her associates left to start Tunheim Santrizos, their own PR agency, and sold their services back to Honeywell on an outsourcing basis (see chapter 2). Since then, they have built a long list of blue chip clients.

"We were inside a $7-billion company at high levels during a very dynamic time [when Honeywell was restructuring in the late eighties]. As a result, we know how to marry the PR expertise with the insider's sensitivity to the dynamics of corporations in turmoil.

"The best compliment I've gotten was from another client, in an industry very different from any I'd worked in directly myself. He and I sat and talked about some strategic problems in his organization, and how Tunheim Santrizos might be able to help. We agreed to work together. A couple of days later my phone rang and he said, 'I just had to call you, because I've been thinking all day long, I have never worked with an agency that thought like I do. I know that you're thinking of things I would think of if I had the time.'

"I've been on the client side, and I know the client is always thinking, 'Can this agency get up to speed and understand my problem, and can they make it easier for me rather than more difficult?' We all know situations where for the client to get the consultant up to speed to be able to do a job takes more effort than doing the job yourself. Our responsibility is to get into a position where our clients conclude it's easier for them to have us do it than to do it themselves."

2. An Insider's Ability to Talk the Talk

Having run the media function for the cosmetics firm Fabergé, Pattie Garrahy knows what the client wants to hear from its media buyer, and that insight makes her a more effective media-buying consultant (see chapter 7).

"You can't be a media nerd and stand up there in front of the client with a batch of overheads and do technical talk," Pattie says. "You need to fit into the bigger realm of things. We started the agency presentation to UNUM [the insurance company] by saying to the chairman, 'You're trying to reach 3.5 million people who have buying power for your product. Here's how your competition's reaching them. Now here's how we're going to beat the competition and spend only a third of their budget.' By bringing it up that way, rather than launching right into the details of reach, frequency, and gross rating points, we got his attention." She also got his business.

3. An Insider's Track Record

When Bryan Robertson created his company Subsidiary Services International (see chapter 10) and needed his first client, he called on Eastland, a company in the footwear business that knew him by his reputation at Adidas and G.H. Bass.

"They had made some mistakes trying to go to Europe. They kind of knew what they shouldn't do, but they didn't know exactly what they should do. I came in and said, 'Here's me. Here's my company. Here's what I do.' They liked my idea, but more important, they liked my track record and they trusted me." Eastland signed on with a three-year contract and gave Bryan the initial fuel and credibility he needed to build his business.

In each of these examples, what the client values is a consultant who comes with an outsider's perspective and freshness and an insider's ability to connect to the client's own situation.

A Voice for the Forbidden Questions

A first responsibility of consultants is to ask why are things the way they are. Once you understand the answer, you're a big step toward helping the client make them be other than as they are.

I approach jobs with something my friend Bob Walker refers to as my "Boy Scout routine." Basically, I stand up in front of groups and ask questions about their business, how it's structured, and why they do things the way they do—who is their customer, what's their product or service, or how do they make and distribute it, how do they get paid, where's the profit, and so on. I'm after two things: understanding the basics of their business, and uncovering inconsistencies that reveal the competing forces behind decisions they have made. A naive chain of logic often leads to questions the client hasn't considered—such as asking those bankers how they evaluate the profitability of their products.

I accept politics as a legitimate answer for why things are done the way they are. If you're trying to solve a political problem, you work in different ways than when you're trying to solve a financial or technical problem. The top manager of a corporate division, the CEO of a bank, or the president of a hospital couldn't stand up before his managers and ask the same simple questions that I can ask. For one thing, he's supposed to know the answers. And for another, he's part of the politics and a principal reason why things are the way they are.

A consultant has to search for consensus; an executive does not. One of my clients is fond of saying that he's found the most effective way of getting buy-in is to sit down with his managers and say, "I hear what you're saying, but the consensus on this thing, goddamnit, is that we're going to do the following." He knows I can't do that, which is one of the reasons I am useful to him as well as to his management team.

Results Without a Head Count

During times of stress when corporations are laying off managers, a department head with an opening seldom has the luxury of filling it with the person of her choice; it gets filled by someone who was on the excess list. Paying a consultant even at a daily rate that's three or four times what it would cost for an employee to do a similar job is a bargain because the manager gets to hire the consultant of her choice, the consultant gets paid for results and goes away when the job is done, and the consultant does not present a long-term salary and benefits liability.

All of these roles clients often expect of consultants net down to one idea: your job is to make it easier for the client to do business. As long as you define yourself in that capacity, you will not stray far from what the client wants to see when she looks at you.

Ideas to Take Away

- Every client has a preconception of your role, and the better you know what it is, the more effective you can be.
- A consultant is more like the midwife than the mother: you can help the client solve the problem, but you can't solve it for her. Accept the mantle of accountability that lies within the limits of your control.

- Expand your accessibility to clients, but limit your accessibility to others. Under pressure, remember that less sooner is better than more later, and give the client something to hold.
- Borrow against the future to get results faster, but budget time to recover, and charge on the basis of value.
- Being a consultant means being a partner with your client in her situation. Show the objectivity of an outsider and the understanding of an insider. Learn to work with the client's team and be a voice for the forbidden questions.
- Get results and be gone until the next time you're needed.

Making it easier for the client to do business is the organizing principle of Verne Severson's practice, described below. Verne brings the perspective and objectivity of an outsider to his client's new product ideas and functions as part of his client's team, bridging the gulf between engineers and marketing people. He thinks like the client, accepts the accountability burden, and spends himself to add value by shortcutting the development cycle. Even in the gee-whiz world of microcircuits and electronic wizardry, the fundamentals of consulting still apply.

MAKING IT EASIER FOR THE CLIENT TO DO BUSINESS
Profile
VERNE L. SEVERSON
Electronics Engineer, Eden Prairie, MN

The back rooms of large computer and electronics companies are staffed with engineers who can take a product idea from the marketing people and figure out whether it can be built, how, and at what cost. They can design and assemble prototypes, and they can debug and refine the prototypes into successful, marketable products. Smaller firms traditionally turn to outside engineering services like Forward Research, Verne Severson's sole proprietorship, to buy the engineering expertise they need without the expense of supporting it on the inside.

Verne is thirty-nine, tall and thin. His curly salt-and-pepper hair looks like it might blossom to Einsteinian proportions if it ever got free rein. He and his wife, Sue, have two children. He's been a consultant for nine years, a little longer than he's been a dad.

Verne sees the bigger companies trying to get leaner, focusing on what they're good at, such as marketing, and buying more of their engineering on the outside. That's the good news for people like him. The bad news lately is that with all the layoffs, there's a lot of qualified people out on the street, and they're looking more and more like competition.

Before he went independent, Verne was an engineer and manager at several Twin Cities electronics firms. The most recent was a firm called Wordtronix which he helped create to develop and market a new word processor. Wordtronix's product was a technical success but a marketing failure as the market shifted to word processing based on the IBM PC architecture.

When word got around that Wordtronix wasn't going to make it, Verne started getting calls. "A couple people I knew in other companies called me and said, 'While you're looking for a job, how about doing this little design project for me?' I figured why not, and began free-lancing part-time while I was helping Wordtronix close the doors. Next thing I knew, I was too busy with free-lance work to look for a job."

He decided to take consulting seriously. He developed a brochure and cover letter and sent them to a hundred local technology companies. None bit. "The only response I got was standard rejection letters from personnel departments," he says. "It was like they thought I was asking for a job."

After his mailing drew a blank, Verne picked up the phone and called people he knew, engineers and executives acquainted with his work. "I told them I'd gone on my own and would like to do some short-term technical investigations and feasibility work. I couldn't believe the response I got. 'Great! Come by tomorrow!' If I've learned one thing, it's that personal contacts and referrals where there's knowledge of your work are the only ways to market yourself in this business."

The first call Verne placed was to an executive at DataCard Corporation. He paid a visit the next day, and the executive introduced him to a colleague down the hall. The colleague had an engineering problem that was an exact fit with Verne's background, and Verne got the project.

The DataCard experience was typical of Verne's early calls. Another came through a former manufacturer's rep who had gone to work with a technology company to develop a new form of computer-controlled manufacturing machine. Verne called him, learned about the project, and got a contract for the electronics engineering. It was the start of a series of jobs in robotics. "I had no idea how I would do it at the time. I'd never done motor controls. But I knew I could do it, and my confidence gave the client confidence, and he hired me." How did he know he could do it? Verne shrugs his shoulders. "I guess I'm just good at figuring that stuff out. I always have. It's the creative side of this business that I really enjoy."

Verne's consulting services involve tapping his clients' creativity and his own to make advances in the electronic brains that go into a variety of small communications devices from credit card verification terminals to ele ronic lettering machines, motor controls, and protocol converters that enable computers with different operating systems to recognize each other and communicate. His know-how lies partly in understanding how to work effectively with his client's team to develop an innovative and practical product concept, and partly in knowing the latest applications of technologies in a wide variety of fields that he can put to work to turn the concept into a successful prototype.

Verne's consulting projects can involve one or all of the following seven phases of work. (1) Many begin when he's hired to listen to a client's product need and help brainstorm solutions. He bridges a gap that exists in most companies between the marketing people and the engineers. His experience with Wordtronix gave him insights into what makes a business successful and gave him considerable respect for marketing. "It's the marketing people who know what the customer needs, and the engineers who know whether it can be done."

For most of his clients, Verne is there to function as the project engineer, but he works with his client on both sides of the equation, leading the brainstorming to a point where marketing and engineering intersect. Then he addresses the technical questions behind the product idea: can it be done, what would it cost to develop, what would it cost per unit to manufacture.

Verne sees himself as his client's partner. "It's a lot easier for an engineer to tell a marketing guy his idea isn't feasible than to spend the effort figuring out how to make the idea work. There are always technical problems, but they're never the first thing out of my mouth," he says. "I feel that negative thoughts and comments only hinder the creative process. I start by reinforcing the positives to help generate as many ideas as possible. Then look at where we need to focus our creativity. It's an attitude thing, being positive, enjoying the challenge."

(2) If the project goes to the next step, Verne writes formal specifications describing the product's characteristics and produces a quote to develop a set of prototypes.

(3) Next he develops a wiring diagram and parts list, using special software on his computer to help. (4) Then he lays out a printed circuit board on his computer. When he starts, there's a pile of parts at the bottom of the screen, and an outline of the circuit board above. He picks out the parts one by one and puts them on the circuit board where he thinks they should go. The computer connects them, and then he overrides the computer wherever he thinks he can reduce the product's noise or enhance its performance. The output is a floppy disk, which he sends to a printed circuit board manufacturer. They make the board and send it back.

(5) The next step is to build the prototype, soldering a clutter of chips, diodes, capacitors, and resistors onto a plastic board that looks like a green miniature street map. "I'm a degreed engineer, but I still solder. The customer's in a hurry. I could send this out to a contract shop, but I'd have to wait in line. The customer is willing to pay my rates to do it so he can get it built and tested as soon as possible." Verne is acutely aware that when his client is in a hurry providing fast turnaround counts.

Since the customer usually wants five to ten prototypes, Verne builds the first one himself. Then he piles the remaining boards and parts into a box along with some instructions and farms them out to a retired electronics assembler who builds them at home. "She's inexpensive. She loves the work. She's seen it all before. If my instructions aren't clear, she figures them out."

(6) The next step involves testing and debugging the device. Included in this step is testing it for compliance with FCC regulations regarding electromagnetic emissions and for UL safety certification—and making the changes to comply with both. This involves driving forty-five miles to a special lab. He brings much of his workshop with him, so that if the prototype fails the tests, he can redesign it on the test room floor until it works, rather than taking it back to the shop and scheduling a second set of tests. Again, this compresses time for the client.

(7) The final phase involves working with the customer to figure out how the prototype could be improved, and then going back to the lab and reengineering it to make it meet or beat the customer's specs—delivering on the accountability he accepted when he took the job.

From a financial standpoint, Verne's practice has been a success since the first year. He puts in about fifty hours a week, thirty of which are billable. He charges by the job, but he is careful to make the client know his hourly rates, so that if and when add-on work is requested, the terms are known in advance. "I will not negotiate my rate. A discount this week just leads to trouble next week when they come back for more."

On the other hand, he charges on the basis of value, which means his rates vary depending on what services he's providing. Assembly work is billed at a lower rate than computer-aided design work, which in turn is billed cheaper than time spent working directly with the client on the client's premises.

He differentiates himself from in-house electronic engineers in several ways: his creativity, his breadth of knowledge, his can-do attitude, his short turnaround time. Verne sees himself as an engineer's version of a generalist; he lacks the technical depth of an engineering specialty and replaces it with a breadth that specialists typically lack. Through professional journals, he stays current on a weekly basis with breakthroughs in the application of many related technologies, so that when a customer describes a need, he knows what's available to address it. This gives him considerable value. Clients often call and say, "Tell us what's out there that can do this." But taking the generalist route makes him insecure around other engineers who spend more time following scientific advances. And while he feels he lacks depth, he also knows that the combination of his breadth and currency enable him to solve problems, which is what counts with customers.

An important difference between Verne and other free-lancers is that he can take a customer's project from the concept stage all the way through to production of a prototype, whereas most firms that rely on outside electronics consulting have to march their projects around town from the designer to the draftsman, then to a printed circuit board layout house, on to a board fabrication house, assembler, testing facility, and so on.

These are important differences that add value. Consulting—meaning the sum of Verne's methods and services to meet the needs of his customers—adds up to much more than a free-lance version of an in-house electronics engineer, and is worth considerably more to his clients.

7

BRINGING OTHERS IN

Don't build an empire
unless you want to feed one

The Bottom Line Is What's Left Over

When you go from operating solo to having an employee, you may think you've done the world a favor—you know, job creation and all that. My advice is to think twice.

A sole proprietor who works alone or in cahoots with contract associates isn't of much interest to the government. Make your quarterly tax payments and fill out 1099s for associates at year end, and you're square with the world. But hire an employee and hoo-ha, you get an employer number and a bureaucrat from every state and federal agency under God waving forms at you: W-4s, W-2s, SS-8s, SS-4s, FICA, FUTA, worker's compensation, quarterly withholding returns, compliance with immigration and human rights laws, and who knows what.

I once was driven to write a letter to a lady in the bowels of the Minnesota state government saying I was going out of business, so she could unplug my name from the electronic lists of former employers whom the state suspected might in a weak moment hire again, and *the state would want to know*. It was the only way, she said, if I really wanted to stop this constant badgering for reports, even though I was willing to swear on my grandmother's grave that I hadn't had an employee in eighteen months and would never have one again. Maybe Cheeta was on salary and that's what Tarzan meant when he told Jane it's a jungle out there.

Still, every successful consultant faces the question of whether to grow his practice, and if so how. There are good reasons to grow a consulting practice—to broaden your capabilities, dominate a market, make more money, build the team you've always wanted to work with, and provide some backup for times you take off. But when you hire to grow your practice, you will pay for growth in two ways.

First, your focus will shift from consulting to managing staff and from hustling contracts so you can make payroll. The more people you're feeding, the more business you need; the more business you need, the more marketing you must do; the more you market, the more you have to manage.

Second, you pay for growth by subordinating yourself to yet another claimant on the firm's gross revenues. A business owner is at the end of the food chain, and every time you hire, you move yourself down the line another notch, behind everybody in your shop who works for a wage or salary that is not somehow pegged to revenues. In other words, yours is what's left over after you've paid your employees, creditors, suppliers, and landlord. Look at the financial projections in chapter 11 and imagine what would happen if Lucy B. added a $1,500-a-month secretary-receptionist to her fixed monthly expenses, and you will get a good idea of what a commitment even this small can mean to the bottom line.

If your sense of self-worth and job satisfaction depend on managing a big organization, don't head into consulting, go get yourself a management position.

Three Approaches to Growth

If you want your practice to grow, and client work is what you really enjoy, you can choose among at least three approaches.

Get Big

One is to be really aggressive and grow the business large enough so that you can afford to pay somebody else to manage the staff and hustle contracts. If this is your game, here are some tips.

- Prepare financial projections to estimate what critical mass of clients and staff will work financially, what kinds of reserves you will need in order to weather slow periods with high overhead, and what it will take to support a business manager, freeing you to work with clients.
- Use contract workers and temporaries to meet peak periods without adding to fixed costs.

- Peg at least part of staff consultants' salaries to financial performance or their ability to bring in business.

Grow Your Bottom Line Instead of Your Business

Channel your compulsion to build in ways that translate into direct financial benefits without the costs and risks of adding to overhead. The following ideas are treated elsewhere in this book.

- Enhance the quality of your networks and client base (chapter 4).
- Reduce marketing expenses and increase billable hours by turning transactions into relationships (chapter 4).
- Review your pricing structure (chapter 5).
- Convert unpredictable, project-based revenues into sustainable revenue streams (chapters 5 and 10).
- Leverage your know-how into equities (chapter 10).

Opt for Variable Costs Over Fixed Costs

Salaried employees are fixed costs, meaning overhead that must be fed regardless of volume and earnings. Variable costs are those you don't incur until you get the business that will pay them: for example, a secretary from a temporary-help agency whom you hire when you win a contract, and release when the contract ends.

When Verne Severson needs special equipment for an electronics engineering job, he rents it and passes the costs through to his client. If he were to buy the equipment, the investment would represent sunk costs that would add to overhead, requiring him to increase fees or eat a share of his profit margin.

The same principle can be applied to some kinds of employees—people on the client-services side of your business—by tying a significant share of their compensation to their productivity. Since consulting is a labor-intensive business where clients pay by the hour and servicing is selling, it may be reasonable to tie compensation to billings. A typical approach would be to establish a targeted number of hours the employee is expected to bill, which represents his base compensation, and then to structure incentives for every hour billed over the base.

Whatever you do, don't grow your business simply because you can. Do it for a reason.

Len Smart, a data communications consultant, summed up the issues nicely: "One advantage to building a practice with employees is that ultimately you can sell them the business. In a one-person consultancy, when you stop paddling, the boat stops. On the other hand, you need to have something like half-a-dozen people before you can make as much money running a larger organization as you can in a one-man shop. You have to sell the work, manage the work, monitor quality, swallow cost overruns, pay the secretaries, pay the rent. In my business, I don't have a secretary, I don't have to pay rent, I can put 80 percent of my income into my pocket."

How the IRS Defines an Employee, and Why You Should Care

Merrily you roll along, just you and Jack B. Nimble, your fleet-of-foot secretary, doing a land-office business in consulting. You pay Jack as an independent contractor because he's agreeable to the arrangement and you want to avoid all the hassles of having an employee. No withholding, no benefits, just ten bucks an hour and he takes care of his own taxes, insurance, and whatnot. Jack keeps regular hours that you define, does exactly what you want, works in your offices at a desk you own and on a word processor that belongs to you. Just like any normal secretary. And then one day you get a phone call.

It's Rowena May Getcha from the state department of revenue and taxation. It has come to Ms. Getcha's attention that a Mr. Nimble, for whom you've been filing 1099s the past three Januarys, may in fact be an employee. If so, Ms. Getcha breathes, you are personally liable for a penalty equal to 100 percent of the taxes you should have been withholding over the years and didn't. This, you're thinking, is somebody's idea of a *joke*.

Where you have the choice of hiring an employee and taking on the daunting burden of government paperwork, or hiring an independent contractor without the paperwork but the potential for big penalties should the IRS deem your contractor an employee, you are between a rock and a hard place. It really pays to know the difference between the two when you decide on your hiring strategy.

Factors Distinguishing Employees from Independent Contractors

Following are some excerpts from what the IRS says on the subject ("Tax Guide for Small Businesses," Publication 334, Department of the Treasury). Let me add a caution. Even the IRS is not in agreement within itself on the interpretation of these rules. If you're bringing people into your business and you aren't sure if they're employees or independent contractors, consult your attorney.

Independent Contractors   The general rule is that an individual is an *independent contractor* if you, the employer, have the right to control or direct only the result of the work and not the means and methods of accomplishing that result.

You do not have to withhold or pay taxes on payments you make to independent contractors.

Common-Law Employees   Under common law rules, every individual who performs services subject to the will and control of an employer, as to both *what* must be done and *how* it must be done, is an employee. It does not matter that the employer allows the employee discretion and freedom of action, so long as the employer has the *legal right* to control both the method and the result of the services.

Two usual characteristics of an employer-employee relationship are that the employer has the right to discharge the employee and the employer supplies tools and a place to work.

If you have an employer-employee relationship, it makes no difference how it is described. It does not matter if the employee is called an employee, partner, coadventurer, agent, or independent contractor. It does not matter if the payments are measured, how they are made, or what they are called. Nor does it matter whether the individual is employed full-time or part-time.

You must withhold and pay taxes on wages you pay to common-law employees. In addition, if you have a worker "who works at home on materials or goods which you supply and which must be returned to you or to a person you name, if you also furnish specifications for the work to be done," that person is a "statutory employee," and you must withhold and pay Social Security and Medicare taxes. You do not need to withhold and pay taxes for "leased employees" (for example, workers you get from temporary-service agencies) because they are not your employees, they are employees of the firm that provides them to you. Again, from IRS Publication 334:

> *Penalty for Treating an Employee as an Independent Contractor* If you classify an employee as an independent contractor and you had no reasonable basis for doing so, you will have to pay employment taxes for that worker. . . . Further, if you do not withhold income, Social Security, and Medicare taxes from his or her wages, *you may be held personally liable for a penalty of 100% of such taxes* if you are the person responsible for the collection and payment of withholding taxes. [Italics mine.]

Influential Factors

Since the IRS definition seems less than precise and the question can have significant repercussions, I have excerpted and adapted additional information on how to tell an employee from an independent contractor. The following material is from two sources. One is "A Guide to Starting a Business in Minnesota," published in 1991 by the Minnesota Department of Trade and Economic Development. The second is a questionnaire I received from the Minnesota Department of Jobs and Training just this week, trying to ascertain whether work that I performed for one of my clients over a period of several months in 1990 was performed as an employee or as an independent contractor. The information is not specific to Minnesota but is generally applicable under the IRS code.

- *Control:* The most important factor determining whether somebody works for you as an employee or an independent contractor is the extent of your legal control. Do you control *when* the work is to be done? *Where* it is to be done? *Methods* for completing the work? If the answer is yes, the worker is likely to be considered an employee. If your control is limited to defining the *result* of the worker's work, and the worker controls the manner in which he achieves that result, he is likely to be considered an independent contractor.
- *Terms of a contract:* While both employees and independent contractors can work under contracts, a contract that clarifies the nature of your relationship by addressing the issues listed here can support your case that a worker is an independent contractor.
- *Mode of payment:* Workers who are paid on a regular basis are more likely to be considered employees than are those who are paid a fixed fee for a specific service.

- *Materials and tools:* A person who furnishes his own materials and tools is less likely to be considered an employee than one who uses yours.
- *Control of the premises:* A person who works in her own office is more likely to be considered an independent contractor than one who works in an office you provide.
- *Right of discharge:* A person is more likely to be considered an employee if you have the right to set terms of employment and to fire him (compared, for example, to a person you get from a temporary-services agency).
- *Continuity:* A person you use on a continuous or frequently recurring basis is more likely to be considered an employee than is someone you use on a irregular basis.
- *Ability to realize a profit or loss:* Someone who can make a profit or loss as the result of working for you is more likely to be considered an independent contractor.
- *Services available to the public:* Somebody who markets himself to others at the same time he's working for you is more likely to be considered an independent contractor.
- *Investment in facilities:* Somebody who has put her own money into equipment and facilities to perform her work is more likely to be considered an independent contractor.
- *Employment benefits:* If you provide benefits like worker's compensation, insurance, or vacation pay to a worker, she is more likely to be considered an employee.

Employee Tax Withholdings and Filings

Chapter 14 presents a twenty-one step checklist to identify and comply with withholding and filing requirements of employers. Note that *twenty* of the steps involve complying with the paperwork required where you have an employee, and only *one* applies to filings required for payments you make to independent contractors.

There is very little in the way of work that you cannot contract out in place of doing it yourself or through employees you hire. I know one consultant whose revenues run into seven figures, yet he hasn't a single employee. He buys services from businesses who have employees. If you decide to hire, know the rules and follow them. If you need advice, call your accountant or your attorney.

In addition to making sure you correctly classify anybody who works for you, make sure you are taking all the appropriate steps to be deemed a consultant *yourself*, and not an employee. To make sure that taxpayers who report consulting income are in fact consultants and not employees, the IRS is scrutinizing their returns. My accountant says that this will continue to be a hot issue in the nineties, because so many people are consulting with their employers following retirement and so many are leaving their jobs to go independent and outsource to their former employers. These people may consider themselves to be consultants, but they will not meet the IRS test unless they are aggressively pursuing other clients, pricing and billing on the basis of projects, signing agreements, and exhibiting the other characteristics of independent contractors.

Buying the Milk and Not the Cow

Here are three alternative strategies for meeting your needs without resorting to hiring employees.

Collaborate With Other Consultants

When I have a client who needs market research support, I bring in Diane Page (see chapter 5). When a job calls for financial expertise, I know a finance consultant I can bring in. If there a program-evaluation component, I sweet-talk my mentor, Bob Walker, out of retirement to take a piece of the project. In each case, the associate and I jointly work up the project bid, define the scope of work, agree on each party's responsibilities, and agree on the distribution of proceeds before the project begins.

When I initiate the collaboration, I take the lead in working with the client. When I am brought in as a collaborator in another consultant's project, the other consultant takes the lead. An important distinguishing characteristic in a collaboration is that once each of us has committed to the deal, we are committed to seeing it through at the quoted price, sharing in the project's risks and rewards. Whoever brought the project in might take a finder's fee or mark up the others' fees to the client. But if the budget runs over, it will come out of each of our hides in the same ratio that the project was bid. And if we come out ahead, we share in the profits in the same ratio.

Advantages

- I have access to really good people without having them on salary.
- Collaboration leads to referrals and enables me to take jobs I would otherwise have to pass up.
- Fixed-price deals limit my financial exposure to overruns and provide an incentive for the others to meet project budgets and timetables.
- For those of us who usually work alone, collaboration seems like a party.

Where to find potential collaborators? Networking is the best way I know, but state and local chapters of trade associations can also provide referrals. Another possibility, if you use data base services, is to post a query on an electronic bulletin board.

Buy the Services of Contract Workers

This option involves using independent contractors as temporary staff. You are not asking them to share in the risks and profits of the job, simply to do their part at the price you agree and be gone. This kind of arrangement is common when you are bringing in support staff and suppliers like researchers or survey workers. You might also bring in an expert as a contract worker for a short but critical part of a job.

Advantages

- You treat staffing as a variable rather than fixed cost.
- You avoid the paperwork associated with employment.

Caveat: a contract worker who stays around for long may begin to look like an employee in the eyes of the government. Make sure the relationship meets the tests of an independent contractor.

I was recently asked by a corporate client to downsize and revamp a comprehensive policy manual that had grown too thick and become obscure because of bureaucratic language. The job involved interviewing users of the manual to find out what they wanted it to contain and how they would like the material organized, and then updating and simplifying the contents. I couldn't afford the time to do the job and my rates would have been prohibitive, so I called an ace copy editor I know who had just retired.

We met with the client to pin down the specifics of the job, and then the copy editor gave me a fixed price for doing the work. I turned around and quoted a price to my client, marking up my colleague's fee by 20 percent, and adding in some hours of my own to oversee the project.

From time to time you may need to contract for the services of a highly focused specialist or an expert. How to find one? Try an information service like Teltech Resource Network Corporation in Minneapolis (1-800/833-8330) whose Network of Experts contains the names of 2,500 of the top technical professionals in the country. Other possibilities: conduct bibliographic searches in the field of expertise and get authors' names; contact national trade associations; use bulletin boards on data base services; check out the book *Lesko's Info-Power Source Book* published by Matthew Lesko, which contains a section featuring some 8,000 experts in various levels of government.

Nest Your Practice Within a Larger Organization

This is the sort of arrangement where you set up shop in a spare office of an established firm and pay a monthly rent that includes, in addition to the space, heat, and lights, certain support services like clerical, receptionist, and research services that you would otherwise have to buy on your own. This assumes that your host has staff on board with time available to meet your needs. I have nested my practice in two different organizations, and it has been an exceptionally simple and satisfying way to minimize overhead while getting access to the resources of a much larger organization, and companionship in the bargain.

Following are examples of how several consultants profiled in this book have expanded their businesses—by hiring employees, forging partnerships, collaborating with other consultants, hiring contract workers, and nesting their businesses within other organizations.

Brizius & Foster, Public Affairs Consultants to Governors   Jack Brizius and Sue Foster have expanded their business by collaborating with other consultants and by hiring. As their business evolved, Jack and Sue established relationships with other independent public policy consultants who were working at the state level. Eventually, they formed a loose-knit collaboration called State Research Associates, a network of ten consultants managed by two of their members in Kentucky who handled clerical support, billing, and other administrative tasks.

The notion behind the association was partly to get marketing leverage by tapping one anothers' strong relationships in different states, and partly to create a larger presence in the market able to take on more complex jobs requiring a team approach. The members of the association agreed to adjust their fee schedules so that they all billed at the same daily rate, and to pay the association 10 percent off the top as a commission.

Brizius and Foster has two employees, a secretary and a research assistant. For the first four or five years, they hired clerical services on an as-needed basis, gradually reaching a point where they needed their own part-time secretary. When they published "States in Profile," their support needs grew and they made the position full-time. To provide research support and handle administrative tasks, they hired their part-time research assistant three years ago for three days a week.

Though having employees poses its own pitfalls, Jack feels that they are essential to free Sue and him from the details of the business in order to be creative. "If overhead gets too high, you spend all your time trying to support it. Ultimately, you come to realize what your minimum level of support needs are, and how to contract out to handle peak periods."

Louisa Casadei, Communication Consultant   When a client's needs are bigger than Louisa can handle on her own, she brings in other consultants as associates. She has structured her relationships with associates in various ways but now prefers to function like a general contractor, meaning she negotiates with the client and assumes responsibility for the job, and pays her associates an hourly rate.

"I used to work in partnerships, but I ended up being the one who managed the job, handled the money, filled out 1099s at tax time, and so on. So now I make sure I get paid for that administration by negotiating a fixed rate with my associate that will support a modest markup to the client." She also found she needed more control over the product, and she didn't often feel the benefits of a partnership approach to jobs were entirely mutual.

Verne Severson, Electronics Consultant   Verne consults with his clients on their product ideas through a sole proprietorship called Forward Research, but when he has a product idea of his own, he develops and sells it through a corporation he and a friend created named Comm-Star. When Verne decided he needed an employee to support his consulting practice, he hired a technician to work in the lab, freeing Verne to spend more time with clients.

Although the technician works for Verne at Forward Research, he is actually employed by CommStar, the corporation, which sells the employee's time to Forward Research. Sounds complicated, but it actually simplifies Verne's life. Being a corporation, CommStar provides liability protections that Verne doesn't have in a sole proprietorship. Also, CommStar has another employee and is already set up to handle the paperwork associated with employee taxes and withholding. Verne's accountant set up the record keeping and tax filing system for Comm-Star, and Verne's partner in CommStar maintains the system, issuing paychecks, handling withholding, and filing returns. (Read more about the differences between a sole proprietorship and a corporation in chapter 11.)

Verne has structured his technician's salary in two parts, base plus bonus. The bonus is paid quarterly and tied to the financial performance of Forward Research, providing an incentive to the employee to help keep costs down and revenues up. Their employment agreement spells out the base salary and the equation for calculating quarterly bonuses. Benefits include a combined vacation and sick pay allowance, and cash in lieu of health insurance.

Verne's partner in CommStar is a former colleague with a strong marketing and contract negotiation background that complements Verne's technical expertise. They created CommStar to design and produce products of their own, capitalizing on opportunities that arise in the course of Verne's consulting practice (see chapter 10). CommStar is incorporated both to provide liability protections and to establish a means for the two to share ownership. Neither draws a salary from CommStar, although they may sell consulting services to the corporation from time to time to drain off surplus cash.

Diane Page, Market Research Consultant   Diane has used three techniques to expand her business without adding to fixed costs or bringing on employees: she has formed a partnership with other consultants; nested her business within a larger firm; and made a practice of using contract workers for support services.

She and two other independent consultants in related fields—advertising creative and copy writing—discovered an opportunity to capture business that they saw their clients giving to other firms. They had to team up to get it, so they formed Leapfrog Associates. "Leapfrog is a way to work together on an as-needed basis without establishing serious overhead," Diane says. Leapfrog's legal form is a partnership. Through Leapfrog, Diane and the other partners help consumer packaged goods companies name new products, invent new product concepts, and develop promotional programs. "We learn about these opportunities in our individual consulting practices, but a solo consultant just can't get the bigger projects. You have to create an *organization* if you want to bid against the big shops. It gives you a positioning you don't have as a free-lancer." Leapfrog brings in other consultants on a fixed-price, job-at-a-time basis depending on the nature of the assignment.

Leapfrog accounts for about a third of Diane's consulting income. Its only employee is a part-time business manager who handles client scheduling, arrangements with outside consultants, billing, and administration. The business manager also takes care of all the withholding and paperwork associated with her own compensation. "Having a hired manager makes the arrangement work. Not just because she handles the details, which is essential, but because she's the neutral party we need to represent the best interests of the partnership."

The balance of Diane's consulting is practiced as a sole proprietor out of an office at a firm called N. K. Friedrichs & Associates, Inc., a survey research firm from which she sublets space. Diane's monthly rent covers her office, heat, lights, receptionist services, and coffee. She pays by the hour for secretarial support and by the sheet for photocopying.

Diane says nesting works best when you co-locate with others related to your field ("but not competitors") because the proximity creates synergy and moral support. "When you walk across the hall to visit, they know your business, your language, your issues." In some cases, she says, you can swap services to keep your overhead down, as she did in an earlier setting where she traded focus group moderating for rent.

Diane has been in business for herself more than twenty-one years and has never had to hire an employee. She goes outside for tape transcription services, word processing, focus-group recruiting services, filing, and bookkeeping. "You look for people who are underemployed, and hire them at an hourly rate. There's an awful lot of people out there who have terrific skills and are eager for the work."

These examples are testimony that there are a lot of ways to grow your business short of bringing in employees. Nonetheless, sometimes hiring *is* the best option, as in Verne's case. If you're planning to bring in employees, here are some thoughts about employment benefits, contracts, noncompete agreements, and the like.

Employment Benefits

Employers commonly provide some form of health insurance, sick leave, vacation, and retirement benefits to employees. At the time of this writing, employers are not *required* to provide these or any other fringe benefits to employees. However, mandated employment benefits—particularly health insurance—may become a fact of life before long. Chapter 13 provides tips for getting access fringe benefits in a small or one-person consulting practice.

A retirement plan that you have set up for yourself must be extended to employees you hire, or it will be deemed discriminatory and no longer eligible for favorable tax treatment. An alternative is to amend the plan when you bring on employees so that it suits your changed circumstances. Note, too, that in certain situations it may be preferable for you to negotiate cash in lieu of a fringe benefit that is important to an employee but difficult for you to provide.

Employment Agreements

Something called the "employment at will" doctrine states that an employment relationship can be terminated at any time for any legal reason, or for no reason, by either the employee or the employer, with or without notice. In Minnesota, this doctrine applies in the absence of another written or spoken employment agreement. It may apply in your state as well (check with your state's department of labor to find out more about your rights and obligations as an employer).

For boilerpate employment contracts go to the library or check software like Home Lawyer, published by MECA. You may want to run any agreement past your own attorney before executing it.

Assignment of Patents and Inventions

In some states, including Minnesota, employment agreements are required to exclude inventions that are developed entirely on the employee's own time, that do not result from employee's work for you, do not draw on your equipment or resources, and do not relate to your business.

Noncompete Agreements

A noncompete agreement has to be aimed to protect your legitimate business interests and limited in time, or it will not hold up. It must also be supported by "adequate consideration," meaning that the employee is given something of value in exchange for signing it. Adequate consideration could be the initial job, a promotion, cash payment, or it may be something else. But you cannot spring a noncompete agreement on an established employee without providing something of value in exchange, or it will not hold up.

When You Decide to Hire

Here are six pointers from the consultants I interviewed, to help you make the right moves when you decide to become an employer.

Before You Hire

1. Know the objective that hiring will enable you to achieve, and satisfy yourself there isn't a preferable way to achieve the same end—say, buying support from a temporary services agency, contracting it out, teaming up with another consultant.
2. Try to find out whether you and the new employee are compatible. The best way is to work together. If possible, bring him on as an independent contractor at the outset so you can get a feel for what a long-term association will be like.
3. Read through the twenty-one steps in chapter 14, "Checklist for hiring an employee," for a taste of the government paperwork you're letting yourself in for. Make sure the person you hire has the ability to handle these tasks, unless you'd rather fill out forms than work for a living, or you have somebody else on board to handle this.

When You Negotiate the Deal

4. Write an employment agreement that spells out the objectives of the relationship, expectations and responsibilities on each side, and how the relationship can be terminated.

5. Make sure you and the new employee both understand what's required to make this financial commitment pay off for your business. For example, if you hire someone to sell for you, set targets that will more than offset the added overhead, and peg some of the compensation to financial performance. If you hire some to handle administrative work so you can spend more time with clients, figure out how many additional hours you need to bill to break even, and hold yourself accountable for it. If you hire to bring complementary expertise into your business, figure out how you're going to charge for that expertise, and then set targets and track results.

After You Hire

6. Pay attention to your management style. You can't skulk in a corner like you could when you worked alone. Be sensitive to your employee's needs, let him know what's on your mind, help him see how he is contributing to the success of the business. Communicate.

If you hire employees to cope with a surge in business that doesn't sustain itself, you'll have to let them go eventually, to survive, or increase your reserve to ride out lean periods (see chapter 12). On the other hand, if business stays strong and you need the extra hands, you might look back and bless the day you made the decision to hire. Ultimately, you may even find yourself transferring an equity position to an employee to cement a close relationship and share the rewards of building the business.

Ideas to Take Away

- When you hire your first employee, you open yourself to a whole new world of paperwork and taxes.
- Every time you hire, the further you move down the food chain, and the more you will be marketing and managing in place of consulting.
- Control overhead: opt for variable costs over fixed costs, tie compensation to performance.
- Alternatives to hiring include collaborating, contracting out, nesting your practice within a larger organization, growing your bottom line instead of your head count.
- The IRS imposes stiff penalties for treating employees as contract workers and failing to pay employment taxes. The more you con-

trol *how, when,* and *where* a worker performs his work, the more
likely he will be deemed an employee.
• When you decide to hire, make sure you and your employee both
know what's required to make the decision pay off for your business.

Pattie Garrahy's business grew like topsy. She was lured into consulting by a network of former clients and associates who knew her capabilities and wanted her help. Her business multiplied at nearly every turn, and the same network proved a godsend for finding the people to help Pattie meet her commitments. Today, she relies on a mix of collaborative and contractual relationships to extend her reach without building herself an empire. And yet, as successful as these arrangements have proven, the notion of bringing in a partner has an appeal of its own, quite separate from the need for helping hands. See her profile, which follows.

COLLABORATORS IN A "FAIRNESS SYSTEM"
Profile
PATTIE GARRAHY
Media Consultant, Providence, RI

Pattie Garrahy and her friends are reinventing how to be in business in the nineties.

PGR Media (Pattie's business) and four other firms have taken over most of the third floor of a prominent Providence office building where they share equipment and support services, giving each of them access to the companionship and resources of a big organization without the overhead or management hassles.

Pattie is an advertising media planner and buyer. Another tenant is a well-known advertising art director. Another is a copywriter. Another an account director. Another is Pattie's husband, Bryan Robertson, with his young export marketing business. Even the receptionist is an independent contractor, billing her time for various support services as they are used by the different tenants of the space. Some of the tenants are incorporated, the others do business as sole proprietors. One holds a lease with the landlord and sublets to the other four. For the most part they all work independently, but given the complementary nature of their backgrounds, it's not surprising to learn that they have taken advantage of opportunities to collaborate as well.

There is another aspect of Pattie's business that seems especially right for the times. Instead of hiring full-time employees, she has tapped into a reservoir of part-time talent that is going overlooked by most employers: women like herself who have bailed out of the executive suite in order to raise a family and have evolved into consulting because it provides an opportunity to blend motherhood and career. *Flexibility, fairness,* and *common sense* are words that characterize these arrangements. And so is *profit.*

Pattie is thirty-seven, a wife, a mother of two children, and president of her own firm. Through PGR Media, Pattie will not only help you develop a media plan that outsmarts your competition, she'll also go out and drive a hard bargain with the people who sell the space for your ads. What's the difference? Planning services are billed by the hour, whereas media buying is a business of commissions. Her first client for media buying practically had to beg Pattie to place their multimillion-dollar media order to implement the plan she'd developed for them, and pocket the five-figure commission. ("I was consulting. I wasn't in the media-buying business.")

Pattie and I first met in the sitting room of her suite at Boston's Ritz Carlton, which stands at the edge of the Public Garden, stolid as old money. She and her husband were in town for the Boston Ad Club's annual black-tie charity auction the night before.

"I bought a guy playing the piano at a party," Pattie said when I asked how the evening had gone. "My husband said, 'Gee, three hundred dollars. What a bargain. All we need now are a piano and a party.'" There is something dramatic about Pattie—strawberry-blond hair swooping up from a slender face, big eyes, a straight-cut navy dress with big gold buttons, topped off by a navy scarf dappled in orange and pink and yellow flowers. She offered me a juice from the minibar, and a chair in the corner, and she settled into an overstuffed sofa to let me begin the interview.

Like many people who ultimately migrate into consulting, Pattie had a stroke of good fortune early in her career that gave her a practical education on a subject that costs businesses a lot of money.

She was only a few years out of college, with limited experience working in the media departments of several Providence ad agencies, when she was offered a position as media supervisor for a start-up agency called Leonard Monahan Saabye. She joined LMS on the ground floor and rose in the agency as their billings climbed from $3 million to nearly $20 million less than six years later.

During that time, Pattie developed a media department of nine people, established computer systems with on-line research, was named vice president at age twenty-six, and met the man she would marry—Bryan was a Leonard Monahan Saabye account director. In addition to what she learned during those years with LMS, the professional network she developed proved invaluable several years later, bringing her clients and leading her to the other professionals with whom she would eventually join forces.

Pattie and Bryan left Leonard Monahan Saabye when Bryan got hired away by Adidas in New Jersey. Pattie took a position in Manhattan as media director for Fabergé, working in the Trump Tower in the "wild business of cosmetics." Within eighteen months she was pregnant. She took maternity leave, and her feelings about career were quickly eclipsed by her feelings about motherhood. As the time approached to return to the corporate life, she couldn't face the prospect of leaving her daughter, Laura. "I said, 'This is what I should be doing.' I was completely following my heart. I resigned from Fabergé and cut our income by 60 percent."

This is when consulting first poked its nose into her tent. "Some Fabergé product people asked me to do projects, review media plans, not big jobs. Pretty soon I had a low-level flow of media consulting in and out of my home."

By 1988, Bryan took a job with G.H. Bass in Falmouth, Maine, and they moved to Portland. "Once I got back to New England, my old network became active. Bob Saabye, one of the founders of LMS, was now working on his own and called to ask if I wanted to do some of the 'business' work with his clients. His thing is the creative side. I was flattered. And I was ready for the work."

They worked together under the name Saabye & Company. Pattie says this was the point when she started getting serious about consulting. "It got me back into pitching the business, doing a little more than media work, helping companies with marketing positioning, which really did tap into what I'd learned at Fabergé."

It was while she was pregnant with her second daughter that she took her next big step in consulting. She "played spouse" on a trip to the Super Bowl with Bryan and met Bud Guthrie of the Guthrie Group advertising agency. Through Guthrie, Pattie began doing media planning for UNUM, the big Portland-based insurance company, and her consulting practice became a concerted livelihood. She hired a "household manager" four days a week and worked two days as media director at the Guthrie Group, and two days with Saabye.

And then she got a call from a former LMS client named Betsy Richardson. Betsy had joined a corporation called Lifeline as vice president of marketing, heard Pattie was consulting, and called because Lifeline needed help.

Lifeline was using a large media-buying company and Betsy didn't feel comfortable with the level of expertise and service. Pattie contracted to look at the situation. She agreed that Lifeline wasn't getting what they needed, and she recommended an entirely new strategy. Pattie thought that the new media strategy would be executed by Lifeline, through their agency.

But Betsy Richardson had a different idea. "She said, 'You don't realize how good you are. Why don't you must pitch our whole business?' I didn't think I was set up to handle it—I didn't have forms, I didn't have credit, I didn't have a computer—but Bryan said, 'Of course you can do this.' He got fired up about it, and Betsy was all fired up, and I figured if I wimped out of this one, that would be pretty pathetic. So I made up a name for myself, PGR Media, a mission statement, some presentation boards, and went into Lifeline's executive offices and pitched their account. Two days later I had the business—several million dollars."

When she discovered she'd won it, she had to move fast to turn PGR Media into more than a mission statement and a few presentation boards. At the time, Bryan had left G.H. Bass to set up *his* own consulting firm, and they were moving back to Providence. "It was wild," Pattie says. "Stress overload."

Bryan's decision to go into business for himself was one of the forces that propelled Pattie to pursue the Lifeline media account—"the money looked good!" She got a $20,000 line of credit from a bank, bought computers, phones, and trade directories. Her colleague Bob Saabye had space on the third floor of a Providence office building, and some of that space was being vacated, so Pattie and Bryan moved their fledgling companies into adjacent offices in Saabye's space.

Pattie needed to bring some people on board and get to work. "I had this client who was waiting for me to do the work, and I had to get my business together quickly. I wanted it to be clear and simple, and I went to a lawyer for advice. He said to work as a sole proprietor and bring in support people as independent contractors. 'We can always change it later.' "

Pattie called around to people she knew from her days at LMS and asked for names of people who might come to work immediately on the Lifeline project. She found a woman named Terry McGrath. Terry had been a senior executive at the Hill, Holliday and also at Young & Rubicam agencies, and wanted to work three days a week while she raised her two children.

"We worked out an estimate of the time involved and agreed on a rate. And that's when we worked out what I call the 'fairness structure.' We had a problem, and the fairness structure was our solution. Media planning work should be compensated, in my opinion, at a higher rate than execution, because it takes a lot more skill. Once the media plan is figured out, the execution is basically mechanical. I could have had Terry work with me on the plan and then gone out and gotten somebody else to execute it at a lower rate, which I didn't really want to do. Or Terry could have a sliding rate that would be higher or lower depending on the work she was doing. That was my preference, and it was hers, too."

Terry went to work for PGR Media as an independent contractor, paid one hourly rate for media planning work and a lesser rate for execution.

Pattie also felt she needed help limiting her financial exposure and handling administrative details while she focused on serving clients and making money. She worked her network to find somebody with a finance background and connected up with Fran Lemire, a CPA and former coemployee and officer at LMS. Fran had three kids and wanted part-time work. Pattie hired her as an independent contractor two days a week to handle finances, billing, cash flow, and administration. Again, Pattie applied the "fairness structure," negotiating a higher rate when Fran is doing complex financial analysis and planning, and a lower rate for billing and administration.

The entire arrangement has worked well. "I have these two very senior women who could be making six-figure incomes but who would rather have the flexibility of blending work and family."

By joining forces as independent contractors, they have had a chance to get to know one another and better judge how they want the professional relationship to evolve. Fran has fairly low visibility at PGR Media because of the nature of her work, but Terry has a lot of client contact. Involving her in the Lifeline account as a collaborator rather than employee left Pattie important options if the relationship didn't gel.

"I had a chance to see how we worked together, how she handled presentations, how she related to the client. She's terrific. We really bonded on the Lifeline account, and when I landed the next client, I felt comfortable introducing them to Terry. And not long after that, Terry brought a client into the firm." When that happened, Pattie and Terry sat down and negotiated terms that provided Terry financial recognition for bringing in a client.

At this point, Pattie is thinking of incorporating PGR Media so that she can share ownership at some level with Terry and Fran. She wants to provide a financial incentive for them to be mindful of the firm's overall profitability. "Making them partners and coinvestors is a way of vesting them in the success of the business. They can keep things going while I'm off with clients. By the same token, as the business grows and requires more staff support, we can meet that need through other independent contractors. So we build our base at the same time we preserve our flexibility."

Pattie admits that bringing Terry and Fran into the business isn't strictly a dollars and cents issue. She really likes the idea of sharing the excitement of growing the business. "In a funny way it's like that joy of being parents. Sharing the experience with somebody you like makes it doubly rewarding."

8 WORK, MONEY, AND PRIVATE LIVES

Consulting notes from the interior

Breaking Rules

Making it on your own in the marketplace changes the way you see yourself. One day you're a stable sort with a regular job and regular hours slugging it out like regular people. An employee. A player in a system of reporting relationships, performance reviews, grade levels, pay ranges. It's a system with definition and known expectations, a place you belong. In America, especially for men, what you do and how you're paid is who you are.

Now chuck that to go on your own. Suddenly you're hanging out there naked hawking yourself to anybody who's fool enough to make eye contact. No rules. No boss. No grade level. No title or big-ass company name on your business card. Just you. And people are actually *buying*.

It's an eye opener and one hell of a good feeling. It's a feeling of power and freedom. With it comes a big dose of free-floating anxiety, because you know it's not supposed to work out this way—for years you've defined your future by the kinds of *jobs* you could get, and you can't help but suspect this early success at independence is really just a string of lucky breaks or the doing of sympathetic friends, and that you are tripping lightly down the garden path to financial ruin and humiliation.

Some years ago I was struck by research results I read in a magazine for entrepreneurs. The research was designed to answer the question "What kinds of people make successful entrepreneurs?" and it revealed that many very successful entrepreneurs often feel like shams waiting to be exposed.

The reason, I think, is because they've gone against the grain, trading on common sense and good people skills, and when you do that in our society, when you're not an expert or a Harvard MBA, you have no rightful claim on success. If in addition you're a woman or a minority, if you're physically disabled or someone who's been laid off because the company doesn't need you anymore, how could you *possibly* expect to succeed in the market on your own?

Going on your own is about breaking these "rules," redefining who you are, redesigning your life. In *Swim with the Sharks* (Morrow, 1988), Harvey Mackay says that the typical corporate compensation system is structured in a way that has you spending the bulk of your career being paid less than you're worth so the company can make money, and the last years being paid more than you're worth so there's an incentive to hang in there.

When you go on your own, you are opting out of that system. You are taking yourself into the open market, charging fair value for your time, and finding clients who will happily pay and feel themselves fortunate to have found you. This changes your relationship to work and opens a world of possibilities that you'd never seen before. The sense of affirmation—of being desirable—extends to every facet of your life, including the very personal.

Redesigning Your Life

The effects are profound not because of the significance of the work you do, but because, like all of us, so much of your life is defined by the way you make your living. Salary and position underpin decisions about the mortgages we sign and the cars we drive. Nine-to-five jobs carve our days into patterns and our years into forty-odd weeks of work, eleven holidays, a few days of hooky, and company-sanctioned vacations. When you go on your own, you have an opportunity to unplug from those patterns and design your life to fit what works best for you.

Sometimes the most important changes are invisible. Kathy Tunheim, president of the PR consulting firm Tunheim Santrizos (see chapter 2), is thirty-six and married with children ages eight and four. Having left as vice president of Honeywell to run her own shop, she finds one of the biggest differences is simply who decides her priorities.

"When you're a senior staff person in a company like Honeywell, it really isn't for you to decide if you can live with the implications or not. That's for the company to decide, and as much as you might resent it and think, 'Don't they want everybody to have a life?', well, that's why you get paid an extremely significant amount of money, because they actually do get to decide. Having left, I don't work a lot fewer hours, but I do have the opportunity to make choices that weren't mine to make before."

For some people one of the best rewards of independence is the opportunity to work out of phase with the rest of society, leaving them free to shop when the stores are quiet and vacation while others work. For Louisa Casadei (see chapter 1), leaving her job as a manager at Bain and Company to run her own business as a communication consultant, redesigning her life means escaping the ranks of management to work directly with clients, and striking a better balance between her career and other interests. She makes good money by anyone's standards and could make more, but, she says, "one of the reasons I went into consulting was to get more personal time."

Since I initially interviewed her, Louisa and her husband, Eric, started a family, and when I caught up with her again she was eight months pregnant and remanded to her sofa by her doctor. We talked about balancing work and motherhood. "I hope I've learned some lessons from running my own business that I can bring to mothering in the nineties—like how to manage my time and resources. How to manage stress.

"I think a nineties mother is going to have to do more balancing. A typical fifties mother had one main priority: family. It's okay for a nineties mother to have self as a priority, too. And career, and maintaining your relationship with your husband. A nineties mother looks more outside the home for help than a fifties mother did. I have a cleaning person, for example. I used to ask myself, Why would I have to have a cleaning person—I'm capable, I'm healthy. Well, it's because I have other priorities."

Louisa has scheduled three months for maternity leave following the baby's birth, a month longer than most mothers with jobs. She has made arrangements with an associate to work with some of her clients during that period, but other clients where she does senior-level consulting have agreed to postpone the work they need until Louisa can return and do it personally. Meantime, those clients are calling and sending notes and bonbons to help her pass the slow month she's spending on her sofa. "I get very excited about those calls, and as much as I'm looking forward to this baby, I know my work is really important to me."

When she's back in commission Louisa will have someone come into her home to help with the baby. Louisa expects to be working outside the home at her clients' offices two to three days every other week, and at home during intervening weeks. "We'll need to ease into it and find out what works for the baby, what works for me, what works for my husband. And there's also the stress of what other people are thinking of me. My mother-in-law. My mother."

I asked Louisa what messages she gives herself that this is okay. "The first one that comes to mind is financial. But that's not most important. I really believe work is a part of me, and I'm fortunate to love what I do. I'm going to be a better mother when I have been contributing to the bigger world. I feel lucky that I can make that choice."

A friend of mine in the employment counseling business once told me that the most important factor is getting the unemployed back to work is to internalize what he called their locus of control. He explained it this way. If you feel that other people determine whether or not you get a job, you have little chance of getting one. If you feel that you control whether or not you get a job, you probably will.

The idea of a locus of control appeals to me. When you leave a job and go on your own, the locus of control shifts from your employer to you. If you don't like the way things are, you have the power to change them. If, like my friend Joan Solomon, the synapses in your prodigious brain just won't fire before noon, organize your business to open its doors after noon. Challenge your assumptions about work and its place in your life. A business that works for you, builds on your strengths, resonates with your cycles and attitudes, is a business that will add to the fullness of your life. If you go into consulting and do not take the opportunity to redesign your life, either you have been not listening to your own needs for too long, or you are missing the greatest jewel that consulting offers.

In their book *American Couples* (Morrow, 1983), Philip Blumstein and Pepper Schwartz report on how attitudes about work, money, and sex affect the relationships of four kinds of couples: married men and women, cohabitating men and women, gay couples, and lesbian couples. It is a fascinating study dealing with the most intimate issues of income and power, money management, trust, equality, job satisfaction, relationship satisfaction, and sexual behavior and fulfillment. The authors find that for most of us self-worth is strongly affected by the work we perform and our income, but only gay men judge their success by comparing it to what their partners have achieved.

> We believe that when men evaluate their success they look for someone to measure themselves against. The likely comparisons have traditionally

been other men—co-workers, people in similar jobs, friends, or neighbors. Gay men have another man close to them—their partner—who
can become a basis for comparison. Heterosexual men do not feel especially successful when their female partners make little money. They
have not been accustomed to competing with women because it is difficult for women to achieve the same level of earning power as men do in
our society.

Blumstein and Schwartz also find than an employed woman is likely to
be happier with her marriage if she is happy with her job. Wives, hus-
bands, and cohabiting women all tend to be happier in their relationships if their partners are successful in their jobs, but male cohabitators
are too competitive with their partners for the women's success to enhance the relationship.

While Blumstein and Schwartz find that fighting about the intrusion
of work into the relationship can undermine a couple's satisfaction, the
authors don't draw direct links between job satisfaction, self-esteem,
and sexual activity. My premise is simply that (1) when you change the
work equation by going on your own and internalizing the locus of
control, you change how you feel about yourself, and (2) in breaking
with convention you open yourself to new ways of living and relating to
others.

You discover you can leave behind some of your obsessions about
time and structure and competition. If your self-worth is no longer influenced by your position and salary, and your priorities are no longer
influenced by the mission and goals of an organization, you have to
apply within for the answers. What you hear first is "make money,
buster," but as that gets easier you come to trust your financial security, relax about you·r competence and self-worth, and hear other messages from within about what you want from your life and your ability
to get it. Your needs and interests change with success, and since you
have the locus of control, you have the power to change your life to
meet them.

In this era when couples are too busy to take time for each other, I
will wager that those of us who have broken away to create our own
rules spend less time with relationships that are not important to us
and invest more in the relationships we care about. If it has never
crossed your mind to make love for an hour on a workday afternoon
while others toil in the vineyards, go into consulting. It might give you
ideas.

Why Breaking Rules Is Harder for
People of Color

Alexs Pate is a black man who left a management position at Control Data to go on his own. He ran a successful consulting business for two years, but the further he strayed from the rules of convention the more he was drawn to his true passion, which is writing. Over the past six years he has created a new life for himself as a writer, poet, and performance artist. When I worked with him at Control Data, Alexs wore Armani suits and shirts by Ralph Lauren. Today he wears dreadlocks and denim. We went to lunch and talked about how throwing over a successful mainstream career to reinvent life on your own terms is different for people of color than whites.

"The concept of running against convention being legitimate does not exist in the minority community," he told me. "It is a very, very big risk for a person of color because their whole thing and their parents' thing before them has been to conquer the system as it's set up. We're raised for it. 'You be *better* than them! You do what they need you to do, so you can get yourself a good job.' It's like what Robert Townsend says in his film *Hollywood Shuffle*. The theme is 'there's always work at the post office,' meaning, yeah, you want to write films, but if you ever get lost here, you gotta go back to the job at the post office to reclaim your legitimacy.

"So the risks aren't just economic. You risk both your credibility *and* your viability. There's a way in which we trade in the currency of success to overcome being marginalized: the more expensive our suits, the nicer our cars, the nicer our houses, the better we as minority people are able to move about unfettered in a white society.

"For a person of color—especially a black person, Hispanic, Latino, a Native American—to get into the system and succeed to the point that you have marketable skills to support a consulting business means that you really had to invest yourself and work hard to get to that point, and you're not just risking viability when you decide to leave all that.

"It's not only a huge risk, it's also easier to screw up. There are a lot of really competent consultants who are persons of color. But I think minorities often misinterpret their ability to get business as a mandate to *grow* their business, hire people, build an organization. The ability to get business may be a mandate to be selective and charge more, not to hire and get overextended. Growing the business is a greater temptation for minorities because it brings back all the trappings of success: the office, the employees, the things that signal credibility. But trappings can become traps.

"What I'd like minorities to understand is that if by leaving you get to define your life the way you want to live it, then you discover something new that's really more effective against marginalization: self-esteem."

Sometimes it's easier to see your own issues when you can look through somebody else's eyes. I see a lot of myself in Alexs's story, across the gulf of race. Succeeding at self-employment has been easier for me as a white male than it will be for many people. But I know even from my own experience that you cannot overcome the external barriers to independence until you reckon with the barriers within.

Helping Your Best Self Win

There is a book called *Meeting the Shadow* (Tarcher, 1990) edited by Connie Zweig and Jeremiah Abrams that I find revealing. It is a collection of essays that have helped me understand how my shadow side— the appetites and fears I repress, parts of me that I consciously or subconsciously choose not to acknowledge—is as much who I am as the side that I like and acknowledge.

One premise is that by recognizing and accepting our dark side, we free ourselves from the struggle to repress it. A corollary might be that it is easier to control our insecurities and forbidden appetites when we embrace an externally imposed structure—say, the conventions of dress, behavior, time use, and so on imposed by the terms of conventional employment. Every organization requires adherence to its culture. And when somebody else sets the rules, you don't have to.

Unplugging from that external structure, giving birth to an enterprise, and introducing your enterprise with all its appetites and uncertainties into a household, can upset the equilibrium in your life in surprising ways.

"When you set up shop, you're thinking, 'Now I'm in control,' " one consultant told me. "But then you discover you still have all your personal hang-ups, you still have the government and taxes and your in-laws and the recession. Now you're at home, and what you really get is, you get to practice all your vices. So, while it is true that consulting gives you the potential to create a well-engineered life, there are lots of opportunities for things to go wrong. If you set up your business at home, it can be like adding a child. The dynamics of your marriage can get confused. Money issues get multiplied because you don't have a regular paycheck. Anxiety gets multiplied because when things go haywire there's nobody else to blame."

This is the dark side of being on your own. It is real and I don't want to soft-pedal it. When there is a marriage involved, the complexities between business and marriage reverberate. This is when having clarity about the expectations and risks of your new business and separating them from your personal life are make-or-break factors for survival.

When I interviewed Kathy Tunheim, she talked about her own philosophy toward change and taking personal risks. "Thinking of anything in your life. Could it be better? The answer is just about always, 'yes.' So what are we so stuck on staying the same for? Change is never as traumatic as you think it's going to be, and in my own experience, it's just about always good. As long as you understand the implications of your action, then it's not so risky. Understand the implications, and then be willing to live with them. If the worst happens, well, you anticipated it and you decided it was still worth the risk. So don't beat yourself up."

Taking a cue from Kathy, others I interviewed, and what I've learned from my own experience over the past twelve-plus years in a marriage and a business of my own, I've come up with these six points that can help your best self win.

To Help Your Best Self Win

1. *Know yourself:* Know your strengths and goals and what you are setting out to build for yourself. Recognize how your appetites and insecurities will compete for your attention in an unstructured situation.
2. *Create a structure* for your business that will help you focus on your objectives and accentuate the positive. For example, if you have trouble with food or alcohol, if you're easily distracted at home or tend to be a loner to a fault, don't put these weaknesses in the path of opportunity by officing at home. Set yourself up in professional space, co-locate with others, keep regular hours.
3. *Negotiate with yourself* the worst that can happen by going on your own, and whether you can accept it. If you are in a committed relationship, have this discussion with your partner and make the decision together. (If the worst that can happen is a financial setback, use the financial forecasting tools in chapter 12 to define your limits and protect the downside.) When you have defined and accepted the price you may have to pay, you will be freer to focus on the factors that will help you succeed.

4. *Refuse to set unrealistic targets* when you start out. Set goals you can achieve, and then meet them. This will whet your appetite for success, fuel your personal power, trigger your best qualities, and help keep self-defeating behavior at bay. How to know if your targets are realistic? Review them with your accountant and your mentor for candid feedback.

5. *Don't mistake your ability to sell for a mandate to grow.* It might be a sign to stay small and prosper.

6. *Loosen up as you find success.* Don't suffocate in a structure you needed in order to get started but is no longer appropriate. Trust your instincts. Change your goals, experiment with different structures, take risks, tap your creativity to keep the business fresh and rewarding.

Keeping Your Business in Its Place

One consultant I met as I interviewed for this book was unusually reluctant to tell me his story. He was reaching the end of a long, wrenching struggle with his business. He wanted to tell me about it, but he couldn't decide if I could be trusted not to report the details in this book. Finally one day nearly a year after we met he phoned and told me the business was going to make it but his marriage wasn't. He had gambled the marriage to save his business, and lost the marriage even as the business was turning the corner. The issues were complicated, but in looking back he could see how he had let the business come into their lives and confuse the relationship.

The business was located in their home to save money, and he was so consumed in making it go he would work through the weekends and get out of bed and go to it in the middle of the night. When he was with his wife elsewhere in the house his mind was upstairs working. The business was a financial drain, and his wife finally asked him to give it up and get a job, to make a choice between the marriage and the business. He couldn't bring himself to choose. His wife ultimately made a choice of her own and moved out.

I don't know whether that marriage was doomed to fail anyway. Though business and marriage are fundamentally different institutions, they both play off your strengths and weaknesses and must be distinctly separated in order to remain healthy. That doesn't mean a husband and wife can't have a successful marriage and be partners in a successful business. It does mean that there must be lines between the two so that you understand when you are negotiating your marriage relationships and expectations, when you are negotiating your business relationships and expectations, and which comes first.

Three kinds of separation are especially important. One is physical, another is financial, and a third, perhaps the hardest of the three to achieve, is separation of the day-to-day struggles of the business from the day-to-day business of your marriage and personal life.

The importance of separation applies even if you are not married, assuming you want a life other than your work. My own philosophy on that question is simple, although I don't claim to set a great example. I believe in the value of escape. I get more out of my personal life when I can leave my business behind and come back another day. And I think I do better in my business when I can leave my personal preoccupations behind. Perhaps the issues are as simple as focus and presence.

Separate Spaces

Don't conduct your business in the same spaces where you lead the rest of your life, or the two will become indistinguishable. If you have your office in your home, confine it to a distinct place and establish a pattern so that when you go to that place you are going to work, and when you leave that place you are leaving your work.

My office is a room over the garage. It is a wonderful space with skylights and a western view, its own bathroom, lots of bookshelves. Here I am surrounded by the tools of my work. The room is a haven from the rest of the household, and yet it is my connection to the outside world—by telephone and fax, messenger services and mail.

Occasionally I'll take my business reading down to the screened porch. I have a client who likes to meet with me on the porch during summer. In winter we'll meet by the fire in my living room. But other than those occasions, I work in my office. (The tax laws provide another reason why a home office should be used exclusively for business. See "The home office deduction" in chapter 11.)

For ten years or more I located my business in professional space, first in downtown Minneapolis and later in downtown St. Paul. When you have to drive to get to your place of work, I think it is easier to leave your personal life behind at the start of your workday and to leave your business behind at the end of the day.

If you are obsessive about work and have a hard time leaving it alone, locate your business away from your home. If cost is a problem, look for nesting and co-location opportunities like those described in chapters 9 and 11.

Separate Accounts

Financial anxiety gets ratcheted up several notches in any relationship when one partner gives up a salary and starts a business. Uncertainty is at the heart of the problem. Some of the uncertainty stems from the unpredictable nature of a start-up: how much money we are going to put at stake to get this business off the ground? When will it start making money? How much could we lose if our assumptions prove wrong? Chapter 12 gives you some tools to answer these questions before you take the plunge.

It is extremely important that you and your spouse discuss your financial projections and the assumptions behind them and agree on the amount of money you will put at risk, where it will come from, how you will know when you have reached the end of your rope, and what you will do to recover. For every one of these questions that you do not answer, you expose yourself financially and you open your marriage to the corrosive effects of uncertainty. And, from your spouse's point of view, you set the well-being of the business into competition with the well-being of the marriage.

There is another kind of financial uncertainty that comes from consulting, and it is the disjointed nature of your receivables. Unlike a salary, business receipts come in fits and starts. You hit long dry spells of hard work and no money when you spend down your balance keeping the mortgage paid and food on the table. Your spouse gets edgy and so do you, the bank hits you with a service charge, you put off buying some things you need. Finally the dry spell is ended and you're awash in cash. You feel fat and rich and you get the urge to go buy something really big, maybe a new car. This feast and famine pattern throws off your best money management instincts, throws your prudence out the window.

Whoever is accustomed to managing the household accounts is put in a hard position by the unevenness of your earnings. In the first place, he or she can't predict cash flow. In the second, he or she can't count on money being in the bank when it's needed to pay the bills. The person who manages the money needs to know what's coming.

A simple solution to this problem is to have separate business and personal accounts. This separation not only simplifies your tax reporting job, but it also enables you to absorb the financial ups and downs in the business account, and to pay yourself a regular monthly draw. This is how my wife and I work out accounts. At the end of every month, I write a check of a fixed amount to our personal account, which my wife deposits and draws against to pay our mortgage and personal bills. She deposits her own earnings into the same account.

Since I know that we will have to pay income tax of approximately 40 percent on money we draw out of the business (this surely will rise with changes in the tax laws), I have set up a savings account into which I make deposits directly from my business for purposes of building a tax fund. I keep this fund separate from our personal savings so that we don't delude ourselves into thinking the money is ours to spend. When it's time to file quarterly income taxes, I pay them out of my tax savings account. This idea is very similar to the tax escrow account that your mortgage company keeps.

I also keep a cushion in the tax account that I can draw against from time to time when I run into a temporary cash shortage in my business. The only other way short of borrowing that I could cover a cash flow gap in my business account would be to hold back my monthly contribution to our household account or to draw some money out of that account back into my business, but those options defeat the goal of building a predictable household revenue stream. So I find the idea of a modest cushion in the tax savings account preferable. Financial advisors have told us that we would do better if we invested that money rather than let it sit in the bank, but we ignore the advice because the peace of mind is more important to us than juggling accounts to get the highest yield.

I asked other consultants how they deal with financial issues and was stuck by something Eric Mitchell said (see chapter 10). "When I first started, I starved and the business grew. And then my accountant taught me this is a *business* and encouraged me to incorporate it so that the business spends its money and I spend mine. He put me on a salary and told me to keep to it. He taught me to look at my business's profit and loss statement the same way I would if I were on the board of Xerox."

You don't need to incorporate in order to put yourself on a salary. You don't need to keep a cash balance in a bank account in order to cover cash flow shortages; a lot of businesses negotiate a line of credit with the bank that they draw against. There are also things you can do to take some of the hills and valleys out of your receivables (see "Sustainable revenue streams" in chapter 10). The key points are (1) to be aware that the cash flow of your business will be uneven and that the ups and downs are normal, and (2) to find solutions that keep your personal cash flow predictable.

Open Lines

There is always a question about how deeply you should involve your spouse in your business. A husband or wife can be your best ally in analyzing business problems and brainstorming solutions. Sue Foster and Jack Brizius represent one extreme: going into the business together (see their profile at the end of this chapter). But if you're married and in a business of your own that does not directly involve your spouse, how much should you try to keep your spouse informed? The answer depends on what kind of a marriage you have and what makes both of you comfortable.

My advice is to keep the lines of communication open. One simple rule of thumb is to make a special point of involving your spouse in aspects of your business that potentially affect your personal lives. In my judgment, these include the following talking points.

Talking Points

- *Decisions about the kind of business you're in.* What you do still very much reflects who you are in our society, and the kinds of consulting you do will affect your earning power and your personal financial future. This is a decision where your spouse's view should count for a lot.
- *Significant capital investments.* Decisions about how you invest to grow your business are yours to make, but when they involve personal resources or guarantees, they need to be made jointly with your spouse.
- *Location decisions.* If you plan to work at home, you need to negotiate what that means in terms of separation of business and personal lives. If the separation seems to work for you but not for your spouse, accept that it doesn't work and find another location where it works for both of you.
- *Decisions to bring in a partner.* By a partner I don't mean somebody with whom you collaborate from time to time, but somebody with whom you plan to strike a close, long-term business relationship. If your spouse is not comfortable with your business partner,

the partnership will create tensions and resentments that could damage both your marriage and your business.

- *Significant time commitments.* Commitments to major new projects and clients have repercussions on your personal time and should be reviewed with your spouse before you make them.
- *How you're doing.* Because going on your own involves risks both to your financial well-being and your self-esteem, your spouse has an enormous stake in knowing how the business is going for you. Talk about it.

Of all these areas, the last is most often taken for granted. Men in particular have trouble separating professional and personal issues, and an erosion of self-esteem is where the troubles of a business can work their worst effects on a marriage. When things are going well financially in your business, it's important to let your spouse know, for his or her peace of mind. When things are not going well, you need to talk about it directly or your negative feelings will spill into your relationship in unforeseen and painful ways.

My wife has stayed out of my business, but she's had a lot of influence on my choices and survival. For starters, she accepted my decision to go into consulting despite her own misgivings, because she could see it was something I needed to do. She worked at a job that paid a good salary, enabling me to build my consulting business without our having to make sacrifices. Over the years she's given me marketing ideas, helped me think through solutions to client problems, acquainted me with experts when I needed outside help, celebrated my successes, helped entertain clients, and eventually come to believe that consulting was not the misadventure that her fears had supposed it might be.

Ideas to Take Away

- Going on your own gives you license to be different.
- Taking control and taking risks reveal new dimensions of who you are and what you are capable of accomplishing.
- Each of us has a shadow side of anxieties and suppressed appetites. By understanding these, you can negotiate limits to the risks you are willing to take, structure your business to build on your strengths, set objectives you can meet, and adapt the business to let your best self win.
- A business and marriage need boundaries in order to succeed in proximity: space, money, and day-to-day focus and presence.

- You need to involve your spouse in aspects of your business—such as significant investments and time commitments—that have an impact on your personal lives.
- With success, your needs and interests will change. Remember that you have the power to change your business, too.

When a husband and wife are in business together, the boundaries between work and family blur. Put the business in the home and add a couple of kids to the mix and the relationship becomes a complex dance in which each partner searches out his own rhythms in the changing harmonies of work, family, and spouse.

Sue Foster and Jack Brizius, profiled below, are a married couple who left government jobs in Washington, D.C., to make a new business and a new life in the mountains of southern Pennsylvania. The years that they have been in business for themselves have seen a gradual integration of their professional lives with their community work, and a subtle redefinition of how each of them best balances work and family, marriage and business.

WALKING THE TALK TO CHANGE YOUR LIFE
Profile
SUSAN E. FOSTER AND JACK A. BRIZIUS
Brizius & Foster Public Affairs Consultants, McConnellsburg, PA

Sue Foster and Jack Brizius left the Sturm und Drang of Washington, D.C., for Pennsylvania hillbilly country, only two and a half hours out by car, but fifty years back in time by the feel of it.

There on 155 acres of fields and woods under the shadow of Scrub Ridge, where Patterson Run spills into Licking Creek, they have painstakingly converted a century-old hillside dairy barn into a breathtaking home and place of business. Nine-foot windows frame a broad sweep of valley—rolling hills, creek bottoms, a few homes, a forgotten farm implement waiting for spring in a fallow field between two woods.

In this setting, with the gradual addition of daughters Alison and Erin, cat Jake and pooch Ellwood, Sue and Jack have built a nationwide consulting practice whose clients read like a list of presidential hopefuls and *Who's Who* in American public policy development. I flew into Washington and drove up to McConnellsburg to interview them in early February 1992.

Jack and Sue have backgrounds in public sector management and policy development at both the state and national levels. Sue entered consulting first, in 1979, leaving a job at the Department of Health, Education, and Welfare in Washington where she was deputy undersecretary of intergovernmental affairs. She saw consulting as a way to buy time, maintain her contacts, and sort through her choices. In her post at HEW she had gotten to know the new governor of Arkansas, Bill Clinton. When Clinton learned of her plans to leave, he urged Sue to join his administration. Instead, she worked out a consulting relationship, selling him a third of her time to help set up his Washington office and develop a rural health initiative in Arkansas. This base gave her the confidence and credentials to build her practice.

"Getting that first contract on your way out the door is critical. Quoting a credible job you have gets you more work." Through her contacts, Sue landed another consulting job, this one with Price Waterhouse providing advice on a federal program with which she was familiar. The consulting practice began to blossom. Sue says she had mixed feelings at the time, not so sure she wanted to turn consulting into a full-fledged business. Yet she went with it, worked her network, and got more business.

A year and a half after Sue had put out her shingle, Jack decided to do the same. He negotiated a half-time consulting agreement with his employer, the National Governors' Association, and that gave him the base he needed to get started.

"At this point we were looking at a life-style change, too," Sue adds. "We figured we could run a consulting business from anywhere, so long as there was an airport." A health problem had forced Sue's dad to put his property in McConnellsburg on the market to finance his retirement, so Sue and Jack bought it and moved up. "All my life growing up, I couldn't wait to leave," she says. "And here I am." Back she may be, but clearly on her own terms.

Brizius and Foster, as they call their practice, defined its niche as public affairs consulting for governors, governors' staff, state offices, and regional governors' groups, drawing directly on Jack's and Sue's experience and contacts.

They helped Governor Bruce Babbitt develop a children's initiative for Arizona. They helped Governor Kit Bond develop a program for maternal and child health in Missouri. They worked in Rhode Island, helping Governor Joe Garrahy develop children's services. Their early projects lasted five or six months, but before long their focus shifted to larger, more complex projects like education reform in Mississippi, a $200,000-plus project involving teams of consultants and on-site staff.

In 1982, they started a family. "I felt particularly strongly that since I was in my midthirties before I started this child-rearing business, I didn't want to hand it over to somebody else," Sue says. She cut her work load back one-third and found ways to be a mother and a consultant at the same time.

"When Ali was young, she was very portable." Sue took her along to meetings. Once they were part of a small group of advisors meeting with Ohio's first lady Dagmar Celeste. Celeste delivered some passionate remarks about mental health, and in the pause that followed, Ali shoved her fist down her throat and gagged. Sue had a moment's panic, but the first lady took the critique in stride.

Over the years Sue and Jack have found other ways to make time for the kids. Jack drives them to school. When the kids get home, Sue and Jack take a break from work to visit with them about what's happened during the day and what they have to do that evening to be ready for the next day. "Sue is better than I am about making sure we have some time that's just family, no business," Jack says. "We're driving down to Wal-Mart on Saturday morning and I'm blathering on about my office checklist, and Sue will look at me and I'll know that this is not the time to do business because she wants to shut that out for now." Other times, according to Jack, the kids will tease them about it and they'll knock off the office talk.

How long did it take before they were satisfied with the money from consulting? "Six or seven years," Jack says. "It took time to build volume. Also, we set our rates too low when we started, and it takes time to recover from that. And, when we had kids, Sue cut back her billable hours, and that had an impact." Psychology plays an important part. "You have to separate judgments about the value of your services from your sense of modesty and quote a price that will support a business."

Their business and family have grown up together, and perhaps for that reason the lines between them are flexible and not always distinct.

Asked for some thoughts about being married and partners in business, Sue says, "For starters, you can never get away from your work. It's integrated not only into your living space, but into your relationships. It heightens the highs and deepens the lows. On the good side, when one of us gets frustrated, the other understands. We can support each other in ways that other couples can't."

Sue also says that, in their case, each wants to take the lead and not be relegated to a second position. "Jack and I work together on every contract. He's the creative side, marketing, good with data. I'm the implementer and the public speaker."

Jack says they had an advantage when they started because they had worked together in earlier jobs, and as a result they had come to appreciate each other's talents and discover how to complement each other's work. Just the same, each has an idea about how things should be done, and it has taken a long time to get comfortable with different work styles.

"I used to think that if she didn't do marketing, the whole business would dry up and we'd blow away," Jack says. "But as we've gotten older and all the bad things you imagine will happen didn't happen, we've gotten mellower."

They've also developed different schedules. Sue has drawn a line around weekends to save them for personal time as best she can in a business where, when a governor calls on a Saturday with a question, "you don't want to say, 'Call back Monday, we're not open weekends.' " She keeps a steady pace during the week, whereas Jack will take a break during the week and make it up on Saturday. "I have to trust Sue to meet her commitments to the business and remind myself not to meddle in the way she does it," Jack says, "and she has to do the same with me."

One area where they had to do some serious work was in reconciling their attitudes about money and living with the unpredictable cash flow of a consulting business.

Jack: "Sue grew up with the idea that needing to borrow money is a shameful thing. So here we were, doing business at the local bank where her father at the time was a trustee and attorney. We were running a business where the cash flow seesaws up and down, and we'd get into situations of financial extremis where American Express practically had snipers in the airports looking for us, but Sue couldn't bring herself to go the bank and take out a loan. I'd tell her that banks *like* to lend money, we're doing them a *disservice* by not borrowing.

"We worked it out eventually. Now we have a large line of credit at the bank, we don't think twice about borrowing, and that's behind us. But I would offer this bit wisdom: a lot of people will borrow money from Mom and Dad for the house, but when you borrow to start a business and you have a cash flow crisis and you have to decide between paying your American Express or her mom, that's a choice you don't want to make."

While the business has been very successful, Sue admits that ten years into it she faced a midlife crisis. "I got to the point where I was questioning whether this was where I really wanted to be. I just wasn't happy with it anymore, and I began looking for a way to figure out what I wanted. I'd say to myself in that kind of rigid way we're taught, Here are your skills, here are the opportunities that you could create for yourself, do you want A, B, or C, or some combination? But I was getting nowhere. I finally figured that what I needed was to take a break from the business and see how it felt."

I asked Sue whether she felt trapped because her work was her life, everything was connected: *"Everything* was connected," she said. "I had to break the connection, so I just stopped working. For the first time I really carved space out to come to terms with who I was and define myself separately from work, and to figure out how I was going to be happy regardless of what I was doing.

"Going through that period of reflection was scary. I had no idea how I was going to come out of it. If I let go of all this work stuff that I've used to define myself, what if I looked within and there wasn't anything there? And I was still clinging to this question, What am I going to do with the next phase of my life? And I finally just had to let go of that, too.

"The wonderful thing was that after several months of reflection, I did come to a sort of peaceful resolution with myself, and I came back to the business. Now I'm not so concerned what I do for a living. I really enjoy the work again. It's the same work. The reason I enjoy it now is that I feel better about me. I have a better understanding of myself."

I asked, "Was part of the value of your process the fact that you gave yourself the choice of coming back or not, and in coming back you were saying, 'I'm coming back because it's what I *choose* to do, not because it's what I *have* to do'?"

"Yes. You come back with a very different attitude. I'm making the decision, it's not being made by circumstance. I have a much better sense of how to evaluate the jobs that I want to do and the one that I don't. I'm better able to say no to work that I don't want to do. And, as a result of this, I've become much more involved working in the community on issues that I have dealt with professionally for years."

The upstairs of the Foster-Brizius house contains the bedrooms. The main floor contains the living area and Jack's office, and half of the walkout level is dedicated to Sue's office and space for two support staff. Jack says, "One of the joys of having our business in the house is that we have a lot more unstructured time to work things out. I like being able to crank up the computer if it's late at night and I'm having trouble sleeping. On a Sunday morning Sue might say, 'I've figured out how to get this chapter done,' and we'll discuss it. So all of that doesn't have to be crammed into the weekday period, and I think that's a major advantage."

Is there any part of the business they wish wasn't so present in their lives? Possibly the support staff. Jack says if he and Sue ever build the garage with offices above it that they have in mind, they'd probably move the support staff out there. "You have to be able to have a good argument in a marriage, and it's hard to do that with other people in the house."

The business has evolved as they have become successful and their interests have changed. Consulting to governors has required grueling travel schedules, and they've taken several measures to cut that back. One is to turn the data and knowledge they have developed through consulting into products they can sell from their home (see chapter

10). Another has been to market their services to the mayor of Harrisburg and other clients within striking distance of McConnellsburg.

After her sabbatical, Sue redoubled her volunteer work, serving on boards of the library, the local hospital, and a community college, as well as the school board and several advisory groups. She and Jack developed an economic recovery plan for the county as a consulting engagement, and Sue has been volunteering a lot of time to help get the plan implemented.

They have also helped create a community organization called the Fulton County Center for Families to bring a lot of the programs that they've been advocating in other states into their own county. Once a month the Center for Families meets at their house to do business over a lunch that Jack prepares.

The group started a "parent as teacher" program to help prepare young children for school. The PAT program serves fifty-three families, all poor and many headed by single parents. The county has no day care, so the group created an afterschool latchkey program that serves ninety-six children. The group has also worked to set up a school-based health clinic. In a separate effort, Sue and Jack organized an enriched summer school math program for sixteen kids and hired a local woman with a master's degree in statistics to teach it.

"Sue and I know how to raise funds," Jack says, "and we've written grants to the tune of about $1 million for this community in the last year. I just wrote another one to take the old Fulton House, which was the 1765 inn and get some federal money to refurbish it as a center for tourism. You pick those things and go and do them, and you can apply the skills you've learned over the years. It's highly satisfying."

Jack reflects on the last twelve years. "It's been an evolution. A coming to terms with ourselves." He says he still worries about the financial side of the business, but not as much as he used to. "I was having my monthly money fit last night. But we have the business booked up for about six months, so we have a chance now to go out and do a few proposals for stuff we really want to work on. And to look at doing some other things with the community and the kids."

What are some rules of thumb for making a marriage and business work together? Jack: "One, learn to trust each other to get the work done and don't meddle. We've tried different experiments with 'you be the manager and I'll be the worker,' but our patterns are much more collaborative. We meet and adjust what we're doing at least weekly, sometimes daily.

"Two, go with your strengths instead of pressuring each other to do things you're not good at. That way you'll produce better for your partner and get along better.

"Three, don't draw artificial lines between work and family that you'll constantly violate because they're not right for you. Try different things to find out what boundaries really work, and recognize there will be differences.

"Four, make time to be parents. Your eyes are screwed to columns of numbers on your computer screen and your kid walks in and says, 'Daddy, I have to write this tall tale for school about how the solar system was created. You type and I'll dictate.' You know, the numbers will keep."

Sue: "The most important thing is to give yourself time to find your soul—who you are, how you fit, what it is you can contribute."

9   KEEPING YOUR BALANCE

How the choices you make
will help you stay in control

Hedging Your Bets

A Fish Tale

John Niles cast his line into the waters only once. He was practicing his cast, you might say, not actually out to land his dinner. To his utter surprise, Control Data Corporation rose out of nowhere, grabbed his bait, breached, and gave John a run for his life.

A man with a fish on the end of his line must be a fisherman. A man with a client—a big and successful client like Control Data—must be a consultant. So that's what John became. A solo practitioner with one huge and hungry client who kept reupping every time the contract came due for renewal. For *eight years.* Until the mideighties, when Control Data's earnings hit the skids, its vitality began to flag, belts were tightened, new managers were brought in. And John lost his client. John began to get hungry and looked around. He'd been so busy with Control Data, he hadn't thought to put any other lines in the water. He oiled up his fishing rod and put it back to work. And that's when he discovered that one lucky cast does not a fisherman make.

Here is a quick sketch of how John's experience with Control Data came about, and some of the lessons he learned.

John grew up in Detroit during the time of the civil rights riots and developed a strong interest in social issues and public service. His dream was to become a city manager or join the staff of a big city mayor.

After graduate school and the navy, he landed a job in the office of Walter Washington, the mayor of Washington, D.C., working in a division whose staff functioned like internal consultants to improve the efficiency and effectiveness of various city agencies. He liked the projects and ideas, being a change agent, but after four or five years he grew impatient with the bureaucratic aspects of the job. He'd also had a chance to see the kinds of jobs that people moved into when they rose up the government hierarchy—jobs that represented his future—and the way those jobs were limited by politics and bureaucracy. The notion of becoming a city manager stopped appealing to him.

"It seemed very much a rat race. What began to appeal to me—really what always appealed to me—was the notion of structural change. That the key to our future on this planet is revisions to the system. Analyzing what's wrong and fixing it. I came to see that was not easy to do as a manager. What I really wanted to do was to work *with* line managers to help them make change, not to *be* one."

John left government just as Marion Barry was elected. One reason for leaving was to write down what he'd learned—that there was a lot of innovation going on in state and local government across the country, but people inside local governments couldn't find out what was going on. There was no system to transfer the technology.

He wrote up the idea as an article for the *Washington Star:* city governments ought to share ideas. It was published on a Saturday and read by a local manager for Control Data Corporation who called John to say, "Our company is interested in computer systems for technology transfer." The CDC manager showed John some software the company had developed to support technology transfer. John said it was a start but would need modifying, and asked, "How can we work together?" The manager suggested he write to Control Data's CEO. John clipped the article and sent it off with a note. In response he got an invitation to fly to Minneapolis, which he did. "I'd quit my job in late October, and by the middle of January I was on a plane to Minnesota and launched my career as an independent consultant on that one visit."

He hadn't intended to go into consulting. On that visit he was engaged first for three months, then renewed for three, then for six. He worked for Control Data as a writer and thinker based in Washington, helping sort out how technology transfer could help city governments everywhere, and how CDC should structure and market is Local Government Information Network (LOGIN). In effect, he functioned as LOGIN's eyes and ears in Washington, and helped them land their first contract, selling the service to the Department of Housing and Urban Development.

Over the next eight years, Control Data accounted for about 90 percent of John's revenues. "I viewed the Control Data headquarters as my target market."

When John's wife, Elizabeth, finished her Ph.D. in 1981, they decided to leave Washington and relocate where she could get a job. They ended up in Seattle. With this move, John was no longer able to function as the "Washington office" for LOGIN, and it is his sense that this change was probably the first step in his becoming less essential to Control Data. "As new managers came in, I think I was perceived to be of less and less value."

Within a year or two, Control Data entered a period of significant losses that persisted through the eighties and precipitated a string of management changes. A new manager came in over LOGIN. "I think he saw me as more of a cost than a benefit. The people who eventually cut me out I never met. That was a change. For quite a few years running, any time my client ended up with a new boss, we'd gone to dinner together to cultivate the relationship." Meanwhile, John hadn't made any prospecting contacts in Seattle. "I was not conscientious about marketing." When Control Data went away, most of his consulting practice went with it, and John found himself forced to start over, rethink how he intended to make a living.

Years later, he has refocused his consulting business and built it into Global Telematics, the Seattle-based telecommunications strategy planning firm. And he carries with him some valuable lessons from his earlier life.

Some Pearls of Wisdom from John's Experience

- *On angels and sugar daddies:* "Finding an angel is a great way to get into business. But what are you going to do after your angel dies? You had better find a way to hedge your bets. And that's not something you can do one month before the contract ends. You have to get other things going *before* you need them."
- *On marketing:* "Writing and speaking are good ways to get your name out, but they rarely lead directly to new business. The experience I had with Control Data based on my newspaper article was a total fluke. And I operated for eight or nine years thinking that when Control Data ended, all I'd have to do was write a couple of articles and snag a new Control Data."
- *On endings:* "In consulting, the way relationships end is very interesting—they just don't return your call, you don't get renewed. Nobody has to say anything. That's the easy thing about consul-

tants. There is no particular expectation. Everybody knows the rules when you start."

The manner in which John got involved with Control Data may not be common, but the tendency for solo consultants to get swallowed up by big organizations is not uncommon at all.

When a big organization needs to strike out in new directions, those within seldom have the personal experience or contacts to lead the way; somebody is needed from the outside like John. A large number of the consultants I interviewed face this dilemma, and so do I. A stable relationship with a large company that pays you well and appreciates your contribution can be a wondrous thing for a consultant, but you alone are responsible for hedging the down side. In the profile in chapter 5, Len Smart describes how he gradually scaled back his 100 percent commitment to one client.

How did John recover? By dint of sheer will, drawing down his reserves, calling on old relationships, perseverance, luck, and eventually creating a new focus that fit his skills and addresses an emerging market for consulting support.

Staying Out of the Victim School of Consulting

The Victim School of Consulting is a figment of my imagination. I dreamed it up one night a few years ago as I lay awake fretting over the commitments I'd made. Consulting was becoming a lead weight around my neck. Whoever called, I said yes. Whatever they wanted, I did. My problem wasn't unreasonable clients, but my own failure to discriminate which and how many clients I let in the door. I operated from some fifties' notion that success in a service business required that people like you, and getting people to like you meant doing whatever they wanted, only twice as fast and twice as well. (I always fancied myself as Cubby on the "Mickey Mouse Club.") Lying there, it struck me that my way of practicing consulting was the "victim school." No job is too big or too small, the customer is always right, and when called, you serve. If you're one heck of a nice person, and nothing pleases you more than pleasing the customer, and you just can't bring yourself to say no, the Victim School of Consulting is pleased to make your acquaintance.

So there it is. Consulting as one of those codependent things. There are more constructive ways to approach this business. Following are four of them.

Remember That It's Only a Business

There will be plenty of times in life when you're called upon to suffer sainthood and "no thanks" isn't an option. Families and close friends have that claim on you. But clients don't.

Cultivate the ability to scope out and deflect opportunities that look as if they won't measure up. Don't let the power of "no" rest solely with the client. Chapter 4 talks about the importance of finding out how the customer defines success so you can develop a consulting approach that achieves it. It's just as important to know your own definition of a successful engagement, and to turn away jobs that don't have promise. You can always tell a prospect you're fully booked. Or you think he'd do better with someone who specializes in the sort of thing he wants to get done, and here are a couple of people he could phone.

I'm not saying you should hold back when a client needs you to go the extra mile. I'm saying be careful about what commitments you make. I will inconvenience myself for any client. The dividends I look for are compensation, a stronger relationship, a good reputation, and insights that will enable me to make the client happy without inconveniencing myself quite so much in the future. I may not get them all. But however well I perform, I know that ultimately we will part ways, because it's only business.

Know Your Limits and Powers

I used to panic in the early days because whenever I said yes to a client, I felt that I had accepted accountability for solving his problem. When you've done that a few times and discovered that often the *client* is the problem, you change your way of thinking about your role. Now I see my job as helping the client solve his problem.

As a consultant, even if you are an expert, the success of your contribution is going to be influenced by many factors beyond your control—how aggressively the client pursues the solution, the extent to which it is embraced by his team, and so on. The keys to successful implementation are held by the client.

In my practice, *process is the product, and discovery is the process.* By this I mean simply that any kind of problem-solving requires a journey. First you recognize a problem of some sort does in fact exist. Then you define and describe its manifestations. You look behind the manifestations to poke at possible root causes.

If this is a group discussion, everyone weighs in with examples of how other parts of the organization contribute to the problem and make life hell. You go out and gather information—how others have solved the problem, what competitors are doing, what trends might make the problem get better or worse, how customers feel about possible changes, and so on. You get back together, look at what you learned, and then start brainstorming solutions. The energy turns. People start building on one another's ideas. You get up a list of criteria for ranking ideas and setting priorities. You settle on a plan of action and ask around the room for commitment. You agree on what'll happen over the next couple of months, and you set a date to check in on progress.

I've seen this process unfold in one form or another time after time. It starts as a wary, frustrated discussion, descends to the depths of people's darkest feelings, acknowledges truths, and, in moving on, begins to rise.

The *process* is what moves people beyond the limits of their divisiveness and frustration to rediscover their common ground for collaboration and solution. This journey, in nearly any field, is of tremendous value. Few organizations can make it without a neutral facilitator who makes it safe for people to state what's on their minds and offers a framework for moving the dialogue forward. Without the journey, organizations cannot solve problems, develop shared vision, collaborate to change what is. The lessons for me in this have been many.

- The client must own the problem.
- It's less important for me to have answers than to know how to find them.
- The journey is as important as the destination, because it is only by traveling together that people can arrive at the same place.
- In an organization, it is the opportunity to discover common ground that provides both the path and the energy for solving problems.

To me, this knowledge is very freeing, because it reveals both my limits and my powers, and knowing both is a key to staying within my depth and focusing on the things I can do to be of most value to my client.

Your area of consulting may be entirely different, but the basic point remains: time and experience season you in your field and make it easier to get your bearings in new situations, to set limits, and to contribute to the client's success without neglecting the half of the equation that has to work for you.

Have Goals and Make Choices

You cannot judge an opportunity unless you have a vision to which you can compare it. Keep in mind why you've gone into consulting, and make the kinds of choices that will lead you into the life you want and help achieve the goals you've set. Know what kinds of clients and assignments you want, and don't take others unless they can help you to get where you want to go.

If you don't know what kind of consulting you want, take all kinds of assignments until you do. Then focus.

If the industries you want to work in aren't buying what you want to sell, find out what they will buy and sell it to them. Get a better feel for the market and reassess your strategy: can you repackage what you want to sell so that people will buy? Can you redefine your focus to fit the market and still be happy? If the answer to both is no, go after a different market.

If you have a string of clients in an industry that doesn't suit you, keep your head down, take your money, and don't feed the network, or you'll get more.

Leave Yourself an Out

In high school driver training we were taught always to leave ourselves an out in any driving situation. The same advice applies in consulting. I find it a lot easier to get past disappointment and insecurity if I don't feel owned by my business—that is, knowing I could *move* on makes it easier to get over the bumps and *hang* on.

For most people, going into consulting isn't an all-or-nothing gamble: it doesn't usually involve risking your life's savings; it is based on reinforcing your networks and relationships, not burning bridges; you can work your costs close to the bone without looking like a cheap operator. If while you build your consulting business you can keep some money in the bank and maintain your reputation and professional relationships, you've left yourself the time and raw materials for a good job search.

If the prospect of honest work isn't your idea of an "out," you could dedicate yourself to community work, or train somebody younger to perform your magic and then sell her your practice, or just grab your cat and move to the desert and live out of an old trailer with Jose Cuervo and a case of decent cigars.

Whatever is right for you, simply knowing you are not dependent on consulting is the first and best strategy for beating a sentence to the Victim School. Come up with a contingency plan you can live with, keep some cash in the bank, and you'll be in a stronger position to negotiate when the other party is the insecurity within you.

Embracing Consulting's Cycles

The two best times in consulting are when you're busy, and when you're not.

Maybe that's obvious. If not, consider that when you're busy in consulting, you're raking in the dough and pleasing hell out of a lot of clients, which produces two enviable rewards, profit and self-affirmation. But when business is slow, you get an even more precious commodity: free time. Any business that brings you, in the course of its natural cycles, money, self-affirmation, and free time, is a business whose cycles are worth embracing.

In a job, you are insulated from the cycles of your industry by the security of a paycheck and the predictability of regular hours. Leave your job for consulting, and the peaks and valleys that are the natural cycle of this business loom strange and alarming. Where's the control? How can you live off something so unpredictable?

One guy I talked to in researching this book got out of consulting because, as he put it, you're either too consumed with client commitments and deadlines to think of yourself, or too consumed with worry over where the next nickel's coming from. (For him, the two *worst* times in consulting were when he was busy, and when he wasn't.)

I feel that way sometimes, but not as a rule. When I do, I remind myself that the power to change the way I practice consulting lies with me and not with my clients. That simple idea works for me. Then I can focus on the potential of consulting to help me refresh my life in new and interesting ways. If you can do that, it will help you to see in the rhythms of consulting opportunities you never had as a nine-to-fiver.

You never entirely overcome the panic that sets in when you hit the downward slope of a new valley, but you do learn there's a bottom, and after the bottom another rise.

You can mitigate the peaks and valleys somewhat by cultivating sustained relationships, developing new offerings, broadening your network, building collaborations. But the ebb and flow of work will persist to some degree, and you can find ways to take advantage of it.

My work usually slows down in December and January, so I take three weeks off at Christmas. I like to write, and I usually have several stories in various stages of development to which I turn when the phone is still. My wife and I have a van we outfitted for camping, and we like to sneak away now and then to make up for those Saturdays and Sundays we spent slaves to deadlines. Every practice will have its own rhythm. You need to listen for the rhythm of your business and make it work for you. Loosen your grip. See what comes.

Ideas to Take Away

- When the balance of power shifts from you to your business, you have entered the Victim School of Consulting.
- To stay in control:
    Set goals and make choices.
    Don't let the power of *no* rest solely with your clients.
    Know your limits.
    Let the client own the problem.
    Leave yourself out.
- Everybody panics when the phone doesn't ring. Peaks and valleys are the natural rhythm of consulting; adapt to them and they will bring your money, self-affirmation, and free time.
- The power to change the way you practice consulting lies with you, not with your clients.

Susan Stevens (profiled below) was a social worker when she set out to change her life. After the dust settled, she discovered she'd become a financial management consultant. If something doesn't work for her, she changes it. So far, with some adjustments here and there, her consulting business has toed the line. But the day it doesn't, she'll either rearrange it or move on to the next phase of her life.

FINDING HAPPINESS IN WHAT YOU CREATE
Profile
SUSAN KENNY STEVENS
Financial and Management Consultant, St. Paul, MN

Susan Stevens is living testimony that in this dog-eat-dog world of unemployed MBAs, even a social worker from a humble nonprofit agency can leave her job and make a prosperous new life in consulting. She is also testimony to the power of a simple idea: for those of us who set our own course, the better share of happiness lies in the choices we make.

Susan is forty-five, a wife, mother of two, gardener, adjunct graduate school professor of finance (sans MBA), avid amateur musical satirist skewering local politicos on public television, and, since 1982, owner and president of the Stevens Group, which today is a stable of seven consultants providing management and financial services to nonprofit corporations and foundations across the country.

How well is she doing? By financial standards, she's very comfortable, taking home an income most corporate managers would consider more than ample. The firm has a spacious suite on the ground floor of an older, low-rise office building midway between St. Paul and Minneapolis. The space is well appointed but not lavish, the colors muted and inviting. Susan sits in a large office at the rear of the suite, where we meet around a glass top coffee table. Her walls are not covered with accolades and trophies. You get the sense her surroundings are important to her, but only in the way clean air is important to a long-distance runner.

Where Susan rates her success highest is on the job satisfaction scale. "I could take any old job and not be happy in it," she says. "But for pity's sake, if you create your own company and you can't be happy in it, then there's something wrong." Consulting has given Susan what she most wants from a career: good relationships, hard work, variety, and a chance to make a difference.

The secrets to Susan's success lie both in her personality and in an unusual pairing of interests: social work and finance. It's a combination that sets her apart from most consultants and, as it turns out, makes her particularly well attuned to the needs of the nonprofit and foundation marketplace of the eighties and nineties.

After earning a bachelor's degree in social work in the late sixties, Susan took a job working in the justice system with juvenile delinquents. She did well, changed jobs, and got promoted several times through the seventies. At about the same time Ronald Reagan went to the White House and began cutting funds for social services, Susan hired on as the administrator of New Connection, an agency helping youth overcome alcohol and drug abuse.

New Connection was entirely dependent on public funding, which had suddenly come to look rather perishable. "We knew we had to get fee income, and the logical place to turn was insurance companies for third-party reimbursements." With considerable salesmanship, Susan and her boss converted New Connection to 99 percent private pay. While this was a major move to financial stability, it also created an administrator's nightmare. "We now had multiple sources of referral instead of one. We had a horrible receivables problem, had to learn to manage *sixteen* funders. They all allowed different costs. We were doing it by the seat of our pants. I had never had a single class in finance. So one day my boss said, 'Get yourself trained.' "

Susan applied for and won a Bush Foundation summer fellowship. She lined up a neighbor to help look after her two toddlers and, with her husband's blessing, headed off to Cornell University. "Instead of enrolling in a program that was targeted at New Connection's specific situation—like how to manage Medicare reimbursements—I took a huge leap of faith and applied to a broad course in finance and economics. I figured I only had one shot at a Bush Fellowship, so I might as well go big with it instead of doing some kind of micromanagement program."

When she got to Ithaca, there were 120 people in the program. Susan was one of only seven women, one of only a handful of participants under age forty, and the only employee of a nonprofit corporation. "I was sitting there with IBM on one side and big oil companies on the other, and they would ask, 'What's New Connection?' They probably thought I was from the plumbers and pipe fitters' union. I wouldn't tell them it was a social service agency. I was already feeling swallowed alive at this place, and I thought, I cannot let myself get psyched out here. I've got to be able to do this work."

The finance and economics course opened a whole new world to Susan. "All of a sudden I was no longer a little girl from Nebraska walking along this preordained path. The world was my oyster. I understood how money worked. And the break had gotten me out of all my roles. I was thirty-two years old. I'd been a hard worker since I was in sixth grade. The only thing you *did* in my family was work. That's how we grew up. I was the oldest of five. Our father died in a fishing accident when I was seven. We worked because we needed the money, but work was also how we got reinforcement. So here I was, without work for the first time I could remember, and my mind was being opened up. I was not anybody's *wife* at that school, nobody's *mother*—I didn't have babies in diapers there like I had at home."

She returned to Minnesota resolved to do something new with her career.

She put in six months at New Connection to pass along what she had learned and then resigned. She took a series of short-term assignments with other organizations. She would finish one and something else would come along, and it was during this period that the notion of going into business for herself took form.

"I thought, Why not get into something where I could control my own destiny and get the benefits of my own hard work?" Around this time Susan also got a call from an executive in a large corporation—one of her acquaintances at Cornell. He was calling to offer a management position. She thought long and hard about the offer, but turned it down. She says she had come to see that jobs have limits, and to feel that no job could ever give her the latitude or opportunities she could give herself. "I didn't formally weigh out the risks and possibilities of working for myself. It was more a matter of opening myself to the opportunity. I think because I felt secure in my marriage and personal relationships, I didn't have to spell it all out. I have always trusted that if I ever got myself into a jam, I could get myself out of it. My mother used to tell us there was no point to worrying about things because we'd already survived the worst thing that could possibly happen."

Susan decided to start the Stevens Group. She told friends that she was going to sell management and financial services to nonprofits. "They said, 'You mean you're going into fund-raising?' In those days, nonprofits didn't know about *managing* money," Susan remembers. "Controlling it, developing new sources of income, looking at the liability side of the balance sheet. I also set out to bring *business* principles to the sector."

It was the next logical step to independence, and it crystallized what had become a fundamental change in Susan's attitude toward responsibility, caretaking, and opportunity. "I had always been one of those diaper-bag-in-the-briefcase mothers; couldn't separate work and family. When I stopped being tied into all of that, I ended up being a *better* wife and mother. So, I'm not the 'oldest daughter' anymore. I'm somebody else now. It was the beginning of *me*, the first time that I ever really let go."

She targeted the nonprofit sector because it was the world she knew. "It's always risky to serve nonprofits in the sense that everybody *needs* what you can do, but who can *pay* for it. I'd had enough experience of everybody needing me when I was a social worker. So if somebody said, 'Oh, we really need you,' my first reaction was, 'Well, great. How are you going to pay for it?' In ten years we've had only one client who did not pay us. Part of it is that when you're working with organizations on their financial situations, you know who you're going to be able to get the money from. On at least two occasions, I've required clients to advance our fee into a separate bank account before we would begin, and then the client and I would cosign to get the money out."

Many of the Stevens Group's nonprofit clients pay directly for consulting services. Others get a foundation to put up the money. "In the early years, we built our business on solving financial problems and making organizations whole again." They also filled the function of what Susan calls a roving CFO. "With money being so short, agencies were cutting out middle-management positions. So we would go into a client's offices and help put together a financial strategy for the organization, and return once a month to conduct a review and develop a plan for the coming month. There was a tremendous need. The marketplace was just slightly behind what I had already gone through."

Today the Stevens Group does three things: consulting (both strategic and problem solving), helping foundations set up and manage loan funds, and training nonprofits and foundations in finance through seminars conducted across the country. At age ten, the Stevens Group comprises three full-time professionals, four contract associates, and three support staff. Susan owns the corporation "wholly and solely."

Besides having a fundamental understanding of money, Susan attributes her success to her social work background and her family upbringing. "I can't tell you how important that has been for me. We all find ourselves over and over in situations that build on who we are and what we learned early on in our life experiences. I like people, and I was raised in a family where you always tried to bring the best out in people. I was raised to know that if this is somebody else's show, then stay out of the limelight. That's been one of the major secrets of our success as a firm. As consultants, we understand that we're always in the role of supporting cast."

As her practice has matured, Susan has faced a different set of issues than in the early days. One is learning how to select the jobs they want and turn down others that come their way without building a reputation for being unavailable.

"Managing your time is *the* issue in consulting. It's the issue in the beginning, when all you have is time and no clients; and it's a killer down the road when you've got more clients than you have time. When you're booked up, can't possibly take on another commitment, and you get that call from an old client, you have to say 'yes,' because this is a business of relationships."

Susan has also begun to look outside the business for more of her creative challenges. "Some of the routine things I do aren't fun anymore. How do I get variety and stimulation? You learn that you don't keep your company in crisis just so that you can have something new to do."

She has been drawing a sharper separation between her business and her personal life, and turning increasingly to her personal life for new sources of stimulation. "I've stabilized the company, I'm finding other ways to have fun, taking more time for my family, my music, books. I have a *fabulous* garden," she says with a sudden laugh, as if the very thought of herself kneeling in the dirt and cultivating relationships with her plants surprises her.

Susan is at the point where she is beginning to think about how to build assets in the business. "We're doing more product development so that we have materials we can sell that aren't just based on our time. Books, articles, seminars, audiotapes. Another idea we're looking at is owning a building and putting the company into it. Besides being an asset in its own right, there's something about bricks and mortar that increases the perceived value of the organization. I'm also trying to get more and more contracts that others here can execute, and more contracts that are ongoing, building a sustained revenue stream that is not dependent on me." Susan has had three bona fide offers to buy her company, two from accounting firms interested in product expansion. One is a standing offer. "But why would I sell? This isn't about the dollars. What am I going to do if I don't have this business?"

The only way she would sell, she says, would be if she took herself up on the offer she makes herself every year when she goes on vacation. "I tell myself that if I want to bail out of this, I can do it now. Then I spend the rest of my vacation thinking about what would I rather do than what I'm doing. In ten years, nothing's looked as good."

✓ 10   DISCOVERING YOUR RESIDUALS

How to tap the equity in your consulting practice to sell more than your time

Consulting's Hidden Annuities

This chapter is about leveraging what you've built and tapping the equity in what you've learned. When I talk about equity in this chapter, I'm talking about residual value. Equity is like the big flywheel on an old-fashioned cider press. You bend your back into the crank to get the mechanism turning, and when you finally get it up to speed you can ease off a little because the work you've put in keeps paying you back. Equity is the residual value in your consulting business that pays you back when you take time off or sell your business.

Traditionally, consulting is a business of selling time. It's an independent life, a good life, but no matter how high you ratchet up your rates and no matter how strong a base of clients you build, there are only so many hours in a day to sell, and when you shut the door to go fishin', ain't any money gonna be earned.

By leveraging and tapping equity I mean making your assets work harder for you; finding ways to sell the same hour's work to more than one client; building a business that keeps making money while you take a break; transforming what you've built into something you can *sell off* to finance your next career, play the market, or set yourself up in that artsy little villa with a Deux Chevaux in the wine country.

In most successful consulting practices, the ingredients for leverage and equity already exist in the form of potentials that I call "hidden annuities." Here are four:

1. Sustainable revenue streams.
2. Convertible assets.

3. Corporate equity.
4. Clients' equity.

Sustainable Revenue Streams

Revenue that comes in a consistent stream is better than the unpredictable kind because it reduces anxiety, helps you plan, makes it easier to control cash flow, and gives you an asset you can borrow against to grow your business.

Big projects that unfold over many months or several years can be structured for predictability: when you negotiate the project's price, suggest to your client that the fee be prorated over the life of the project and paid out at a regular monthly rate. Most clients prefer the predictability of such an arrangement, but if your client is hesitant, suggest a modest holdback to be released at key progress points and on completion.

Many consulting relationships begin as project-focused engagements and evolve into ongoing work for any of several reasons: to support implementation, serve as a trusted advisor, execute a series of related jobs. A time comes when it makes sense to convert your billing from job-by-job bids or time-and-materials billings to a monthly retainer. You may not want to use the word *retainer* because I think it scares some clients. It sounds like you're going to become a fixed rather than variable expense, but that's not the case. You're simply going to make the billings predictable.

If you have an ongoing relationship, figure the average monthly volume and propose to your client that you bill a constant monthly fee, with an annual or semiannual adjustment to reconcile your billings with the actual workload. This is what Alice Lucan did with her *USA Today* client when she left her law firm job and set up shop on her own (see chapter 1). Most clients will welcome the predictability: it simplifies their budgeting and makes your monthly invoices simpler to approve and pay.

A sustainable revenue stream can be established by contracting to provide an ongoing service in your area of expertise. Susan Stevens's main business is providing financial management consulting to foundations and nonprofit organizations. But since 1983 she has also had a contract with the Minneapolis Foundation to administer a nonprofit community loan program called the Minnesota Nonprofits Assistance Fund. The fund has made over $15 million in loans during the time

Susan has been running it. In addition to providing a source of sustained income, the contract has given the Stevens Group a base from which to help set up and administer loan funds for other foundations.

Eric Mitchell, a pricing consultant, generates sustainable revenues through subscriptions to his newsletter and membership dues in an association of pricing professionals.

Convertible Assets

There are two kinds of assets in consulting, the kind that you can sell off, like furnishings and equipment, and the kind you can't sell off because they are a part of who you are—assets like your reputation, your know-how, your strong client relationships. I call the first kind convertible assets because you can convert them to cash. I call the other kind intrinsic assets because they are an intrinsic part of who you are. A typical consulting practice is high in intrinsic assets and low in convertible assets, which means you can make a pretty good living as long as you stay at it, but when you're ready to retire, there's not really a business there to sell because you are it.

You can build equity in your consulting practice by transforming intrinsic assets into convertible assets. Two examples of this are turning your proprietary knowledge into products, and turning your name and reputation into a brand.

Turning Your Knowledge into Products   The notion here is simply that by turning your distinctive knowledge or processes into products—whether books, newsletter, seminars, software, or electronic devices—the result is something you can sell to multiple clients, which creates both equity and leverage.

On the plus side, products can become significant money-makers and an effective way to turn years of experience into equity. On the minus side, developing, marketing, and distributing products is a different world from consulting. It can consume substantial up-front time and capital, and it is inherently riskier. As a general rule, the closer you stick to products and processes you know, and to markets you know, the less likely you are to miscalculate.

In addition to the following examples, I recommend reading about Eric Mitchell's experiences with seminars and conferences in the profile at the end of this chapter, and about Skip Pile's work on product development in the profile at the end of chapter 14.

Jack Brizius and Sue Foster, the consultants to governors (see chapter 8), have consciously looked for product opportunities from their consulting work in order to get more leverage and reduce travel associated with consulting.

One of their first products was a book called *States in Profile,* a state-by-state reference volume of demographic, economic, and government tax, spending, and program data. The book has sold well, and they have published the data in expanded form on diskette, making it possible for users to manipulate the information. They developed a diskette called "State Policy Trends," which presented the same data in a time series to illustrate trends. They have subsequently repackaged the state data for sale to businesses in a print- and diskette-based product called "Perspective," which buyers can use to help make business decisions such as where to expand.

Sue and Jack joined up with two partners to develop "Perspective." In order to provide for shared ownership, they created a Subchapter S corporation called U.S. Data on Demand, Inc. U.S. Data on Demand is now producing products in three categories. One is a category they call "dataware," which consists of easy-to-use data bases and accompanying users guides. "Perspective" is the first product in this category and was introduced at $129.95.

The second category, the "Governor's Accountability Presentation System" (GAPS), is a data-based computer program that enables someone like a governor's aide to call up data on any community in a state and compare it with other communities or states. GAPS costs $75,000, and for this U.S. Data on Demand will build a custom data base, train the client to operate it, and update the data. The third product category consists of a series of books that Brizius & Foster anticipate publishing for consumers, using their data to address specific topics like picking a place to relocate your career or to retire.

Early in my own practice, I developed a methodology for helping nonprofit organizations identify opportunities to increase their earned income through mission-related venture activities. What made the methodology good—that it was careful and deliberate—also made it too expensive as a facilitated process, because nonprofits simply don't have the money to keep consultants around for extended periods.

The experience taught me a thing or two about sizing up a market—which, of course, is what *I* was teaching my clients. I turned to greener pastures but kept getting calls from organizations that had heard about my work and wanted help. So I approached a foundation with a proposal: if they would be my partner and pay for the time required to do it, I would convert what I'd learned into a self-help process, write a workbook, look for a publisher, and split royalties with the foundation. They agreed. I wrote the book, sold it to an international publisher, and today we are still sharing royalty income.

Turning Your Name and Reputation into a Brand   Possibly the most powerful intrinsic asset a consultant develops is her reputation and the goodwill of her clients.

A strong reputation enhances the earning power of any business. In a consumer products firm, brand equity is the price premium that a brand with a strong reputation can command over the average selling price for products in its category. A brand is a name with associations that communicate a benefit to the buyer—in effect, a promise.

In consulting, your name is your brand, and your reputation is its promise. In a smaller consulting practice, a strong reputation is usually tied inextricably to the person, and while it is clearly an asset, unless you find ways to transfer it to others, the only way to cash it in is to sell more of your own time—the client wants *you.*

If you think of your reputation as a halo, leveraging it would mean finding a way to make the same halo appear over your entire business as you grow. If all of your products, services, and employees carry the same promise in the eyes of your customers, all can command a premium price in the market without the customer requiring your personal involvement. For evidence, consider these prominent names: Arthur Andersen; Peat, Marwick & Mitchell; McKinsey; Yankelovich; Booz Allen. Every one has become a distinctive brand in the consulting business.

For an example more relevant to the scale of your practice and mine, consider Susan Stevens. When I interviewed Susan, I asked her why the Stevens Group hires most of her financial consultants as employees instead of as independent contractors.

"The answer lies in what the community has come to expect from us in terms of quality and standards," she said. "When I first started using associates, people would call and say, 'It's not that they didn't do a good job; they just didn't do it the way that, you know, *you* would have done it.' I realized that the value our firm adds is determined not only by *what* we do, but *how* we do it. In a typical consulting association, everybody brings their skill to the table. We go a step beyond that. We hire people with skill, yes, but then we expect them to do their work in a certain way. It has to do with the Stevens Group *style.*"

By understanding the importance of this unique style to her clientele, Susan has transformed her own reputation into a promise to be kept by the entire firm, where it functions like a brand, providing leverage and building equity in the business.

One testament to the value of the Stevens Group brand is the fact that she has had three unsolicited offers to buy her company, two from *accounting* firms. I emphasize who the would-be buyers are because I don't think you would expect an accounting firm to enter financial consulting through acquisition, unless they saw more value in the business than its financial expertise. One of the offers is a standing offer.

To turn your name into a brand, you have to look upon it impersonally, as a property, and give it legs.

How to Turn Your Name into a Brand

- Establish a clear association between your name and a distinctive competency—its promise.
- Treat your name as a company treats a brand asset: invest in building its visibility; be fierce in protecting its use; never allow its value to be eroded.
- Build a business of employees, processes, or products that embody your distinctive competency, carry your brand, and therefore command customer loyalty and premium pricing.
- If the scale of your business warrants, protect your name by registering it with the federal trademark office.

Corporate Equity

If you want to build equity in your business with the idea of someday selling it, consider incorporating. Among the other benefits of incorporation (see chapter 11), this will separate you as an individual from your business as a legal entity, and translate ownership of the business's equity into stock, which can be pledged, traded, or sold.

If you have established your business as a distinct entity, you can sell the business, its name, its proprietary products and processes, the building, even contracts. A buyer will pay a premium for goodwill, if it clearly follows the business.

Goodwill can be generally defined as the excess earning power of a business over and above that which is attributable to its identifiable assets. Brand equity is an example of goodwill. The IRS defines goodwill as including every positive advantage that a firm gets in doing business—the total of all indefinable qualities that bring customers to a business. When you sell a business and a buyer pays a premium for goodwill, that premium is a capital gain to the seller. Recent changes in tax law allow goodwill to be amortized and deducted like a tangible over 15 years. This change will surely increase the price a seller can get for goodwill, although by how much is anyone's guess.

Ways You Can Build the Assets of Your Company

- Establish a track record for showing a profit.
- Retain and reinvest earnings.
- Buy your office building by paying a mortgage instead of rent.
- Cultivate long-term client commitments that can be met without your being personally involved.
- Build strong brand equity.
- Develop profitable proprietary products and services.

Clients' Equity

The idea here is to look for ways of tapping into the financial and market strength of your clients through commission-based pricing, equity positions, or collaborations.

When Pattie Garrahy develops a media plan (see chapter 7), she is generating fee income and building equity in a client at the same time. She taps that equity by winning a contract to execute the media plan (go into the market and purchase the advertising space), a service that is billed on a commission basis.

Traditionally, a company's ad agency develops an advertising campaign for a fee and executes it for a 15 percent commission. Competition has changed that. The media have become more complex, and so has media-buying, and advertisers have become more aggressive about price. One result is the rise of companies that specialize in buying ad space for a reduced commission, typically 5 to 8 percent. In this environment, Pattie offers clients a choice of time and materials for media planning, or a guaranteed ceiling if she gets to execute the plan. In some cases, she has structured a graduated commission, starting at 4 percent for the first three months as a sweetener to bring in business, then moving to 5 percent.

The upshot is, she gets paid at both ends of the relationship, and commissions are typically six-figure invoices, far more than she could make simply selling her expertise by the hour. Pattie adds value to her clients through the know-how to produce a more effective media plan, flexibility in the relationship, and an ability to meet or beat the competition in the pricey realm of execution.

When Bryan Robertson helps a client like Eastland or B.D. Baggies develop a marketing and distribution network in Europe (see chapter 2), he charges a fixed monthly fee until the client's European sales surpass an agreed level, at which point Bryan's fee converts to a percentage of the client's European sales.

Bryan's reward for helping his client succeed is a share in that success until sales reach a volume where the client determines it makes sense to establish their own management structure for Europe and bring Bryan's contract to conclusion. Bryan adds value to his clients through his intimate knowledge of European retail marketing, strong distributor relationships, track record, and a proprietary process for focusing his clients in the right markets and building and protecting their brands in Europe.

A friend of mine who is helping a consortium of Russian companies develop import-export deals works on a modest monthly retainer plus an equity position in any deals she helps bring to fruition. This arrangement enables the cash-poor Russians to get high-powered consulting services for a fraction of the market rate, and enables my friend to tap directly into the client's share of successful deals. She and the client renegotiate her percentage separately for every potential deal as it is identified, depending on the nature and size of the opportunity. When the client does well, my friend does well. In essence my friend brings two critical ingredients to the relationship. One is her contacts and skill for developing and negotiating deals, and the other is a willingness to take most of her compensation at the back end, sharing in the client's risk.

Verne Severson, the electronics engineering consultant (see chapter 6), has found a way to leverage his long-standing relationship with DataCard Corporation, benefiting both parties. DataCard is the leading manufacturer of devices that read magnetically encoded cards—like the credit card scanners on retail checkout counters.

Several years ago, DataCard was in danger of missing a significant sale. One of its products is a machine that hospitals use to make patient ID cards. The machines are connected to a hospital's computers for integration into their management information system. One of DataCard's largest hospital customers was changing computers, and unless DataCard could figure out how to make its machine compatible with the customer's new computer, DataCard's product would be replaced by a competitor's.

Verne offered to design and produce a black box called a protocol converter that would serve as an interpreter between DataCard's device and the hospital's new computer. Verne and a former associate formed CommStar, Inc., a Subchapter S corporation through which to negotiate the deal and deliver the product. DataCard gave them a purchase order for a hundred units, which Verne and his partner priced to cover the development costs. The black box worked so well DataCard has ordered more than six hundred additional units, and CommStar has retained the earnings to fund new product development.

To that end, Verne and his partner recently announced a "reseller agreement" with DataCard. Under this agreement, CommStar will customize DataCard's products by adding software and hardware enhancements, enabling CommStar to resell them for specialized applications. CommStar's first contract is with a firm called Smarte Carte, which has over 80 percent of the airport cart rental business worldwide and wants the DataCard device adapted so that cart rental stands will accept credit cards.

Verne says his understanding of DataCard's product puts him in a unique position to adapt it for other applications. DataCard likes this "value-added reseller" arrangement because it puts their products in new markets without their having to be in the customization business.

Verne maintains his consulting relationship with DataCard and other clients through Forward Research, his sole proprietorship. Through CommStar, he and his partner are able to convert their know-how into new products, tapping equity in the products and market position of clients like DataCard.

Three ingredients must exist for client equity relationships to succeed:

1. Strong underlying trust between the consultant and client,
2. Clear articulation of the terms, and . . .
3. Added value.

Added value is the sine qua non of collaborations like Verne's reseller agreement with DataCard. Added value is also the basis on which a commission like Bryan Robertson's or an equity position such as that which my friend takes in dealing with her Russian clients is considered fair compensation. Value may be added in many ways: special knowledge, special relationships, proprietary processes, sharing of risk.

Tips to Help You Develop the Hidden Annuities in Your Practice

---

Taking Inventory

Here are some places to look for hidden annuities in your consulting practice that can be developed to increase your leverage or help you build equity.

Market presence and client relationships that can be leveraged. Do you have relationships that can be restructured into sustainable revenue streams? Can you get more out of existing relationships by offering new services that address other needs of your clients? Can you team up to get business that your clients normally give to others? Example: Diane Page and Leapfrog Associates (see chapter 7). Can you serve the same clients in more than one way? Example: Eric Mitchell's newsletter, consulting, conference, and professional association all serve the same audience.

Knowledge that can be converted to cash. Do you collect data in your business that could be repackaged and sold to others? Example: Brizius & Foster's dataware products. Have you gained insights into an emerging issue for one client that you could resell to others in noncompeting fields? Would a seminar company be interested in marketing proprietary seminars on the subject? Example: Len Smart's relationship with Infotel Systems Corp. Have you come to understand the unmet needs of a special market that others have yet to recognize? Can you use that knowledge to add value and support higher prices? Example: Pile and Company's consulting to help companies get more from their ad agencies (see profile following chapter 14).

Processes that can be converted into products. Have you developed a methodology that could be packaged and sold to special markets in the form of seminars, software, workbooks, instructional videos? Example: Pile and Company's Marcom Manager software.

Know-how in a field you are abandoning. Are you getting out of a market where there is still interest in what you can offer? Can you cash in on the residual equity by repackaging your knowledge and techniques into self-help materials, or licensing others to deliver it? Example: my how-to book on entrepreneurship for nonprofit corporations.

Ability to add value to a client's product. Do you have special know-how that would enable you to customize a client's product or service for special markets? Could you be a value-added reseller, like Verne Severson?

Channels of distribution or marketing networks. Do you have networks or channels of distribution that would be of value to others, like Bryan Robertson's relationships with European distributors?

Reputation. Do you have a well-known reputation in your field? Could you turn your name into a brand, as Susan Stevens has, and build a business of branded products and services?

Corporate equity. Would incorporating enable you to leverage your business by attracting outside capital? Would it enable you to build an asset with retained earnings, ongoing contracts, employees, equipment, and goodwill that you can cash out or turn into an annuity when you're ready for a change? Example: Skip Pile.

Expenses you can convert to assets. Are you training associated consultants how to use your methodology, then finding they become competitors? Can you train a cadre of employees instead and build a client base that does not require your direct involvement? Example: David Hallowell (see chapter 2). Are you paying rent when it would make more sense to pay a mortgage?

Commissions, equity sharing, cost sharing. Do your services have a direct and measurable impact on the client's sales or profitability? Can you add value to your clients and increase their value to you by structuring a risk-sharing/profit-sharing agreement? Example: Bryan Robertson's pricing system for Subsidiary Services International.

Buying Back Your Time

For many of us, consulting is more like being an artist than a manager or executive. We like getting into the thick of a client's problem, but we're darn glad we're not vice presidents in the client's company. We like coaching managers, but we don't want to be one. We're lousy delegaters, never really satisfied with a subordinate's work. For a lot of us, the beauty of this business lies in the cleverness of a solution, the look of grateful surprise on a client's face. Building a business is the last thing we want to do. Developing products, worrying about packaging, pricing, marketing, and distribution, these things give us knots in the stomach.

In order to go into consulting, you bought back your time from your employer and took it out into the market under your own banner. If you want to develop products and build a business, you'll have to buy back some of your time from consulting to do the work involved. Building your business changes its chemistry and the way you spend your day. Visualize what you're letting yourself into. If it involves the kinds of things that you expect to enjoy doing, you will probably do very well.

Cash, Not Conversation

I have an uncle named Grosvenor who built a business that became the world's largest supplier of aftermarket parts to general aviation. He wears big bow ties, has a bank account that makes Chase Manhattan look anemic, and is fond of saying "cash, not conversation" when he gets the feeling he's being patronized.

I was reminded of my uncle's maxim when Bryan Robertson told me his tale of misadventure raising capital to launch Subsidiary Services International, his export marketing firm. The lesson: don't be a stooge. If you're first in line for the risk, make sure you're first in line for the reward.

Bryan needed to raise at least $150,000 up front to cover salaries, rent, promotional materials, initial marketing costs, and travel expenses. He was introduced to two retired businessmen who had the kinds of contacts Bryan felt he needed in order to locate potential investors. The two proposed a deal in which each of them would put $25,000 into Bryan's new company in exchange for 30 percent equity. Bryan would retain 40 percent. The two would then help Bryan pitch other potential investors, in exchange for which each would take a $25,000 salary in the first year. An expensive way to raise venture capital, but Bryan had no way of judging the terms.

His new associates lined up a meeting of potential investors, and Bryan made his pitch. It was received with interest. Some said they could put up unsecured debt financing, but would expect an equity position. "I started to feel pretty uncomfortable," Bryan confesses. "It was becoming clear that my two partners weren't going to raise as much money as I needed, and that they weren't making a contribution anywhere near worth the equity and salary they'd asked for. I started to think, Why am I doing this?"

About the same time, Bryan had an opportunity to meet with a family friend who was a successful businessman and had started his own company. "I told him what I'd been through and how I was trying to raise capital for this company. He went through my materials. He said, 'A lot of young guys make this same mistake.' He said he'd be more excited about my idea if I had a partner more like myself—enthusiastic, and counting on the business to make it. 'It's your idea, you've got to drive it, you've got to own most of the company.' He said he would give me some money, but that I should go get most of the money from my family, and then come see him again. 'Have it be *your* company,' he said.

"I took his advice, and when I came back and told him my family was willing to put in $100,000, the guy wrote me a check for $75,000—right there. I was overwhelmed by his belief in me. It gave me tremendous confidence. Then he showed me how to structure it. 'You keep 51 percent. Hold aside 10 percent for somebody you might want to bring in someday. Spread out the remaining 39 percent among the investors.' He was so fair, I was just flabbergasted."

Bryan undid the tentative deal he'd put together with the two initial investors, neither of whom had yet put up their money. "It was one of the most awkward things I've ever been through." He ended up paying them each a month's salary and reimbursing any expenses they'd put into the business. "It cost me over $13,000 to get out of the deal. And it was a hell of a lesson. I don't know how I let myself get into it. It was one of those situations where insecurity obscures common sense." With the equity restructured and the capital raised, Bryan formed the company, incorporated, got all the legal documents done, and set up an office. In the process, he landed his first client. "I went to someone in the footwear business who knew my work at Bass, and fifteen days later I had a three-year contract."

For me, Bryan's experience sums up the theme of this chapter: we're all worth more than we think. Turning what we know into a business and making it grow means more than having a good idea and selling it. It means respecting what we bring to the table and leveraging its value —finding the flywheel in the business, and getting it up to speed.

Ideas to Take Away

- Leverage and equity in consulting can come from four hidden annuities: sustainable revenues streams, convertible assets, corporate equity, and clients' equity.
- Sustainable revenue streams reduce anxiety, help you plan, make it easier to control cash flow, and give you an asset you can borrow against to build your business.
- Convertible assets can be turned into cash; intrinsic assets are those you can't sell off because they are a part of you.
- You can turn intrinsic assets into convertible assets by (1) turning proprietary knowledge into products like seminars, newsletters,

and software, and (2) turning your name into a brand that adds value to your services whether or not you are directly involved with the client.

- If you want to build equity in your business with the idea of some-day selling it, consider incorporating.
- Look for opportunities to tap the financial and market strengths of your clients through commission-based pricing, equity positions, and collaborations.
- To develop your hidden annuities, take inventory, buy back your time, assess feasibility, and ask for cash, not conversation.

Eric Mitchell, profiled below, left a corporate staff job and went on his own as a pricing consultant. He asked himself the tough questions about leverage and equity before he even started his business. The an-swers he came up with influenced the way he structured his services as well as his business. The Pricing Advisor, Inc., is a model for the rest of us, who may work just as hard as Eric, but would be thrilled to work half as smart.

BECOMING THE PRODUCER INSTEAD OF THE ACTOR
Profile
ERIC G. MITCHELL
Pricing Consultant, Atlanta, GA

Eric Mitchell left Xerox in 1982 after nine years as a pricing manager, product manager, and region controller in Phoenix. Before Xerox, he'd been a pricing manager at Ford. Since he knew a lot about the subject, he decided to go into business as a pricing consultant. But instead of simply hanging out a shingle, Eric wanted to find some way to set himself apart from other consultants, build his reputation, and build a client base.

He decided that publishing a newsletter that talked to corporate pricing professionals about pricing strategies and tactics would be a good way to get started, so he went down to the library at Arizona State University and spent night and day for weeks on end reading everything he could find about how to start a newsletter.

"I picked up the phone and called newsletter publishers and asked questions until I made people sick." In the process he got a lot of free advice, built colleagues, and got a lucky break. "I was calling a guy who was a board member of the Newsletter Association of America to ask his advice on the best ways to research lists. The guy said, 'Tell me what you're writing about again,' and I said 'Pricing.' He said, 'Well I'm president of a company that publishes books for overseas audiences, and we've been looking a long time for someone to write a book on pricing. Would you write it?' "

Eric wrote the book in exchange for what seemed to him at the time to be a considerable amount of money. "Every day from eight-thirty to twelve-thirty I sat at a desk and did nothing but work on the book. I used the afternoons for phone calls, and spent evenings at the library."

Eric incorporated his business as the Pricing Advisor, Inc. Tax laws related to subscription publications enable him to accrue and defer revenues in ways that made incorporation advantageous. The first issue of the newsletter was published in the United States in 1983, at about the same time that his book was published and marketed in Europe, the Mideast, and the Far East.

"Suddenly I was both a newsletter publisher and an author." His plan was to use the book as a marketing premium to build subscriptions for the newsletter, and to use the newsletter as both a profit center and a base for building his reputation and consulting referrals. And that's just how it's worked out.

How long did the process take? The planning and development phase of the business took Eric nine months. He started promoting the newsletter in the fourth quarter of 1983, and the first revenues began arriving in early 1984. In May of 1986 he moved from Phoenix to Atlanta. "That's the point where I felt I'd reached financial independence and could relocate my business and my life." All told, close to three years.

The business had been self-financed and today has three sources of revenue—the newsletter; consulting, which started in 1984; and an annual pricing conference begun in 1990. Eric maintains twelve to twenty active consulting clients, big companies like Motorola, Merck, AT&T, and Deluxe Corporation. They come to him either because they are subscribers to the newsletter or have heard of him from other sources such as the direct-mail marketing he does to build newsletter subscriptions and conference registrations.

Each of his three sources of revenue produces about a third of the firm's total income. "They're different media, same message—giving advice to people on pricing. I didn't want to become dependent on a single source of revenue."

One lesson he's learned is that he doesn't want to be in the business of writing for publishers. "I compare the book, which I wrote but somebody else published, to my newsletter, which I write every month and publish myself, and while there may be some benefit to doing the book, the financial rewards go to the publisher, not the author. By now, I've written the equivalent of several books on pricing but in the form of a hundred issues of an eight-page monthly newsletter. With the book, the publisher makes the money and pays me a *fee*. With the newsletter, I have a *revenue stream:* four thousand subscribers all over the world, who each pays $200 per year for the subscription."

The same lesson came home to him in another experience, this one having to do with seminars and conferences.

In 1985 Eric received a call from a man who had a seminar business, and the business had a contract to market and conduct seminars for *Business Week.* The man was calling because he was interested in developing a pricing seminar. Eric went to New York to meet him. "He said, 'We'll put you out all across the country. You'll become famous because you'll have the *Business Week* name. The only thing we're going to ask you to do is coauthor the seminar for us and conduct it. We'll do all the marketing, handle all the details. The only thing you don't get, is we own the seminar and materials that you write.'

"I didn't like that, but after much agony I decided to go ahead with the *Business Week* name, even though I wasn't that attracted to the terms and conditions. The guy was a tough negotiator. I remember at the end of the negotiation he said, 'Look, Mitchell, you don't understand. We *produce* the seminar, you're just the actor. We'll make you famous, and we'll pay you a fee. But you do what we tell you, because we hold the key to the *Business Week* name.'"

The first seminar drew forty-two people at $700 each. Eric was getting paid less than a thousand dollars to run it. "Every city I went to, there were thirty or forty people. The guy who owned the seminar company came back and said, 'Look, this thing's grown, we want you to train some other people to run it.' I couldn't be in ten different cities a month and still run a consulting business and put out a newsletter. They brought ten guys in for me to train, and now all of a sudden these guys were pricing experts. I finally left in 1987, but the program continued through 1989." In all, it grossed over $6 million.

Seminars, like plays, have a limited life. When this one had run its course, the seminar operator severed his relationship with *Business Week* and approached a conference company in Hong Kong with the idea of turning the material into an annual pricing conference. The first conference he put on drew about seven hundred people at a fee of about $800 each. Having demonstrated the value of the idea, he sold the rights to the Hong Kong company and retired to Florida on the proceeds.

Eric kept tabs on these developments and saw the money that could be made. "I decided to do the same thing. We offered our first annual pricing conference in Chicago in 1990, and now it accounts for a third of our revenues."

The way I first found Eric was through a mutual friend in Seattle when we were talking about how consultants set their rates. Eric is the person who had opened my friend's eyes to the notion of pricing on the basis of value rather than cost. "He's a pricing consultant. Very successful. Many years as a corporate manager. Midforties. Black." My ears had perked up. Besides looking for pricing insights, I'd been wanting to broaden the cross-section of consultants presented in the book and was looking for more minorities who'd left management jobs and gone on their own. With a little persistence, I managed to catch Eric in his office in Atlanta. Too busy to meet, he said, but he'd be happy to do a phone interview.

"There's a theme here," Eric says during that first interview. "In case you didn't pick up on it yet. It's 'don't be the actor, be the producer.' "

I point out that the producer is the one who puts up the capital and takes the risk. Eric agrees, but says that with his seminar experience and newsletter in place, the risks were not great. "It's a logical extension of my business. The prospect base is right there: the people who read my newsletter." He pauses. "Besides," he says in a confessional tone, "my wife's in her own business, too. Meeting planner. She helps me out."

Being the producer means owning your expertise and controlling your channels of distribution. Being an actor means getting paid for your time while someone else packages your wisdom into a product, markets it, controls its distribution, and makes the real money. Eric is quick to admit to life-style and risk trade-offs associated with leveraging his expertise into multiple channels.

"The good news is, it's all mine; and that's the bad news, too, because it means I'm constantly fighting the battle of which revenue stream to serve today: the newsletter, the conference, or consulting." But that's not stopping him. Before long, he's saying, "The next logical extension, if you have conferences and if you write to people on pricing, is to start an association of people who share an interest in pricing. So we're starting an association of pricing professionals." Listening to Eric, you get a feeling he has a definite handle on making money.

Another theme emerges in our conversation, the notion of leveraging your expertise into sustained revenue streams, rather than simply selling advice through a series of independent consulting engagements.

"Consulting is the least-leveraged activity I engage in. It's a dilemma. How do you free yourself from the sweet bondage of a forty- or fifty-thousand-dollar contract and the time it consumes? It's like a sugar high. The moment they want you, you have to be there, beholden to the customer. The moment it's over, they forget how to spell your name. It's *noncontinuous* revenue. Consulting clients may come back, but they're driven by problems. They hire you to solve a problem, then pay your bill. They may call back in three years with another problem, but you never know when.

"Noncontinuous revenue is unpredictable, hard to track, has a feast and famine character. I always look for *revenue streams.* When I get paid an advance to write a book, that's revenue. But by turning my knowledge into a base of newsletter subscribers, I've turned noncontinuous revenue into a revenue stream. It's renewable. A conference that people come to every year to learn and grow is a revenue stream. A professional association where people network and grow and pay annual dues is a revenue stream. My purpose in going toward the revenue stream is to smooth out the income, control it, grow it predictably, improve it incrementally, and be able to rely on it and pay the rent from it."

Many consultants create a revenue stream by turning their knowhow into a seminar and taking it on the road. Eric could do the same, but for now he is limiting his seminar business to in-house seminars conducted for his consulting clients.

"For reasons of these other pursuits, I haven't built a seminar business. There's just not enough of me. Because I'm not financially leveraged, don't have the time, and haven't developed other experts under me, I'm not doing seminars around the country, and that's foregone revenues and profit."

On the other hand, Eric says he has found it more profitable to design and market in-house seminars for his consulting clients than to mount public seminars, because there is virtually no risk, marketing expense, or registration hassle. The client assembles the audience and pays the tab. There again, that uncanny handle on money.

Our conversation digresses into the personal. I'm curious about how it works for Eric and his wife, both running their own businesses.

"We have some basic rules, like not bringing business into the bedroom. If one of us slips up, we just remind each other." Eric keeps money issues straight by putting himself on a salary and keeping a P and L statement on the business. "My accountant taught me to look at my P and L the same way I would if I were on the board of Xerox." I ask him about stresses during the start-up years. "I was a bachelor when I started the business," he says. "Kids from a former marriage. Workaholic. I spent a tremendous amount of time building my business. It was my wife, actually, before we got married, who laid it out for me. 'You're either going to be a miserable old man married to your business, or you're going to have a life. You tell me which.'

"I decided I wanted to have a life. So I leave the business every day at five. I'm very disciplined about it. It works for me. I can't say that it'll work for everybody. But I can tell you it's a whole lot easier to do when you've got some revenue streams in place."

✓ PART II

Setting Up Shop—

Straight Talk

About the

Nuts and Bolts

11   ESTABLISHING YOUR BUSINESS

Tips to simplify the start-up process

Picking a Name: You Are Your Business

Companies spend fortunes coming up with names, because a name is the distillation of everything they want the business to represent to their customers. Coming up with a name that fits who you are and what you offer, a name that will wear well over the years, build your reputation, and put the customer at ease, takes some rumination. It helps to ask what kind of an image you would want if you were a brand.

Doing Business Under Your Own Name

Many consultants do business under their own names, as in Pile and Company, Wheeler Design, Brizius & Foster, Diane Sims Page, L. W. Smart & Associates. There are some good reasons.

Benefits of Using Your Given Name for Your Business

- *The name of the business tells what the customer gets: the person behind the name.* In consulting, the product is the consulting relationship. If a brand is a promise, then your brand must promise something to customers about the kind of relationship they can expect in doing business with your firm. *Easy:* Use your good name and image to personalize the promise of a satisfactory relationship. *Much harder:* Create an impersonal company name, make people aware of it, and establish in people's minds the attributes you want them to associate with that name.

- *You already own your name, and you have the right to use it.* If you pick a name you do not own, say Quixotic Technologies, you are obliged to conduct a search of that name in the office of the secretary of state in every state where you plan to do business. Where somebody has already registered that name, you may not use it without risk of legal action. However, you have the right to do business under your given name, regardless of whether others are also using that name.
- *Using your own name makes referrals easy, and referrals are the lifeblood of consulting.* Not everyone who wants to send a friend your way will be able to recall that you do business as Quixotic Technologies.

Reasons for Not Using Your Given Name for Your Business

- *Put prospective clients at ease by sounding big and established.* Verne Severson consults under the name Forward Research in part because some of the firms with which he's worked have scaled back their consulting budgets with their belt tightening, and he feels that an executive who sees large invoices from somebody who is obviously a consultant might decide to bring a salaried engineer on board and save a buck. But the same executive is accustomed to spending sizable sums on supplier invoices, and an invoice from somebody called Forward Research could just as easily fall into that category of expense.
- *Build awareness of a proprietary consulting product or specialty.* Example: Eric Mitchell's the Pricing Advisor, Inc.
- *Link your firm to a special market niche.* Example: State Research Associates, the group that Brizius & Foster associated with to do state government consulting.
- *Refrain from singling out one individual's name in a practice with multiple partners.* Example: The Boston Consulting Group.

After you decide on a name and the image you want that name to help establish for your business, reinforce that image in everything you say and do: the design and quality of your letterhead and business card, the way in which you approach prospects and sell your services, the quality, style, and packaging of your written proposals, the way you dress, the way you interact with clients' employees, your reports, your invoices, how you handle mistakes, the way you respond to inconvenient requests.

Some tony corporate marketing communications consultants call the sum total of these impressions a corporation's "voice." It is important that there be one voice, and that the voice reinforce the personality and core values of the corporation. Other marketing consultants talk about the concept of a USP ("unique selling proposition").

Your USP is what sets you apart from your competition—it is your sustainable competitive advantage, the reason your clients come back, the reason they pass your name to their friends and associates. Brand consultants talk about brand personality and brand equity. One definition of brand equity is the pricing premium a product can command because of the intangible attributes (personality) associated with the brand in the minds of buyers.

In my mind, these ideas are all circling around the central truth that to build your professional image, you must:

- Know what attributes are most important to your target customers.
- Determine which of those attributes best fit your strengths and set you apart from your competitors.
- Strive to make everything you say and do work together in a seamless way to reinforce those attributes in the minds of your target customers.

What you call yourself makes a difference in how you're seen. Susan Stevens does business as the Stevens Group, a name that implies both Susan's personal commitment and a sense of size and establishment. When she went on her own, Susan discovered that not only what she called her business mattered, but also how she described herself.

"I learned that the more adjectives you could put before the word *consultant* the better off you are. When you tell people you're a consultant, they figure you're between jobs. But when you tell them you're a *management* consultant, it actually sounds like something. When I started to say *financial management* consultant—then I was treated with *respect!*"

How you're seen makes a difference in how comfortable your client is, too. Pattie Garrahy does business as PGR Media, a name that sounds established and is at once personalized by her initials and focused on her specialty (media planning and buying for advertisers). Pattie carries two sets of business cards. One lists no title, and the other says "President" discreetly beneath her name.

She says, "If I'm talking to a prospect where the management is loaded with people from big companies, they feel more comfortable knowing I'm *president* of PGR Media. They like to know they're deal-ing at the top. It makes it easy for them to introduce me to *their* presi-dent. But a lot of smaller companies are trying to get away from the traditional corporate structure. They're all part of one team. To hand them a card that says 'Pattie Garrahy, President,' would seem preten-tious, so I don't."

If you wish to reserve exclusive right to your business name, you must register it with the secretary of state in each state in which you plan to do business. Businesses are unlike trademarks, patents, and copyrights, which are federally protected and registered at the federal level. Busi-nesses are creatures of the states in which they are located, and there is no way to register and protect a business's name at the federal level.

If you do business as a sole proprietor using your given name, you may do business in any state. If you do business as a corporation, you will be required to file articles of incorporation with the secretary of state in the state in which you choose to incorporate. The filing must include the name of the corporation, and the name may not be the same as another company name or trademark on file with the secretary of state.

If you file under a corporate name that is already reserved by some-body else, your filing will be returned. (Increasingly, states are estab-lishing a standard of allowing names that are distinguishable in any way from that of an existing business. Rainbow Consulting, Inc., will be ac-cepted even though Rainbow Paint, Inc., is already registered. But not every state uses the same standard.) If your name is accepted, it will be reserved in that state from use by another business.

Unlike a sole proprietor, a corporation must qualify for the right to do business in any state other than that in which it is incorporated. You call the secretary of state in the state in which you want to do business, and ask for the forms for qualifying to do business in that state. If your business name has already been reserved by another firm in that state, you must do business under another name (a "DBA") in that state. You keep your own name in your own state.

You can check a name's availability on a state-by-state basis by con-tacting the secretary of state's office in each state where you wish to do business. Nearly every secretary of state's office will tell you over the phone whether the name you wish to use is already taken in their state. (A few require you to request in writing.) Qualifying to do business as a corporation in numerous states is expensive, because it involves annual filings and fees and a registered agent in each state.

If you are not incorporating but plan to do business as a sole proprietor or partnership, you are not required to register with the secretary of state, but you may want to do so to reserve your rights to your business name. You can fill out a "certificate of assumed name" and register the name with the secretary of state.

In Minnesota, such a certificate costs twenty-five dollars to file and protects the business name for ten years. If the name is already taken, you will be notified. While states do not take legal action to protect your reserved name from use by others, the fact that you have reserved the name with the state establishes your rights to exclusivity, enabling you to sue for relief from infringement.

Picking a Location

There are four criteria to consider in evaluating office-siting options: costs, professionalism, location advantages, and personal preference and productivity. Given those criteria, here's a quick take on the most frequent options for siting your office.

Working at Home

Pros

- Lean, comfortable, profitable.
- Integration of personal and professional lives.
- Tax write-offs.

Cons

- Isolating.
- May not be suitable place to meet clients.
- Muddying of the distinction between personal and professional lives.
- Family interruptions.

Leasing Private Space in an Office Building

Pros

- Professional and impressive.
- Quiet place to work.
- Can pick advantageous location.

Cons

- High monthly overhead requires more capital for your business and undermines staying power during lean times.
- Multiyear lease commitment.

Sharing Space in an Office Building

Pros

- Professional.
- Companionship and expense sharing.

Cons

- Overhead high notwithstanding expense sharing.
- More commitments (lease; cotenants; "joint and several liability"—see below).
- Affected by changing fortunes of others.

Nesting Within Another Organization and Tapping into Their Support Services

Pros

- Letting them be landlord, receptionist, copier-repair person, while you focus on making money.
- May be quite inexpensive.
- Seldom requires lease.
- Provides companionship.

Cons

- Very low profile; your name not on door.
- No control over space use or conditions.
- Affected by changing fortunes of others.

I have been a consultant since 1981. Over the years I have sublet space from larger organizations where I have gotten access to their support services at a nominal charge, I have signed a lease with two other consultants for a three-year period, sharing support services and equipment, and, since 1991, I have had my office at home. Of the consultants interviewed for this book, about half have offices at home, and half in professional space. Many who have their office at home are not known to do so by their clients; some even put suite numbers on their business cards.

Costs

Professional space costs more than you'd think. In my experience, whatever you pay for rent, you can add 50 to 100 percent in related costs. As the financial scenarios in chapter 12 illustrate, renting professional space can have quite an impact on the amount of capital you need to launch your business and your staying power through lean times. Having your office at home not only saves money, you get to deduct as a business expense a pro rata share of the operating costs of your home, and depreciate a pro rata share of your capital investment in the home—as long as you are scrupulous in following the rules set forth by the IRS (see below).

What I Saved by Moving Home

Following is a comparison of some of the costs I incurred in my first year of having my office at home versus one of the preceding years sharing professional space in a downtown St. Paul office building.

The difference between the two? Nearly $1,600 a month. That's the equivalent of more than one day a month I don't have to spend consulting, which in turn frees me from nearly a day of marketing, and since I'm not spending forty-five minutes a day commuting, there's the equivalent of two more days' time released from the hungry jaws of overhead.

What to do? I can keep my nose to the grindstone and put that money in my pocket, or I can grant myself an extra month and a half of vacation

	Office Expenses	Phone	Rent	Receptionist/ Bookkeeper	TOTAL
My share of prof'l office:	$4,845	$3,514	$8,897	$5,455	$22,711
Home alone:	$2,690	$1,104	0	0	$ 3,794

during the year to contemplate why it took me ten years to arrive at this epiphany.

Office expenses include postage, supplies, and messenger services in both cases, as well as copier lease and postage meter lease in the shared office. (At the end of the copier lease, I bought the machine for $200 and moved it home with me, so the shared-office figure in effect represents capitalizing the copier through the lease; now I am benefiting from that investment. To be comparable, the office-at-home option would need to figure capital costs for a copier.) Phone expenses are higher in the shared office for two reasons. One, commercial phone lines are more expensive than residential. Two, working at home with voice mail and other devices described below, I get along with fewer lines.

I had other business expenses besides those listed (travel, promotion, professional fees, software and computer equipment enhancements, publications, insurance), but they did not vary based on where I located my office. However, there are hidden costs of locating in professional space that are not reflected above because they are not legitimate (deductible) business expenses. Among these are the costs of commuting, buying restaurant lunches, and going to work every day in a coat and tie and laundered shirt. Widening the disparity even further is the home office deduction you are allowed on your income taxes when you locate your business at home.

The Home Office Deduction

The IRS allows you to deduct operating expenses that apply to a part of your home, but only if that part is exclusively used on a regular basis as your principal place of business. In a recent ruling, the Supreme Court held that home office space is deductible only if it is the place where your most important work is conducted, *and* where you spend a substantial number of your working hours. In other words, if your most important work is done outside your home office, for example on your clients' premises, your home office is not deductible even if it is your only office—or so the court ruled in the case of an anesthesiologist, whose most important work was deemed to be performed at the hospital.

The deduction is derived by adding (1) all *direct* operating and maintenance costs for the home that you incurred only for the benefit of your business, to (2) a pro rata share of your *general* home operating and repair expenses. The latter is calculated by figuring what percentage of your home's total area is used exclusively for your business, and multiplying that percentage times general household operating expenses like homeowner's insurance, maintenance, repairs and utilities. Additional calculations are used to figure a deduction for a share of the real estate taxes, mortgage interest, casualty losses, and depreciation of the home.

The salient IRS document is form 8829. *Be aware that while depreciation reduces your immediate income tax liability, it also lowers your cost basis in the house,* so that when you sell, your capital gain (if any) will be figured on the net sales proceeds minus the *depreciated* value. In other words, you will have a larger taxable gain.

Professionalism

The need to present a professional image is a good reason to locate in professional space. The questions to ask yourself are (1) will your client know where you have your office, and if so, (2) will having your office at home present an unprofessional image in your kind of consulting?

Ten years ago, running a consulting business out of your home had the image of a shoestring operation. That is no longer true for most kinds of consulting, although it still is for certain kinds, especially image-sensitive fields like advertising and marketing, businesses where clients frequently call on you, and businesses that need to seem large and established in order to win a client's confidence. Thanks to fax, data communications, voice mail, word processing, and courier services, the clients of many consultants who work at home in blue jeans have no idea that their consultants aren't dressed in tailored suits, sitting at walnut desks in office buildings.

Location Advantages

Unlike retailers and restaurateurs, location is not a major consideration for most consultants because they deal principally in information, which travels easily, and because consultants are more likely to meet their clients in the clients' offices than the other way around.

There are plenty of exceptions. Verne Severson rents space in a suburban office park, where he has both his office and electronics lab. He's there because he feels it's advantageous for him to be located in the same area where many of his customers are located, and because he's often visited by people who sell the components that go into the prototypes he builds for his customers. Verne maintains an office at home as well, which is where he handles the administrative side of his business during nights and weekends.

In my business, being close to the customer is not important. A large share of my consulting revenues during a four-year period came from a client in Europe. We did business nearly every day by telephone, fax, and DHL Worldwide Express, and I could have been located anywhere in the world served by couriers and reliable phone service.

If leasing private space in an office building is important from a location or image standpoint, there may be ways to pare costs. Skip Pile's offices are in the advertising and graphic arts section of Boston, in the heart of the Back Bay. Skip waited to get commercial space until he'd been in business a year and had the earnings to pay a lease. Then he picked a class B building and negotiated a reduced rent by investing $25,000 of retained earnings in leasehold improvements as part of the deal.

Personal Preference and Productivity

I came to feel stifled in my downtown office. Working at home, I can move frequently between my office upstairs and the screened porch out back, toting my laptop and cordless phone. I can mow a patch of lawn or take a spin on my bike while I mull over a business problem. When I get stuck or finish one task and get ready for another, movement helps me shift mental gears. I feel freer and more productive. With no commute, I can sit around with my wife longer in the morning and still get to my desk sooner than I used to downtown. I can knock off later in the day and still put my feet up in the den earlier in the evening. I like my home and I feel for the first time as though I'm really getting my money's worth out of it.

Granted, we don't have kids, and my clients seldom come to me. I must add, too, that my wife left her job to go into consulting about the same time I moved my office home. We aren't involved in each other's businesses, but I enjoy the companionship. The solitude of working from home could come to feel like isolation if I were here alone for long.

For some consultants, the strategic and financial aspects of location are less significant than the emotional aspects. Some people find it very difficult to resist the distractions around them at home, or to maintain a clear separation between home and profession. (See chapter 8, "Keeping Your Business in Its Place.") Renting an office and going to work downtown can help you feel successful, reinforce your confidence, and bolster your marketing and pricing, because it adds to your aura of success.

If these factors are important to you, they are certainly legitimate considerations. The daily act of driving from home to office is an essential passage out of the personal and into the professional that enables some people to shut out the demands and distractions of family in order to focus on the demands of making a living and satisfying clients. These are personal choices. You need to trust the kind of person you are, and make the choices that will facilitate your success.

A Word About Zoning

To find out whether zoning prohibits your running a business from home, call city hall and ask. Every city has different regulations. In St. Paul, for example, you can run a business out of your home in a residential area if (1) you live in the home, (2) you don't have more than one employee, (3) you do not store products or conduct services outside of the house. In reality, you can get away with exceeding these limitations, provided the neighbors don't complain.

An Example of Office Sharing: Ladwig, Hoffman, Brown

In 1987, I was forced to move my office and was in a dilemma about where to go. I had been renting expansion space from another organization, and the $300 rent I paid them included receptionist services, light clerical, coffee privileges, access to the photocopier, and use of a beautiful meeting room. The conviviality was wonderful. But they were moving, and their new space was going to be too cramped for hangers-on like me.

About the same time, a consultant friend of mine name Terry Hoffman found herself being ejected from her office because her landlord, one of those executive office suite services, was going bankrupt. Another friend of Terry's, Susan Ladwig, was in a similar fix. Terry brought the three of us together. We'd each had our office in downtown St. Paul and wanted to stay there. We also found out we wanted roughly the same kind of space. We decided to throw in together and set up an office where each of us could pursue his own consulting business but get the benefits of companionship and expense sharing.

Here's What We Did to Forge Our Sharing Arrangement

- Agreed on the kind of space we wanted and the amount of rent we were willing to pay. Discussed our attitudes about space, support services, and sharing.
- Worked with a rental agent who knew about class B office space, would take the time to screen possibilities, and could help us negotiate a lease.
- Hired on an hourly basis a temporary support person to take care of the legwork, like opening a joint office-expense account, and setting up a record-keeping system for expenses that we incurred as a threesome. (Since we were not combining our businesses, we kept our books and accounts separate except for joint expenses. Whenever we needed to indicate a company name, for example to be printed on the checks for our joint account, we used Ladwig, Hoffman, Brown, but this was strictly for convenience, as we were not incorporated and each did business as a sole proprietor.)
- Funded our joint checking account in the amount of $1,000 each to cover common expenses associated with setting up the new office and making initial lease deposits.
- Negotiated a three-year office lease through our agent, including refurbishment of the space and four months' free rent up front. Since we were not doing business as a corporation, each of us had to sign the lease and agree to be "jointly and severally" obligated to its terms. That meant each of us was liable for the entire obligation if the other two were to skip town or get an attitude.
- Rented separate telephone lines, which the local carrier brought into our new office. Negotiated a three-year lease for a shared telephone system (reception set, four desk sets, central processor) and had it programmed to handle calls in a manner we thought would suit us best. Installation and programming were performed by an independent telephone consultant provided by the company that leased us the equipment.
- Negotiated a three-year lease for a photocopier. (We took care to schedule all these leases to expire at the same time as our office lease.)

- Bought matching desks, side tables, and side chairs.
- Bought a fax.
- Moved in, hired a receptionist, and fell in love with our new offices.

Monthly, our secretary paid common expenses out of our joint account (copier lease, phone lease, coffee supplies, postage meter rent, etc.). She gave us each an itemized invoice for our share of the costs, which we paid by writing checks into the Ladwig, Hoffman, Brown account. In that way, joint expenses could be handled efficiently, and each of us had an itemized invoice and a canceled check to record our share in our own business books.

The office-sharing arrangement worked extremely well for us, and the single biggest factor in its success was that each of us made an extra effort to carry his share of the joint expenses. I paid for the fax because I needed it in order to do business with an overseas client. But Sue and Terry each paid a third of the fax phone line and maintenance contract. We split the copier lease three ways, but Sue paid for all the paper and a disproportionate amount of the maintenance agreement because she did far more copying than Terry or I.

Two years into the lease, when Terry left to become president of another start-up company, she continued to pay her share of our leases and receptionist costs. All three of us tried to find someone to rent Terry's third of the space, but were not successful. Eventually the landlord reduced the space and our rent in exchange for a one-year lease extension, which Sue and I both wanted.

Seven Lessons for Office Sharing

Circumstances change, and so must collaborations if they are to be successful. The best collaborations are ones that can be renegotiated. This requires trust, clarity, and a willingness to give to get along.

1. *Don't confuse sharing an office with being in business together.* These are separate decisions, made for different reasons. The former is easier than the latter, giving you cost sharing and companionship without compromising your focus or market identity.
2. *Time your equipment leases to coincide with your space lease.* If that proves impractical, consider writing the equipment lease to expire before the space lease, with the idea that you would purchase the equipment at deep discounts when the lease expires.

3. *Divvy up ownership of any equipment that you buy rather than lease* (e.g., you own the typewriter, I'll own the fax, she can own the reception desk), because this will make it easier for you to depreciate these assets on your business or personal tax return, and will make it easier to decide who takes what with them when the arrangement is done and you dismantle the office.

4. *Keep a master record* of who owns what, all lease and maintenance contracts, the formulas you negotiate among yourselves for expense sharing, and all shared expenses and reimbursements. Down the road, you will forget why things were set up as they were, and this record will enable you to refresh your memories and make it easier to renegotiate as changes warrant.

5. *Agree in advance on how common expenses will be handled if one party opts out before the others.*

6. *Understand each of you is making a legal commitment to carry the others' shares of the lease obligation* when you sign a lease saying you agree to be "jointly and severally" responsible. Make sure you are prepared to hold up your end of that commitment.

7. *Recognize that office sharing won't work for everyone,* and don't pursue it unless (a) you are in reasonably compatible businesses (as defined by factors such as the amount of traffic you generate and the equipment, space, and facilities you need); (b) you all want the same benefits from sharing; and (c) you trust one another.

Whether you opt to have your office at home, throw in with a friend, or lease commercial space, remember that the best place to start your business may not be the best place to locate it once you are up and profitable.

For most consultants, the best place to get started is one that (1) takes the least front-end investment of time or money to set up and is cheap by the month, letting you focus on building initial revenues, and (2) offers mentoring and companionship to help you find your way up the learning curve. The ideal may turn out to be subletting from a friend who will plug you into existing support systems. You can always upgrade a year or two down the road, when you have your cash flow in order, have retained some earnings, and know more about what kind of space you need.

Deciding Whether to Incorporate

Common Organizational Forms for Consultants

In the United States, you have three choices as to what legal form your business will take: sole proprietorship, partnership, or corporation. Every state sets its own rules for doing business in each of these forms, and you must comply with the rules of the state in which you are located.

Central to your decision about what form your business should take are issues of taxation, liability, control, and simplicity. Most consultants do business as themselves (meaning they and their business are the same, which is the definition of a sole proprietor) or through a corporation they establish.

Although corporations are creatures of the states, how they are taxed is determined both by the IRS and by the states. The IRS provides several different tax categories for corporations. Most commonly used corporate forms for consulting are the "S corporation" and the "C corporation." More on each below.

Sole Proprietorship

What

- You and your business are one entity for legal purposes. Even though you keep separate books and bank accounts, there is no legal distinction between your personal assets and the assets of your business. The business's liabilities are your liabilities, and you report your business income or losses on Schedule C (form 1040) of your personal income tax return. (If you wake up one morning, go get a client and start consulting, you are doing business as a sole proprietor.)

Advantages

- Simplest legal form. Not regulated by the state. No specialized filings or reports required. No hassles involved with creating a separate entity, such as establishing bylaws, naming officers, appointing a board of directors, filing corporate taxes, or holding annual meetings.

- Privacy. Since you share ownership of the business with no one, you need not disclose business information or share decisions, and the only government reports you are required to file are your personal tax returns and any tax forms associated with withholding and workers' compensation for employees.
- Business losses transfer to your personal income taxes and can be used to offset other earnings.
- You alone control the business. You do not share control with partners or stockholders.

Disadvantages

- You do not get the liability protection offered by incorporation. Any liabilities and obligations of the business transfer directly to you and your personal assets.
- If you practice as a sole proprietor, you will have to pay self-employment tax (see chapter 14), which is equivalent to both the employer's and employee's share of Social Security.

I practice as a sole proprietor because it is the simplest legal form and I do not need the protections of incorporation. So do Diane Page, Fran Wheeler, Pattie Garrahy, Alice Lucan, Sue Foster and Jack Brizius. Verne Severson performs most of his consulting under a sole proprietorship, which he calls Forward Research, but he and a partner do product development under an S corporation.

Partnership

What

- Two or more individuals (or entities) that join together to carry on a business without forming a corporation. Similar to a sole proprietorship, except involving multiple parties.
- One defining element is an agreement set forth between the partners as to how each will contribute to the assets of the business and share in the profits and losses of the business.
- Income is not taxed in the partnership but passed through and taxed as personal income to the partners. However, partnerships must file an annual informational return reporting their income or losses (Schedule K-1, form 1065), and provide a copy of the filing to each partner, who reports his share on his individual tax return

(Schedule E, Page 2, "Income or Loss from Partnership and S Corporations," form 1040).

Advantages

- Simpler than forming a corporation. No specialized government reports required.
- Control focused with partners.
- Privacy.
- Easier to raise capital than sole proprietorship (partners' personal assets can be pooled to collateralize loans, or additional partners can be admitted to invest in the business).
- Pass-through of business losses to offset partners' personal income tax liability.

Disadvantages

- You do not get the liability protection offered by incorporation. Any liabilities and obligations of the business transfer directly to the partners and their personal assets. (In a limited partnership, limited partners—investors—are protected from liability, but they may not exercise any control over the operation of the business. The general partner is not protected from liability.)
- A general partnership cannot sell stock to raise investment capital.

None of the consultants profiled in this book practice in the form of a partnership.

Corporation

What

- Corporations can take several forms: a regular, for-profit corporation is called a C corporation. The C is a reference to Subchapter C of the Internal Revenue Code. A Subchapter S corporation (or simply "S corporation") is the same in every respect as a C corporation except that it is treated differently for tax purposes and is often a preferable form for a small or start-up business. Both forms are described below.

C Corporation

What

- A separate legal entity with bylaws, stockholders, officers, and a board of directors.
- Earnings are taxed in the corporation, and then taxed again as personal income when they are paid to stockholders in the form of dividends.
- Forming a corporation involves transferring assets to the new entity in exchange for stock, and filing articles of incorporation with the secretary of state in the corporation's state of incorporation. Typical filing fee is $135.

Advantages

- Stockholders are protected from liability for the actions and obligations of the corporation. (Corporate officers are not protected from liability for their actions, and may, for example, be fined by government for breaking laws or sued by stockholders for unfair practices.)
- Ability to sell stock to raise investment capital. (Investment capital is money you receive in exchange for an ownership interest in the business and not an obligation of the business. Debt capital is money you borrow and pay interest on; it remains an obligation until it is repaid, but does not dilute ownership. Unlike a corporation, you cannot sell stock in a sole proprietorship because it does not exist as an entity separate from yourself.)
- Ability to offer an ownership interest as a performance incentive to employees, for example through an Employee Stock Ownership Plan (ESOP).
- Has an unlimited life, whereas the life of a sole proprietorship or partnership is limited to the life of the principals who constitute it.
- Greater flexibility to enter relationships with other corporations, for example, through joint ventures, mergers, or acquisitions.
- Ability to build the business as an asset that can later be sold. (See chapter 10.)
- Consultants may also feel that the act of incorporating reinforces their professional image and sense of commitment to being in business.

Disadvantages

- Less control (control is shared by stockholders).
- Double taxation (profits received by the corporation; dividends received by the stockholders).
- Less privacy; governmental filings are public documents.
- Costs and inconvenience associated with the creation and maintenance of a separate legal entity (writing bylaws, holding annual meetings, filing corporate taxes, filing annual reports with secretary of state).
- Stockholders may not deduct corporate losses from their personal income tax liability.

About two-thirds of the consultants profiled in this book practice as corporations, for a variety of reasons. Eric Mitchell incorporated the Pricing Advisor, Inc., to take advantage of tax laws related to subscription publications, enabling him to accrue and defer revenues. Bryan Robertson incorporated Subsidiary Services International in part to facilitate his raising equity capital. Skip Pile incorporated Pile and Company in part to build an equity he can sell when he's ready to retire.

S Corporation

What

- Same as a C corporation, but also must meet four criteria to qualify for S corporation status: 1. organized in the United States; 2. only one class of stock; 3. no more than thirty-five shareholders; 4. shareholders must be individuals, not corporations or partnerships, and they must be US citizens or residents.
- A company that meets these criteria can be designated an S corporation, in which case it is taxed much like a partnership: in lieu of a corporate income tax, all profits and losses pass through to shareholders to be reported on their personal income tax returns. The corporation files an annual informational return (form 1120S and Schedule K-1). Shareholders get the liability protections of incorporation, and yet eliminate the double taxation of corporate profits and avail themselves of corporate losses to reduce their personal income tax liability.

Advantages Over a C corporation

- Eliminates double taxation.
- Profits and losses pass to the personal tax returns of the shareholders, who report them on Schedule E, page 2, "Income or Loss from Partnerships and S Corporations," form 1040.

Advantages Over Sole Proprietorship or Partnership

- Provides the limited liability protection of a corporation.
- Enables you to bring in multiple investors or owners.
- Has an unlimited life.

Disadvantages

- Same as for a C corporation, except for double taxation.

Additional Notes

- The term *corporate veil* is sometimes used to describe the limited liability protection that incorporation offers. The word *limited* in this context simply means that as an investor you cannot be held liable for losses beyond whatever you have invested in the corporation. Somebody who sues your company cannot go after your personal assets as well.
- I was advised by a representative of the IRS that in the case of an S corporation, it may be possible to "pierce the corporate veil" if you are being sued for liability and a court deems that the S corporation is being run like a sole proprietorship rather than a true corporation—for example, if there is only one major stockholder and no board. The IRS agent allowed that this gets into the realm of business law, where he is not capable of giving advice, but he felt it was an issue worth looking into if you are considering an S corporation for its liability protections.

A small but growing share of Verne Severson's business comes through an S corporation called CommStar that he and a partner formed for the purpose of developing and marketing new electronics products for Verne's consulting clients in situations where the clients would prefer to buy than make their own. The corporate entity makes it easier for Verne and his partner to take the financial risk involved with product development, by formalizing the relationship between them, protecting them from personal losses if the ventures fail, and creating a distinct separation in the client's mind between the product venture and Verne's hard-won consulting relationship under Forward Research.

Under all three forms (sole proprietorship, partnership, corporation), wages and salaries paid to *employees,* if any, are subject to withholding of state and federal income taxes, Social Security (FICA) taxes, and unemployment taxes (see chapter 14). Therefore, there is no advantage to one legal form or another where these burdens are concerned.

Other Organizational Forms

Limited Partnership

This variation on a partnership has a class of investors called limited partners whose liability is limited to the amount of their investment, but who may not participate in the operation or control of the business. This form enables general partnerships to raise equity capital without diluting control. Limited partnerships are complex and governed by many tax and securities regulations and are not useful forms for consultants.

Limited Liability Company, etc.

Some states have established still other corporate forms to promote new-business development. Minnesota, for example, has recently established something called the Limited Liability Company, which combines the benefits of close control offered by a sole proprietorship with the benefits of limited liability provided by a corporation. The limited liability corporation is viewed by some as a coming trend.

To find out what forms are available in your state, call the SBA or the office of the secretary of state. Remember: whatever variations on the corporate form a state may establish, how that organization is treated for federal tax purposes is a separate matter subject to interpretation of the IRS code.

Nonprofit and Tax-Exempt Corporations

The Internal Revenue Code exempts from taxes the earnings of certain corporations that are generally known as charities and are distinguishable by their community-betterment mission.

For example, Don Coyhis created a nonprofit corporation called White Bison through which he sells his consulting services. The organization's mission is to serve Native American youth, and the foundation status of White Bison enables Don to raise grants to supplement the consulting fees he earns to underwrite the organization's programs.

If your principal consulting focus is serving the community, talk to a tax attorney knowledgeable about Section 501(c) of the tax code to see whether you might benefit by doing business through a tax-exempt, charitable organization. This would apply to very few consultants, but where it works, as in Don's case, it provides important benefits, including the ability to raise tax-deductible gifts to underwrite operating and program budgets.

How to Get Established

Steps to Becoming a Sole Proprietor

1. Since a sole proprietorship is not a separate entity, you can begin consulting without taking any steps to establish your business under the law.
2. Decide what name you will use to do business. If the name you choose is your own, you are free to use it.
3. If the name you choose is other than your given name, as in Verne Severson's Forward Research, check its availability by calling the secretary of state's office in your state. If it is available, consider registering to protect it from use by others.
4. Work with your accountant to establish a simple record-keeping system (see chapter 14), and report your income and expenses on Schedule C of your personal income tax return.

Steps to Forming a Corporation

1. Call the Small Business Administration offices in your state, or the office of the Secretary of State, and ask for information on starting a business in your state, including procedures and forms for filing ar-

ticles of incorporation. (The SBA is the better place to call, because it lies within their mission to provide this kind of help, whereas the secretary of state's staff in most states will be more oriented to carrying out the duties of the office than to educating people about the rules, choices, and implications.)

2. Select several alternative corporate names, and check their availability with the secretary of state in each state in which you plan to do business. Consider filing an "assumed named registration" to reserve the name while you prepare to file for incorporation. For a fee, a law firm can both check and reserve the names for you.

3. Review your financial projections with an accountant to determine how much capital the business will need, what percentage will be debt versus equity capital, how much of the capital you will provide yourself versus obtaining from other investors or lenders, and so on.

4. Work with an attorney to prepare the articles of incorporation, addressing such matters as the names of the incorporators, par value and number of authorized shares, bylaws, and so on.

5. Complete the filing documents.

6. Determine all filing fees and submit them with the filing documents.

If you aren't sure which organizational form is best for you, you can always start out as a sole proprietor and expand into a partnership or incorporate at some future date if warranted by the growth of your business.

Controlling Your Technology: Phones, Computers, and Faxes

Information and communication systems are the infrastructure of a consulting business. Without an information system, you have nothing to sell, and without a communications system, you have no way to market yourself or deliver your services.

Information System

To configure your information system, ask yourself these questions:

- What information do I need to have in order to be of value to my clients, and how will I obtain it? This may include subscriptions, manuals, directories, reference tables, supplier catalogues, data bases, trade association memberships. (See chapter 12, "Business plans: when do you need one, what goes in it," for the names of three reference works on data bases and their use.)

- How will I store information (bookshelves, files), process it (computer, software), and communicate it (phone, modem, fax, messenger services, mail)?

The core of most consulting business information systems is the personal computer. With its ability to file, network, manage data bases, telecommunicate and word process, the computer has virtually eliminated the need for a secretary in a one- or two-person office, for a one-time investment of only $3,000 to $5,000. Don't limit yourself by trying to save money on older, underpowered equipment. There is some unnamed law of computer dynamics that will cause you to run out of memory, however much you buy. One reason is because software is becoming ever more powerful: Microsoft Windows and IBM's OS/2, for example, are powerful tools for increasing the computer's value and simplicity, but they take a lot of memory.

I will not try to spec out a computer system or software here even if I could; needs are too individual, and what's available changes too rapidly. Here is some general advice.

Computer

- State-of-the-art personal computer hardware has become a commodity, with terrific price competition and little brand difference in performance and quality. Therefore it is safe to buy generic and clone hardware to keep costs down, provided you buy from a reputable dealer who can support the equipment when something goes wrong.
- Talk to friends who are doing work similar to the work you will be doing, and find out what kinds of equipment and features they recommend.
- Go to a dealer you trust, tell him how you plan to use your computer, and see what he recommends.

Software

- There are large differences in the performance and quality of different software packages, and you will be far better off buying brand name software with several generations of development behind it, telephone support, and automatic upgrades.

- Again, talk to your friends and to a software dealer to learn about the kinds of software you should have, features, and brand name packages.

Communications Systems

The essential communications media are the same whether you have your office at home or in rented professional space: telephone, fax, modem, messenger service, postal service.

Getting the right configuration of phone lines, options, and equipment has gotten tricky. When I set up a shared office with Terry Hoffman and Susan Ladwig, we bought a telephone system for several thousand dollars on a three-year lease-purchase contract, timed to expire with our office lease. We had a dedicated phone line for the fax, and each of us also had two phone lines for our own use, since we were in different businesses. I used one as my principal business line, and the other as a rollover line so that my clients wouldn't receive a busy signal. A receptionist answered our rollover lines and took messages when we were out. We rented a separate line for her, so she could do business without tying up one of our lines. Since we officed in a professional building, the phone company figured we were in business and charged us the business rate for each line, $50 per month. My basic communications cost for phone and fax alone came to something like $160 per month with tax, not including long-distance, plus $375 for my share of the receptionist.

I cut that cost to $32 per month when I moved my office home. I did it by understanding my needs better, researching my options better, and making better use of technology: voice mail, custom ringing, automatic call forwarding for line busy/no answer, and a gizmo that distinguishes incoming fax calls from voice calls.

A word of caution here: since new devices and solutions are being developed constantly but are not universally offered, you need to ask a lot of questions to learn the simplest ways of meeting your needs. In my experience, the most candid and knowledgeable people are the freelance communications consultants that can configure a system as well as sell and install hardware. Find them by referral from stores that sell phones and faxes but do not install. I learned what I needed to know by talking with them on the phone (they make their money from bigger fish than me). As consultants, they have solved this problem for their own shop and understand what you are trying to accomplish with yours and how to get it done simply.

An Adequate Communications System Using Only a Single Phone Line

When I moved my office home, my wife and I had only a single residential phone line. I ordered a second line for my business and set out to accomplish with one business line what I had been doing with three.

Here's how, with a single phone line, you too can eliminate the need for a receptionist, never give a customer a busy signal, keep voice calls separate from fax calls, and leave your fax ready to receive twenty-four hours a day.

You Need

- A touch-tone phone (with memory, to speed dial your voice mail).
- One phone line from your local telephone company. (Since I'm now located in a residential area, the phone company bills me the residential rate, $14.61 per month for one regular private line.)
- Custom ringing. Where I live, this is an add-on service sold by the phone company. It consists of a separate phone number for the same line, which you will give out as your fax number. When it is dialed, you will get a different ring (for example, two shorts instead of a long) in place of the normal ring. ($4.95 per month.)
- Automatic call forwarding when your line is busy or you don't answer. This is also sold by the phone company. You will use it to route callers to your voice mail when you're out or on the line. ($2.60 per month.)
- Touch-tone service, sold by the phone company and needed to retrieve voice mail messages. ($1.20 per month.)
- A fax.
- A gizmo you plug into your phone jack (mine is called Ring Director by Lynx Automation) that discerns which phone number is ringing. It automatically sends voice calls to your telephone and fax calls to your fax ($149.00 one-time expense). (I also sprung for the optional installation at $39.00, which turned out to involve a guy bringing the gizmo to my house, removing it from its box, snapping three lines into labeled sockets, and collecting his money. Trust me, you can do it yourself in half a minute.)

- Voice mail service. (I pay $8.73 per month for this service from GTE because it is not offered by my local phone company.)

Here's how it works. When somebody dials my fax number, the Ring Director at my phone jack sends the call to my fax, which answers night or day. When somebody dials my regular number the Ring Director sends the call to my phone. If I am using the phone line, any incoming call is diverted to my voice mail where the caller leaves a message. When I am away, my fax answers fax calls, but voice calls are forwarded to voice mail if I fail to answer after four rings. One line, three ways to communicate: phone call, fax, voice mail. Cost: about 20 percent of what I had been paying the phone company, and I have eliminated the need for a receptionist to boot.

So, you're thinking, where's the catch? The catch is this: if my line is tied up when somebody tries to fax me, the incoming fax will be routed to my voice mail instead of getting a busy signal. This isn't a problem for me because my inbound fax traffic is not heavy and my clients know to try later, but it wouldn't be suitable for everyone. At residential rates where I live, it would only cost another $14.61 per month for a dedicated fax line, less $4.95 per month saved by eliminating the need for custom ringing, and $149.00 saved by not buying the Ring Director.

Controlling Your Technology

To keep control of your technology, consider the following questions when evaluating whether to expand your information and communications systems.

- What need am I meeting by adding this capability?
- How will this capability make me more valuable to my clients?
- What are the hidden costs? Examples: time required to learn new software; base and use charges for subscription technology like data bases or cellular service; maintenance contracts.
- How will this technology pay for itself? (1) what costs will it eliminate; (2) how can the value that this technology adds be translated into increased earnings?
- Can I reduce the expense of this technology? Example: rent it for the duration of the job and bill the expense to the client.
- Is there a simpler way to meet the need?

In the end, your technology decisions must serve the two masters of consulting: the clients' needs and your financial goals.

Ideas to Take Away

- A business name is like a brand. Consider what promise you are trying to communicate.
- For exclusive rights to your business name, you must register it in every state where you plan to do business.
- Four criteria for deciding where to locate your office: costs, professionalism, location advantages, and personal preference.
- Nesting within an established organization requires little investment and offers mentoring and companionship while you learn the ropes.
- Four criteria for deciding what form your business should take: simplicity, liability, taxation, and control.
- Sole proprietorship is the simplest form and often the most advantageous from a control and tax standpoint; incorporation offers the advantage of liability protection; S corporations blend tax advantages and liability protection.
- You can change your business form as your business grows.
- Information and communications systems are the infrastructure of consulting. Without an information system, you have nothing to sell; without a communications system, you have no way to market or deliver your services.
- To control your technology, understand how it will serve the two masters of consulting: the clients' needs and your financial goals.

Much of the information in this chapter has been drawn from two sources:

- "Tax Guide for Small Business: Income, Excise, and Employment Taxes for Individuals, Partnerships, and Corporations," publication 334 of the IRS, available from the US Department of the Treasury.
- "A Guide to Starting a Business in Minnesota," published by the Minnesota Department of Trade and Economic Development, updated annually, 900 American Center Building, 150 East Kellogg Boulevard, St. Paul, MN 55101.

FINANCES AND PLANS

How to estimate your revenues,
expenses, capital needs, and staying power

How to Buy Time to Succeed

Consultants make money the same way bankers do. Bankers buy deposits from you and me in the form of checking and savings accounts for which they pay a modest interest rate, and then they lend the money back out in the form of car loans, home equity loans, and the like, for which they charge considerably higher interest. The difference between what they pay for money and what they charge for it is the interest rate spread. The wider the spread, the greater the profit.

In consulting you're selling time, and you have at least one advantage over a banker: since all money spends the same, regardless of where you get it, the banker is pretty much stuck competing on the basis of price, but you are not. The greater your value to the client, the higher price you can get for your time.

The limits to your cost-price spread are set at the top end of what you can charge for every hour you sell, and at the bottom end by what your time costs you. The more you can charge, the wider the spread and the more you make. But the obverse is also true: the less your hours cost you, the more money you make, because reducing your hourly costs also widens your cost-price spread.

Owning Your Own Time

When you leave a job to go on your own, you've bought back your time from your employer. If it costs you $60,000 a year to live, and $40,000 a year to support your consulting overhead, you have to earn

233

$100,000—or about $8,350 per month—to pay for your time. Every month that you do not pay for by earning consulting revenues must be paid for in some other way (for example, by drawing down savings). The less it costs you to live and to support your business, the less it costs to own your time and the longer you can endure periods of slow sales.

In starting and operating a consulting practice, you want to invest your time and money in ways that *increase your value to the client* (setting you apart from the competition and supporting higher prices), and *decrease the costs of being on your own.*

The Higher Your Value and the Less Your Costs . . .

- The less capital you will need to put at risk to start your business.
- The more staying power you will have during lean times.
- The more pricing flexibility you will have and the easier it will be to win clients.
- The larger share of your revenues will pass to the bottom line and into your pocket.

Opting for Variable Costs

One strategy to help widen your cost-price spread is to transform fixed costs into variable costs wherever possible. Fixed costs—like salaries, heat, light, rent—must be paid regardless of sales volume. Variable costs are those that you incur only when you make a sale, so when sales decline, costs decline. Fixed cost: a specialist you bring on board as a salaried employee. Variable cost: a contract specialist you pay only when you have work. Fixed cost: specialized equipment that you own. Variable cost: specialized equipment that you rent only when you have a contract that calls for it.

Some other strategies for reducing costs are discussed later in this chapter. Strategies for increasing your value (or perceived value)—and therefore your prices—are covered in other chapters and include such things as enhancing your knowledge, skills, and performance (chapter 3); selling the client what she wants to buy (chapter 4); cultivating the right kinds of clients and understanding your clients' needs (chapter 4); and continually building your reputation and improving your methodology.

When you start a new business, it takes time and experience to learn what works and will make money: who needs what you have to offer;

how to market and price yourself; how to deliver your services; and so on. The more time you can buy for yourself by keeping costs down, the better your odds for success. And the healthier your cost-price spread, the less consulting you will have to sell to break even and make a profit.

Financial Projections to Make Smart Choices

Financial projections enable you to establish and test assumptions about costs and revenues to see their affect on your cash flow and earnings. In this way, you can estimate your revenues, expenses, capital needs, and staying power.

To illustrate, I have developed three financial scenarios for a friend named Lucy B., who is thinking of going on her own. Before presenting the scenarios, let me define some terms:

- *Pre-tax earnings.* The sum of consulting revenues minus expenses. This figure does not include draw (unless you incorporate your business).*
- *Estimated tax.* Self-employed individuals are not subject to withholding, but are required to make quarterly estimated federal and state tax payments. The estimated tax figures in the following scenarios are derived by multiplying 33 percent (an assumed combined state and federal tax liability) times the year's estimated pretax earnings. In the first year, the tax liability is paid in December. In year two and thereafter, it is paid in four installments (April 15, June 15, September 15, January 15). (See chapter 14.)
- *Draw.* Money you take out of the business for personal use, as in a salary.
- *Risk capital.* An estimate of the total amount of capital you must put at risk to fund the start-up of your business to the point where it is generating sufficient revenue to cover expenses and meet your

---

* The following scenarios assume the consultant will be practicing as a *sole proprietor.* This means the business and the consultant are the same entity for tax purposes, and any business earnings or losses transfer directly to the consultant's personal adjusted gross income. If you take more money out of the business for personal use than you generate in revenues (for example, by drawing against a line of credit at a bank), this will not affect your taxable income, which is simply the net of actual revenues and expenses. Likewise, since your business and you are the same entity, any surplus you leave in your business account at year end will be considered taxable as personal income. However, if you *incorporate* your practice, you and your corporation will be separate entities for tax purposes. In this case, the money you draw out of the business for personal use will be subject to personal income tax, and the surplus (or loss) you leave in the business will be subject to corporate income tax.

needs for personal income. *Risk capital* is the sum of two figures below: *working capital* and *reserve fund.*

- *Working capital.* The amount of capital you need in order to fund the deepest point of cumulative negative cash flow in your start-up business.
- *Reserve fund.* The amount of capital you must be able to call upon to fund your monthly operating expenses and personal income needs through an unexpected drought of revenues. This represents your staying power when business is slow. This figure is the multiple of the number of months you want to be able to stay in business without revenue times your monthly operating expenses and draw.
- *Reserve fund multiplier.* The sum of your monthly operating expenses and monthly draw. The nut you have to crack to stay in business every month.

Lucy B. is leaving her job as personnel manager for Digital Components Corporation (DCC) to become a consultant to corporations on how to handle the human resources implications of downsizing and management streamlining. Lucy uses a spread sheet program on a friend's computer to figure out how much money she will need in order to get her practice off the ground. She does some checking around, and she uses the following assumptions about her expenses and revenues to estimate her inputs to the program.

Scenario A Assumptions

Expenses

- $6,000 for equipment and furnishings (computer, software, printer, fax, telephone, desk, chair, files).
- $250 per month for operating expenses like telephone, postage, and out-of-pocket marketing costs.
- $100 per month for operating contingencies, like computer maintenance, software updates, and the like.
- $1,200 per month to office outside the home (rent, parking, and other expenses related to a downtown location), plus a one-time security deposit of $800.

- $3,450 per month draw, which is the minimum Lucy figures she needs as before-tax personal income to keep life and limb together. This includes $3,000 per month to live on, and $450 per month to fund her fringe benefits, as follows: $275 for health insurance and payment of her deductible, and $175 for disability insurance.
- Lucy also plans to open a SEP-IRA and contribute the maximum 15 percent of net earnings, but since she is funding her business start-up out of savings, she does not show a draw-down for retirement. (For more information about insurance and retirement, see chapter 13, "How to provide your own fringe benefits.")

Revenues

- $100 per hour will be her billing rate ($800 per day), which she plans to raise as her reputation and marketing network grow.
- $16,500 is what she estimates she can earn on a typical consulting project, which accounts for almost twenty-one days of billable time at the rate she's set.
- Projects will be invoiced 50% on acceptance and 50% on completion.
- Projects will last 3 months and invoices will be paid in 30 days.
- Out-of-pocket costs will be added to project invoices and are not shown.
- First project to be sold by March.
- Three projects to be sold in her first year, and seven in her second.

Financial Tables

The following tables illustrate how the decisions that Lucy B. makes in setting up and running her consulting business will affect her income and expenses in the first two years of her business, the capital required to launch her business, and the number of months to reach break-even.

Scenario B Assumptions

Same as in Scenario A, except:

- Consultant is working at home.

TABLE 12.1: SCENARIO A

Impact of Expenses and Revenues on Earnings

(Single person leaves job to become management consultant, renting an office outside the home.)

YEAR ONE	JAN	FEB	MAR	APR	MAY	JUN	JUL	AUG	SEP	OCT	NOV	DEC
Expenses												
Equipment & furnishings	0	6,000	0	0	0	0	0	0	0	0	0	0
Operating expenses	250	250	250	250	250	250	250	250	250	250	250	250
Operating contingencies	100	100	100	100	100	100	100	100	100	100	100	100
Office	2,000	1,200	1,200	1,200	1,200	1,200	1,200	1,200	1,200	1,200	1,200	1,200
Subtotal:	2,350	7,550	1,550	1,550	1,550	1,550	1,550	1,550	1,550	1,550	1,550	1,550
Revenues												
Conract revenue	0	0	0	8,250	0	8,250	8,250	0	8,250	8,250	0	8,250
Subtotal:	0	0	0	8,250	0	8,250	8,250	0	8,250	8,250	0	8,250
Pretax earnings	(2,350)	(7,550)	(1,550)	6,700	(1,550)	6,700	6,700	(1,550)	6,700	6,700	(1,550)	6,700
Estimated taxes	0	0	0	0	0	0	0	0	0	0	0	7,953
After-tax earnings	(2,350)	(7,550)	(1,550)	6,700	(1,550)	6,700	6,700	(1,550)	6,700	6,700	(1,550)	(1,253)
Cumulative pretax earnings	(2,350)	(9,900)	(11,450)	(4,750)	(6,300)	400	7,100	5,550	12,250	18,950	17,400	24,100
Cumulative after-tax earnings	(2,350)	(9,900)	(11,450)	(4,750)	(6,300)	400	7,100	5,550	12,250	18,950	17,400	16,147

YEAR TWO	JAN	FEB	MAR	APR	MAY	JUN	JUL	AUG	SEP	OCT	NOV	DEC
Expenses												
Equipment & furnishings	0	0	0	0	0	0	0	0	0	0	0	0
Operating expenses	250	250	250	250	250	250	250	250	250	250	250	250
Operating contingencies	100	100	100	100	100	100	100	100	100	100	100	100
Office	1,200	1,200	1,200	1,200	1,200	1,200	1,200	1,200	1,200	1,200	1,200	1,200
Subtotal:	1,550	1,550	1,550	1,550	1,550	1,550	1,550	1,550	1,550	1,550	1,550	1,550
Revenues												
Contract revenue	8,250	8,250	8,250	8,250	8,250	8,250	8,250	8,250	8,250	16,500	8,250	16,500
Subtotal:	8,250	8,250	8,250	8,250	8,250	8,250	8,250	8,250	8,250	16,500	8,250	16,500
Pretax earnings	6,700	6,700	6,700	6,700	6,700	6,700	6,700	6,700	6,700	14,950	6,700	14,950
Estimated taxes	0	0	0	7,994	0	7,994	0	0	7,994	0	0	7,994
After-tax earnings	6,700	6,700	6,700	(1,294)	6,700	(1,294)	6,700	6,700	(1,294)	14,950	6,700	6,956
Cumulative pretax earnings	30,800	37,500	44,200	50,900	57,600	64,300	71,000	77,700	84,400	99,350	106,050	121,000
Cumulative after-tax earnings	22,847	29,547	36,247	34,953	41,653	40,359	47,059	53,759	52,464	67,414	74,114	81,070

TABLE 12.2: SCENARIO A

Impact of Regular Monthly Draw on Cash Flow and Capital Requirements

	JAN	FEB	MAR	APR	MAY	JUN	JUL	AUG	SEP	OCT	NOV	DEC
YEAR ONE												
After-tax earnings	(2,350)	(7,550)	(1,550)	6,700	(1,550)	6,700	6,700	(1,550)	6,700	6,700	(1,500)	6,700
Draw	3,450	3,450	3,450	3,450	3,450	3,450	3,450	3,450	3,450	3,450	3,450	3,450
Monthly cash flow	(5,800)	(11,000)	(5,000)	3,250	(5,000)	3,250	3,250	(5,000)	3,250	3,250	(5,000)	3,250
Cumulative cash flow	5,800	(16,800)	(21,800)	(18,550)	(23,550)	(20,300)	(17,050)	(22,050)	(18,800)	(15,550)	(20,550)	(17,300)
YEAR TWO												
After-tax earnings	6,700	6,700	6,700	(1,294)	6,700	(1,294)	6,700	6,700	(1,294)	14,950	6,700	6,956
Draw	3,450	3,450	3,450	3,450	3,450	3,450	3,450	3,450	3,450	3,450	3,450	3,450
Monthly cash flow	3,250	3,250	3,250	(4,744)	3,250	(4,744)	3,250	3,250	(4,744)	11,500	3,250	3,506
Cumulative cash flow	(14,050)	(10,800)	(7,550)	(12,294)	(9,044)	(13,789)	(10,539)	(7,289)	(12,033)	(533)	2,717	6,223

Scenario C Assumptions

Same as in Scenario A, except:

- Addition of $5,000 per month retainer from former employer in first year; onset of payments delayed 60 days due to corporate paperwork.
- Revenues from consulting contracts are slipped 3 months to reflect delayed marketing due to demands of retainer work.

Scenario D Assumptions

Same as in Scenario B, except:

- Consultant is eliminating draw and living off spouse's income.

As Table 12.1, Scenario A, illustrates, Lucy's cumulative pretax earnings will reach $121,000 by the end of her second year. By adding to this scenario her $3,450 per month draw (Table 12.2, Scenario A), Lucy can also illustrate her cash flow and estimate her risk capital requirements. She will need $23,550 in working capital to survive the deepest point of her negative cash flow (month five), and she will not break even until the end of her second year. Her reserve fund multiplier (monthly expenses of $1,550 plus draw of $3,450) is $5,000.

She multiplies this figure times three months, which she feels is the minimum time she must be able to survive without revenue in case she has been overoptimistic in her assumptions. This calculation indicates she needs at least $15,000 in her reserve fund. This means she must have available a total of $38,550 in risk capital (working capital plus reserve fund) to underwrite the start-up of her practice, with flexibility to weather an unanticipated earnings drought of three months' duration.

In Table 12.3, Scenario B, Lucy tries to improve these figures by running her business from home, saving the $1,200 per month costs associated with renting an office. In this scenario, she ends her second year with cumulative pretax earnings of $150,600. In Table 12.4, Scenario B, she adds her $3,450 per month draw and sees she will need $17,400 in working capital to fund her deepest accumulation of negative cash flow (month three). Her reserve fund multiplier is now

$3,800, making her three-month reserve fund $11,400, and her total risk capital requirement $28,800, *almost ten thousand dollars lower than in Scenario A.* She will break even in month twenty-two.

In Table 12.5, Scenario C, Lucy analyzes what would happen if she were able to persuade her boss at DCC to give her a one-year retainer when she leaves, at $5,000 per month. To keep things realistic, she assumes it would take a while for the company to get the paperwork completed, delaying onset of her payments by two months. She also postpones other contract revenue by three months, figuring her work under the retainer will cut into time available for marketing. Still, under this scenario Lucy generates cumulative pretax earnings of $194,100 by the end of year two. She needs only $13,600 in working capital, and $11,400 in her reserve fund, adding to a risk capital requirement of only $25,000. She breaks even in July of her first year. She decides this is the best scenario yet, and decides to approach her boss for a retainer.

For the heck of it, Lucy wonders what would happen if she were married and could live off her spouse's income and be covered by his employer's group health insurance during the start-up of her practice. She runs a new scenario (Scenario D) with the same assumptions as Scenario B, working at home but without a retainer (nobody can have it all, she figures). Her net earnings are the same as Scenario B, but by dropping out all of her monthly draw except disability insurance ($175 per month), she makes an enormous impact on her cash flow, reducing her risk capital requirement to $9,150.

If you're thinking that the suggestion Lucy might live off her husband's income is sexist, let me quickly say that this is the approach my wife and I took when I left Control Data to start my practice, and I can recommend it highly where circumstances permit. It won't be practical for a lot of people, and may require scaling back your standard of living, but as the scenarios illustrate, the difference is substantial. Lucy will generate the same $150,600 in pretax earnings over two years as in Scenario B, but she will put nearly $20,000 less capital at risk to do so because, by forgoing a regular monthly draw and taking out nothing but the surplus as it is earned, she only needs to capitalize equipment and operating costs. This provides tremendous staying power during lean marketing times—every month without income costs her business only $525. Elsewhere in this book, experienced consultants will urge you to *keep your overhead low,* and this is the reason why: low fixed costs help you maximize your cost-price spread and enable you to wait out lean months in a business of ups and downs.

TABLE 12.3: SCENARIO B
Impact of Expenses and Revenues on Earnings
(Same as Scenario A, except officing at home.)

YEAR ONE

	JAN	FEB	MAR	APR	MAY	JUN	JUL	AUG	SEP	OCT	NOV	DEC
Expenses												
Equipment & furnishings	0	6,000	0	0	0	0	0	0	0	0	0	0
Operating expenses	250	250	250	250	250	250	250	250	250	250	250	250
Operating contingencies	100	100	100	100	100	100	100	100	100	100	100	100
Office	0	0	0	0	0	0	0	0	0	0	0	0
Subtotal:	350	6,350	350	350	350	350	350	350	350	350	350	350
Revenues												
Conract revenue	0	0	0	8,250	0	8,250	8,250	0	8,250	8,250	0	8,250
Subtotal:	0	0	0	8,250	0	8,250	8,250	0	8,250	8,250	0	8,250
Pretax earnings	(350)	(6,350)	(350)	7,900	(350)	7,900	7,900	(350)	7,900	7,900	(350)	7,900
Estimated taxes	0	0	0	0	0	0	0	0	0	0	0	12,969
After-tax earnings	(350)	(6,350)	(350)	7,900	(350)	7,900	7,900	(350)	7,900	7,900	(350)	(5,069)
Cumulative pretax earnings	(350)	(6,700)	(7,050)	850	500	8,400	16,300	15,950	23,850	31,750	31,400	39,300
Cumulative after-tax earnings	(350)	(6,700)	(7,050)	850	500	8,400	16,300	15,950	23,850	31,750	31,400	26,331

YEAR TWO

	JAN	FEB	MAR	APR	MAY	JUN	JUL	AUG	SEP	OCT	NOV	DEC
Expenses												
Equipment & furnishings	0	0	0	0	0	0	0	0	0	0	0	0
Operating expenses	250	250	250	250	250	250	250	250	250	250	250	250
Operating contingencies	100	100	100	100	100	100	100	100	100	100	100	100
Office	0	0	0	0	0	0	0	0	0	0	0	0
Subtotal:	350	350	350	350	350	350	350	350	350	350	350	350
Revenues												
Contract revenue	8,250	8,250	8,250	8,250	8,250	8,250	8,250	8,250	8,250	16,500	8,250	16,500
Subtotal:	8,250	8,250	8,250	8,250	8,250	8,250	8,250	8,250	8,250	16,500	8,250	16,500
Pretax earnings	7,900	7,900	7,900	7,900	7,900	7,900	7,900	7,900	7,900	16,150	7,900	16,150
Estimated taxes	0	0	0	9,182	0	9,182	0	0	9,182	0	0	9,182
After-tax earnings	7,900	7,900	7,900	(1,282)	7,900	(1,282)	7,900	7,900	(1,282)	16,150	7,900	6,968
Cumulative pretax earnings	47,200	55,100	63,000	70,900	78,800	86,700	94,600	102,500	110,400	126,550	134,450	150,600
Cumulative after-tax earnings	34,231	42,131	50,031	48,749	56,649	55,367	63,267	71,167	69,584	86,034	93,934	100,902

TABLE 12.4: SCENARIO B
Impact of Regular Monthly Draw on Cash Flow and Capital Requirements

	JAN	FEB	MAR	APR	MAY	JUN	JUL	AUG	SEP	OCT	NOV	DEC
YEAR ONE												
After-tax earnings	(350)	(6,350)	(350)	7,900	(350)	7,900	7,900	(350)	7,900	7,900	(350)	(5,069)
Draw	3,450	3,450	3,450	3,450	3,450	3,450	3,450	3,450	3,450	3,450	3,450	3,450
Monthly cash flow	(3,800)	(9,800)	(3,800)	4,450	(3,800)	4,450	4,450	(3,800)	4,450	4,450	(3,800)	(8,519)
Cumulative cash flow	(3,800)	(13,600)	(17,400)	(12,950)	(16,750)	(12,300)	(7,850)	(11,650)	(7,200)	(2,750)	(6,550)	(15,069)
YEAR TWO												
After-tax earnings	7,900	7,900	7,900	(1,282)	7,900	(1,282)	7,900	7,900	(1,282)	16,150	7,900	6,968
Draw	3,450	3,450	3,450	3,450	3,450	3,450	3,450	3,450	3,450	3,450	3,450	3,450
Monthly cash flow	4,450	4,450	4,450	(4,744)	4,450	(4,732)	4,450	4,450	(4,744)	11,500	4,450	3,518
Cumulative cash flow	(10,619)	(6,169)	(1,719)	(6,451)	(2,001)	(6,734)	(2,284)	(2,167)	(2,566)	(10,134)	14,584	18,102

243

TABLE 12.5: SCENARIO C
Impact of Expenses and Revenues on Earnings

(Same as Scenario A, except: (1) Additional $5,000/month retainer from former employer in first year. Onset of payments delayed 60 days due to corporate paperwork; (2) Revenues from consulting contracts are slipped 3 months to reflect delayed marketing due to demands of retainer work.)

YEAR ONE

	JAN	FEB	MAR	APR	MAY	JUN	JUL	AUG	SEP	OCT	NOV	DEC
Expenses												
Equipment & furnishings	0	6,000	0	0	0	0	0	0	0	0	0	0
Operating expenses	250	250	250	250	250	250	250	250	250	250	250	250
Operating contingencies	100	100	100	100	100	100	100	100	100	100	100	100
Office	0	0	0	0	0	0	0	0	0	0	0	0
Subtotal:	350	6,350	350	350	350	350	350	350	350	350	350	350
Revenues												
Retainer revenue	0	0	5,000	5,000	5,000	5,000	5,000	5,000	5,000	5,000	5,000	5,000
Contract revenue	0	0	0	0	0	0	8,250	0	8,250	8,250	0	8,250
Subtotal:	0	0	5,000	5,000	5,000	5,000	13,250	5,000	13,250	13,250	5,000	13,250
Pretax earnings	(350)	(6,350)	4,650	4,650	4,650	4,650	12,900	4,650	12,900	12,900	4,650	12,900
Estimated taxes	0	0	0	0	0	0	0	0	0	0	0	24,024
After-tax earnings	(350)	(6,350)	4,650	4,650	4,650	4,650	12,900	4,650	12,900	12,900	4,650	(11,124)
Cumulative pretax earnings	(350)	(6,700)	(2,050)	2,600	7,250	11,900	24,800	29,450	42,350	55,250	59,900	72,800
Cumulative after-tax earnings	(350)	(6,700)	(2,050)	2,600	7,250	11,900	24,800	29,450	42,350	55,250	59,900	48,776

YEAR TWO

	JAN	FEB	MAR	APR	MAY	JUN	JUL	AUG	SEP	OCT	NOV	DEC
Expenses												
Equipment & furnishings	0	0	0	0	0	0	0	0	0	0	0	0
Operating expenses	250	250	250	250	250	250	250	250	250	250	250	250
Operating contingencies	100	100	100	100	100	100	100	100	100	100	100	100
Office	0	0	0	0	0	0	0	0	0	0	0	0
Subtotal:	350	350	350	350	350	350	350	350	350	350	350	350
Revenues												
Retainer revenue	5,000	5,000	0	0	0	0	0	0	0	0	0	0
Contract revenue	8,250	8,250	8,250	8,250	8,250	8,250	8,250	8,250	8,250	16,500	8,250	16,500
Subtotal:	13,250	13,250	8,250	8,250	8,250	8,250	8,250	8,250	8,250	16,500	8,250	16,500
Pretax earnings	12,900	12,900	7,900	7,900	7,900	7,900	7,900	7,900	7,900	16,150	7,900	16,150
Estimated taxes	0	0	0	(2,107)	0	(2,107)	0	0	(2,107)	0	0	10,007
After-tax earnings	12,900	12,900	7,900	10,007	7,900	10,007	7,900	7,900	10,007	16,150	7,900	6,134
Cumulative pretax earnings	85,700	98,600	106,500	114,400	122,300	130,200	138,100	146,000	153,900	170,050	177,950	194,100
Cumulative after-tax earnings	61,676	74,576	82,476	80,369	88,269	86,162	94,062	101,962	99,854	116,004	123,904	130,047

TABLE 12.6: SCENARIO C
Impact of Regular Monthly Draw on Cash Flow and Capital Requirements

	JAN	FEB	MAR	APR	MAY	JUN	JUL	AUG	SEP	OCT	NOV	DEC
YEAR ONE												
After-tax earnings	(350)	(6,350)	4,650	4,650	4,650	4,650	12,900	4,650	12,900	12,900	4,650	(11,124)
Draw	3,450	3,450	3,450	3,450	3,450	3,450	3,450	3,450	3,450	3,450	3,450	3,450
Monthly cash flow	(3,800)	(9,800)	1,200	1,200	1,200	1,200	9,450	1,200	9,450	9,450	1,200	(14,574)
Cumulative cash flow	(3,800)	(13,600)	(12,400)	(11,200)	(10,000)	(8,800)	650	1,850	11,300	20,750	21,950	7,376
YEAR TWO												
After-tax earnings	12,900	12,900	7,900	(2,107)	7,900	(2,107)	7,900	7,900	(2,107)	16,150	7,900	6,143
Draw	3,450	3,450	3,450	3,450	3,450	3,450	3,450	3,450	3,450	3,450	3,450	3,450
Monthly cash flow	9,450	9,450	4,450	(5,557)	4,450	(5,557)	4,450	4,450	(5,557)	12,700	4,450	2,693
Cumulative cash flow	16,826	26,276	30,726	25,169	29,619	24,062	28,512	32,962	27,404	40,104	44,554	47,247

245

TABLE 12.7: SCENARIO D

Impact of Expenses and Revenues on Earnings

(Same as Scenario B, except eliminate draw and live off spouse's income.)

YEAR ONE	JAN	FEB	MAR	APR	MAY	JUN	JUL	AUG	SEP	OCT	NOV	DEC
Expenses												
Equipment & furnishings	0	6,000	0	0	0	0	0	0	0	0	0	0
Operating expenses	250	250	250	250	250	250	250	250	250	250	250	250
Operating contingencies	100	100	100	100	100	100	100	100	100	100	100	100
Office	0	0	0	0	0	0	0	0	0	0	0	0
Subtotal:	350	6,350	350	350	350	350	350	350	350	350	350	350
Revenues												
Retainer revenue	0	0	0	0	0	0	0	0	0	0	0	0
Contract revenue	0	0	0	8,250	0	8,250	8,250	0	8,250	8,250	0	8,250
Subtotal:	0	0	0	8,250	0	8,250	8,250	0	8,250	8,250	0	8,250
Pretax earnings	(350)	(6,350)	(350)	7,900	(350)	7,900	7,900	(350)	7,900	7,900	(350)	7,900
Estimated taxes	0	0	0	0	0	0	0	0	0	0	0	12,969
After-tax earnings	(350)	(6,350)	(350)	7,900	(350)	7,900	7,900	(350)	7,900	7,900	(350)	(5,069)
Cumulative pretax earnings	(350)	(6,700)	(7,050)	850	500	8,400	16,300	15,950	23,850	31,750	31,400	39,300
Cumulative after-tax earnings	(350)	(6,700)	(7,050)	850	500	8,400	16,300	15,950	23,850	31,750	31,400	26,331

YEAR TWO	JAN	FEB	MAR	APR	MAY	JUN	JUL	AUG	SEP	OCT	NOV	DEC
Expenses												
Equipment & furnishings	0	0	0	0	0	0	0	0	0	0	0	0
Operating expenses	250	250	250	250	250	250	250	250	250	250	250	250
Operating contingencies	100	100	100	100	100	100	100	100	100	100	100	100
Office	0	0	0	0	0	0	0	0	0	0	0	0
Subtotal:	350	350	350	350	350	350	350	350	350	350	350	350
Revenues												
Retainer revenue	0	0	0	0	0	0	0	0	0	0	0	0
Contract revenue	8,250	8,250	8,250	8,250	8,250	8,250	8,250	8,250	8,250	16,500	8,250	16,500
Subtotal:	8,250	8,250	8,250	8,250	8,250	8,250	8,250	8,250	8,250	16,500	8,250	16,500
Pretax earnings	7,900	7,900	7,900	7,900	7,900	7,900	7,900	7,900	7,900	16,150	7,900	16,150
Estimated taxes	0	0	0	9,182	0	9,182	0	0	9,182	0	0	9,182
After-tax earnings	7,900	7,900	7,900	(1,282)	7,900	(1,282)	7,900	7,900	(1,282)	16,150	7,900	6,968
Cumulative pretax earnings	47,200	55,100	63,000	70,900	78,800	86,700	94,600	102,500	110,400	126,550	134,450	150,600
Cumulative after-tax earnings	34,231	42,131	50,031	48,749	56,649	55,367	63,267	71,167	69,884	86,034	93,934	100,902

TABLE 12.8: SCENARIO D

Impact on Cash Flow and Capital Requirements of Eliminating Regular Monthly Draw

	JAN	FEB	MAR	APR	MAY	JUN	JUL	AUG	SEP	OCT	NOV	DEC
YEAR ONE												
After-tax earnings	(350)	(6,350)	(350)	7,900	(350)	7,900	7,900	(350)	7,900	7,900	(350)	(5,069)
Draw	175	175	175	175	175	175	175	175	175	175	175	175
Monthly cash flow	(525)	(6,525)	(525)	7,725	(525)	7,725	7,725	(525)	7,725	7,725	(525)	(5,244)
Cumulative cash flow	(525)	(7,050)	(7,575)	(150)	(375)	7,350	15,075	14,550	22,275	30,000	29,475	24,231
YEAR TWO												
After-tax earnings	7,900	7,900	7,900	(1,282)	7,900	(1,282)	7,900	7,900	(1,282)	16,150	7,900	6,968
Draw	175	175	175	175	175	175	175	175	175	175	175	175
Monthly cash flow	7,725	7,725	7,725	(1,457)	7,725	(1,457)	7,725	7,725	(1,457)	15,975	7,725	6,793
Cumulative cash flow	31,956	39,681	47,406	45,949	53,674	52,217	59,942	67,667	66,209	82,184	89,909	96,702

TABLE 12.9
Summary of Lucy's Scenarios

Scenario	RISK CAPITAL REQUIRED—		MONTHS TO RECOUP WORKING CAPITAL	24-MONTH CUMULATIVE PRETAX EARNINGS
	Working Capital	3-month reserve		
(a) Office outside home	$23,550	$15,000	23	121,000
(B) Office at home	$17,400	$11,400	22	150,600
(C) Add one-year retainer	$13,600	$11,400	7	194,100
(D) Variation on B: Eliminate draw; live off spouse & earnings	$ 7,575	$ 1,575	6	150,600

How to estimate the financial risks and rewards of starting your own consulting practice:

- *Spread sheet.* Get a spread sheet program, or work with your accountant or a friend who has software like Lotus or Microsoft Excel.
- *Cost and revenue assumptions.* Develop assumptions about the cost of equipment and furnishings you'll need, space and operating costs, personal income needs, pricing, timing of contracts, size of contracts, and so on. Plug these into the spread sheet program. Vary the assumptions to find out which will have the greatest impact on cash flow and earnings.
- *Estimated taxes.* For purposes of comparison, you can ballpark a tax bracket for your location, and use it in each scenario. However, when it comes to planning your cash needs and making quarterly tax payments, you should ask your accountant what figure to use for quarterly filing, to avoid year-end penalties for underpayment. (Tax implications of being on your own are discussed further in chapter 14.)
- *Realism.* Don't be overly optimistic about how quickly you will land business. It may take twice as long as you think.
- *Working capital.* When you have a spread sheet that reflects your best estimate of costs and revenues, identify what your cumulative negative cash flow is likely to be at its deepest point. That will be your working capital requirement.
- *Reserve fund.* Figure out your *reserve fund multiplier:* it is the sum of your monthly operating expenses plus monthly draw. Decide how many months of zero revenue you must be able to survive to keep your business flying through rough weather, once you've gotten it off the ground. Three months are a minimum, more are better if you can afford them. Multiply the number of months times your reserve fund multiplier to figure your total *reserve fund* requirement.
- *Risk capital.* Figure your risk capital by adding your working capital and reserve fund requirements.
- *Revision.* If the total risk capital is greater than you are willing or able to commit to the business, review all your assumptions, looking for opportunities to reduce costs and increase revenues, and run the spread sheet program again. (*Remember:* Be conservative with your revenue assumptions, because you are going to have to live on them.)

Four Ideas to Minimize Risk, Increase Gain

1. Review your financial assumptions and projections with your accountant.
2. Reduce fixed costs and invest to increase your value to your clients, so as to maximize your cost-price spread.
3. Price on the basis of value (see chapter 5).
4. Generate revenues at the earliest possible moment: (a) try to line up at least one contract before you leave your job; (b) consider your employer as your first potential client; (c) if you have portables, take them with you (see chapter 1); (d) invoice projects at least one-third upon acceptance by the client.

Ten Ways to Reduce Costs

1. Don't hire employees. If you need support services, buy them by the hour. Where adjunct consulting support is required to meet a client commitment, bring in associates on a fixed-price basis, bill their costs through to the client, and don't pay them until you get paid (see chapter 7).
2. Have your office at home, or rent a spare office in a friend's business where you have access to fax, copier, receptionist.
3. Sign no leases until you know you will be in business for at least the duration of the lease.
4. Share space and overhead costs with other free-lancers.
5. Be your own secretary and receptionist, using word processing and voice mail.
6. Don't do your marketing over meals, meet in the prospect's office—it will save you money and give you better insights into your prospect.
7. Reduce your monthly personal expenses during the start-up phase of your new business: (a) postpone expensive purchases like cars; (b) explore temporary suspension of monthly payments into equity accounts like whole life insurance contracts or savings programs; (c) cut back on expensive forms of entertainment and recreation; (d) pay off credit card loans and other expensive forms of debt.
8. Take care of any deferred medical needs like dental work or prescription renewals before leaving an employer-paid insurance program.
9. Sign up as a dependent on your spouse's employer-paid insurance,

or investigate continuation of your existing coverage under COBRA (see chapter 13).

10. Live within your spouse's income until your business generates earnings.

Where *Not* to Cut Corners

- Computers and software. If you stint in these areas, you may pay a price in quality, capacity, or speed, forcing you into expensive upgrades or premature replacement.
- Communications capability suited to your type of consulting: the telephone, fax, voice mail, modem, beeper, cellular phone, or courier services that you need in order to be accessible to your clients and serve them well.
- Product- and marketing-related expenses, where cutting corners will undermine the professionalism of your image: wardrobe, stylist, dry cleaning, letterhead, report covers, visuals.
- Licenses, taxes, permits.
- Time spent to satisfy the customer.
- Necessary marketing expenses, like attendance at trade conventions and memberships in professional associations, but be sure they really have value for you.
- Periodicals and subscriptions like data base and looseleaf information services (examples: Dun & Bradstreet, Prentice Hall, Commerce Clearinghouse) that keep you abreast of changes in your field.
- Insurance against catastrophic losses (health, disability, life, home owner's).

Where to Look for Risk Capital

Bootstrap Finance

Few consultants need to look beyond their own resources for the capital to start their business. Before you turn to outside investors, heed the findings of Amar Bhide. Bhide is on the faculty of the Harvard Graduate School of Business. In "Bootstrap Finance: The Art of Start-ups" (*Harvard Business Review*, November–December 1992, pp. 109–117), he reports on a study of a hundred companies in the 1989 *Inc.* "500," a list of the fastest growing private companies in the United

States. These are not consulting firms but tend to be software and technology companies, firms that typically take more capital to get off the ground than a service business like consulting. Nonetheless Bhide found that the median start-up capital was only $10,000, and more than 80 percent of these companies were financed through the founders' personal savings, credit cards, and second mortgages.

Bhide reports that having too much start-up capital can backfire, giving the entrepreneur room to turn small mistakes into large ones. He advocates what he calls the "try-it, fix-it approach" in which a start-up business with little capital keeps adjusting its strategies, dropping those that don't work and building on those that do. "Entrepreneurs who are unsure of their markets or who don't have the experience to deal with investor pressure are better off without other people's capital," Bhide concludes.

Among his words of advice for bootstrap finance are these: (1) "Get operational quickly. Bootstrappers don't mind starting with a copycat idea targeted to a small market. . . . Imitation saves the cost of market research." Once you're in the flow of business, he says, opportunities will often turn up that you won't have seen if you're on the sidelines waiting for the big idea. (2) "Look for quick break-even, cash-generating projects. . . . A business that is making money, elegantly or not, builds credibility in the eyes of suppliers, customers, and employees, as well as self-confidence in the entrepreneur."

Potential Sources of Start-up Capital

Following are some places to look for capital, starting with your own resources.

- Personal savings.
- Sale of assets like stocks and bonds.
- Home equity loan (advantage: the interest is tax deductible).
- Loan against cash value of your life insurance (advantage: about 80 percent of the interest you pay goes into your own account).
- Personal loan from family member.
- Small Business Administration loan, especially if you are a woman, a veteran, or belong to a minority group.
- Small business loan from your state's department of economic development.
- Bank loan, secured by personal assets.

- Investors, but only if you are incorporating your business and you need or want equity partners.
- Grants (from foundations, government, corporations, churches), if your consulting services will be focused on addressing community concerns, like combating racism, improving neighborhoods, or starting hospice programs.

Can you borrow from an IRA or 401-K retirement plan? Not from an IRA. You can only borrow from a 401-K for loans to cover hardship, and starting a business is not likely to qualify. However, you can ask your plan administrator, who has responsibility for making this determination. Any loan from a 401-K must be repaid within five years.

Financial Relationships to Keep You Whole

Spouse

If you are married, the most important financial relationship will be with your spouse, because the financial travails of your business will quickly become those of your marriage. This subject is discussed in chapter 8, "Work, Money, and Private Lives."

Investors or Partners

What does each bring to the business, and what does each expect to get from the business? Be clear in your own mind why you're bringing others in—companionship, capital, expertise—and how you will work together to make the business a success. For one perspective, read the profile of Pattie Garrahy in chapter 7. For another, read the experiences of Pattie's husband, Bryan Robertson, in bringing investors into his business ("Cash, not conversation") in chapter 10.

Your Accountant

Are your financial assumptions and projections realistic? What's the best use of your personal assets to get this business launched and up to profitability? How much of your start-up capital should come from equity versus debt? What tax payments will you need to make, and when?

How can you minimize your tax exposure? What kind of a financial record-keeping system do you need?

Your Banker

Many banks offer special packages of checking, savings, and cash flow credit for small businesses. Some will enable you to secure a business loan at a reduced interest rate by pledging compensating balances in personal accounts. If you will need credit, consider getting it before you leave your job.

Your Clients

Determine whether you are working on a fixed-price basis, time and materials, retainer, commission, or some other form (see chapter 5). Establish a billing arrangement that makes the client comfortable and that flows money into your business at the earliest practical moment.

Business Plans: When Do You Need One, What Goes in It

Whatever its format, a business plan spells out the logic and basic elements of your business. These include:

- What services you are going to offer.
- Who the customers will be.
- Why they will buy from you rather than your competitors.
- How you plan to produce, market, and deliver your services.
- How you will get paid.
- What form the business will take.
- How long it will take to reach profitability, and how you will finance it.
- What key assumptions underlie the success of the business.
- Significant risks.
- What you're going to do if your assumptions prove faulty.

Most consultants go into business without any formal plan, probably because they are not putting much capital at risk. As a general rule, *the more capital you are putting at risk, the more thoroughly you should plan*. If you are raising outside capital, the investors or lenders will want to see a written plan as evidence that you have thought through where you're heading and what will be involved in getting there. But even if you don't need a complete plan, at a minimum you should take time to figure out what it will cost you to be in business and how long you can afford to weather a revenue drought.

Following are four elements of a typical business plan:

1. Financial plan;
2. Strategic plan;
3. Marketing plan;
4. Organization and management plan.

Financial Plan

A financial plan answers such questions as how much capital will be required to start the business and where it will come from, what fixed and variable costs will be incurred, sources of revenue, and months or years required to break even and turn a profit. The heart of the financial plan is a set of financial projections and the underlying assumptions on which the projections are based, similar to the projections and assumptions presented above for Lucy B.

Any starting-out consultant should run financial projections. You need to (1) know what your targets are for sales, revenues, and expenses, (2) be able to track whether you are hitting your targets or not, and (3) understand the financial implications of missing your targets. If you are ahead of plan, you need to be able to share that good news with your spouse and financial backers. If you are behind plan, you need to know which of your assumptions was faulty, how to get back on track, and how long you can hold on without getting into financial trouble.

Your accountant can help you develop your projections and give you feedback to make sure they are realistic. Your accountant can also recommend bookkeeping software so that you can track the actual performance of your practice against projections, and make adjustments and midcourse corrections. There's a lot of software on the market to choose from.

Strategic Plan

This part of the plan answers questions about *sustainable competitive advantage.* If you are entering an area with a lot of competition, you should be able to describe your competitors and articulate your advantage: is it price, reputation, superior performance, special knowledge of a niche market? Are your strengths or advantages in areas that customers really care about?

One of the main reasons Eric Mitchell put himself in the newsletter business (see chapter 10) was to set himself apart from other consultants by building a national reputation and subscriber base from which to develop consulting clients. When you read about Susan Stevens's business in chapter 10 ("Turning your name and reputation into a brand") it's clear that the distinctive style with which she and her associates serve their clients is a competitive tool for winning business.

The key point is not necessarily to write a strategic plan but to have a competitive strategy in mind if you are entering a market where you need to compete to survive and prosper. For many consultants, the competitive strategy will grow out of special knowledge, strong relationships, and a strong performance factor (see chapter 3).

Marketing Plan

The more money you are putting at risk, the more important it is to be knowledgeable about the market for your service (How big is it? Is it growing or shrinking? What forces are causing it to change?) and to think through who your target customer is, what factors influence the customer's purchase decision, and how you will produce, price, and promote your service. Here again, it is more important for most consultants to think through these questions and have a plan in mind than to spend much time committing that plan to writing. We can afford to make an informed guess and sharpen our strategies through trial and error ("try-it, fix-it").

In gathering market information, don't overlook data bases as a source. To learn more about data bases and their potential value to you, read:

- "Online Databases," by Carol Tenopir, *Library Journal*, April 1, 1991, pp. 96–98.

- *Journalism for the 21st Century: Online Information, Electronic Databases & the News,* by Tom Koch, Praeger, 1991, 408 pp. (Includes a list of data bases and vendors along with evaluations.)
- *Modem USA: Low Cost and Free Online Services for Information, Databases, and the Electronic Bulletin Boards via Computer and Modem in 50 States,* by Lynne Motley, Allium Press, 1991, 190 pp. (Includes brief bibliography.)

Organization and Management Plan

If your vision is to have partners and employees, you should write an organization and management plan because you need to be clear about how management and administrative responsibilities will be divided, and how you want others to be associated with the business: as contractors, investors, employees, or partners.

If you are raising capital, you will need to write this part of the business plan because investors will want to know the qualifications and capabilities of the management team. If you are operating in league with a close associate, you need to understand how you are dividing up responsibilities, but you probably don't need to spell out the details in a formal plan.

Ideas to Take Away

- You make money on the spread between the price you can charge for an hour of your time and the amount that hour costs you to own.
- Reducing your fixed costs helps you buy the time your business needs to succeed.
- Financial projections enable you to calculate and reduce the financial risks of going on your own.
- Any one of the following measures can dramatically reduce the capital required to start your business: get office space free or on the cheap (by locating at home or with a friend); get a contract with your employer when you leave your job; live off a spouse's income until the business is making money.
- The more capital you are putting at risk, the more thoroughly you should plan.

13

SAFETY AND SECURITY

How to protect the down side

The risks you take in consulting don't ordinarily carry severe consequences because it doesn't take a lot of money to get into the business. But the world being such an uncertain place, a person likes to hedge against setbacks.

In my mind, financial security means protecting my assets and income and building for retirement. Simple objectives, but the tools to help us achieve them are not so simple: business plans and financial projections, financial software, contracts, incorporation, disability insurance, libel and malpractice insurance, errors and omissions insurance, health insurance, liability insurance, property and casualty insurance, copyrights, retirement plans, and so on. These tools are the domain of attorneys and accountants because to make smart choices you need to stay abreast of a complex and changing world of laws, products, and services.

This chapter will give you some ways to think about protecting your financial security but it is not a substitute for the advice of an attorney or accountant. The most important thing you can do for your financial security is to get competent professional advice when you need it. Rule of thumb: *When in doubt, seek it out.*

When to Use Attorneys and Accountants

When to Use an Attorney

I can count on the fingers of one hand the number of times that I've consulted an attorney about a matter regarding my consulting business since I went on my own in 1981. You are more likely to need an attorney's help when your business involves more than one owner, when you have employees, when your compensation and obligations are determined by contracts, and when you engage in activities or sell products that expose you to liability claims.

Consider Getting the Advice of an Attorney When You. . .

- Are not clear what form your business should take—proprietorship, partnership, or corporation (see chapter 11.) An attorney will help you sort through the need for liability protection and whether there are tax advantages to be obtained from one organizational form or another. (Accountants can also help answer this question.)
- Have questions about your liability exposure. An attorney can: (1) assess whether or not you have exposure to product liability, malpractice, libel, or personal injury claims (for example, from business visitors to your home office); (2) advise you how to reduce exposure; and (3) suggest the kinds of insurance you should buy to protect your assets.
- Are planning to sign a lease for office space.
- Are asked by clients to sign contracts (see below).
- Have intellectual property that needs to be protected through copyrights, patents, and trademarks.

What kind of a lawyer do you need, and where can you find her? Alice Lucan, the Washington, D.C., First Amendment attorney (see chapter 1) says you need a corporate lawyer who concentrates in small business and who's in a smaller practice so that you don't pay large-firm fees. How to find one? Alice suggests that you ask a friend for a referral, call a small-business owner and ask for a referral, or call your state or local office of the Bar Association and ask the attorney who heads their corporate law section for some names.

You will also find software on the market like Home Lawyer (published by MECA Software), which provides boilerplate legal materials like employment agreements and independent contractor agreements.

When to Use an Accountant

I turn to my accountant more often than my attorney, but not much more. When I started out, my accountant gave me a ledger and showed me how to keep my books (see chapter 14). Every November, I tell my accountant how much money I expect to have made by year end, and he does a rough tax calculation and tells me whether to adjust my fourth-quarter estimated tax payment. (If you do business through a corporation, your accountant can advise you whether to adjust your withholding before year end.)

In March, I give my accountant a summary of my business income and expenses along with the information for my wife's and my personal tax return. When my accountant has completed our return, he tells me how much I can contribute to my SEP-IRA and what my quarterly estimated tax payments will be for the coming year.

Other than that, we don't have much occasion to talk, unless I have a question about how to handle a capital expenditure or how to evaluate a lease-versus-purchase decision.

According to Alice Lucan's husband, Bob Lucan, who is a self-employed accountant in Washington, D.C., the role of accountants is changing. The growth of computer bookkeeping software has made it much easier for small-business owners to keep their own books, and this is a change for the good. "It's important for people to keep their own business checkbooks so they know where the money's going," Bob told me. "The people who do are going to be more successful. They'll make better decisions, and they'll witness early signs of trouble and be able to adjust their strategies before it's too late."

When You're Starting Up, Get an Accountant's Advice On . . .

- Developing financial projections and financing your business.
- Separating your personal finances from your business finances.
- Setting up your books and record-keeping system, to make sure they are organized to give you the kind of information you need to run your business and file your taxes.
- Tax reporting and filing procedures for the organizational form your business takes (proprietorship, partnership, corporation).

- Structuring a retirement plan (and on how to handle any existing retirement accounts when you leave your job).

When You're Up and Running, Consult an Accountant When You . . .

- Have questions about major expenditures (e.g., does it make more sense to lease or purchase, should you expense the cost or depreciate it, etc.).
- Decide to hire employees. An accountant can advise you whether or not the people you hire will be seen as employees or contract workers in the eyes of the tax code (see chapter 7). An accountant can advise you on employment laws in your state and make sure you are in compliance with workers' compensation requirements, tax reporting, and other rules.
- Experience a significant departure from your business plan or financial projections, or you need help with financial planning, such as pricing or break-even analysis for a seminar you plan to market.
- Need help preparing tax filings and figuring your annual retirement plan contribution.
- Need year-end tax planning.

How to find an accountant? Ask for recommendations from friends who have small businesses. Consider accounting firms that are small enough to value a small-business client, but large enough to have a number of partners and therefore able to stay current with changes in the many areas affecting small business.

How to Provide Your Own Fringe Benefits

Consultants take a backseat when it comes to fringe benefits. Not only must we pay for our own, but when it comes to Social Security, we have to pay twice as much (it's called self-employment tax), and when it comes to health and disability insurance, we have to pay with after-tax dollars. We even get charged higher health insurance premiums because we don't have the clout of somebody who negotiates for an entire group—despite the fact that we file fewer claims. People who are self-employed (that is, people who don't make money when they take time off to see a doctor) have been found to use the health care system far less than their counterparts in the salaried world.

When you set out on your own, you need to be aware of the extra benefits-burden to be carried, and think through what kinds and levels

261

of benefits you really need. You don't want that burden to be heavier than necessary, but you do want to build for retirement and protect yourself from significant financial setbacks.

I look upon insurance as a means of protecting my assets against catastrophic loss. Whether it's car insurance, homeowner's, health, disability, personal liability, or some other form, I try to buy coverage with relatively high deductibles and low premiums, coverage that kicks in when something severe occurs and is aggressive in protecting me from a personal disaster. I can handle the small losses.

Many people seem to look upon insurance not as protection against catastrophic loss but as a means of cost transfer. They file a claim anytime they nick a windshield, get a wet basement, or see a doctor about a sore throat. When it comes to health care, many group policies sponsored by employers provide that level of coverage, and we get used to it very quickly. When you go on your own, you'll find that the rich level of coverage you may be used to, especially in health care, is prohibitively expensive on the open market. You may be able to cut your premium to half or even less simply by increasing your deductible and switching from comprehensive to limited coverage that doesn't fully kick in until you begin to incur heavy losses. Insurance is only one tool in your financial-security tool kit. Before you buy, reassess the role of insurance in your life, and don't buy richer coverage than you need.

Health Insurance

The costs of health care are so high that you simply cannot afford to be without a quality health insurance policy that covers you for major problems. The health insurance situation is changing, but at the time of this writing, depending on your situation, you may have as many as four options for coverage.

Four Options for Health Insurance

1. *Continuation of coverage from your employer.* COBRA (Consolidated Omnibus Budget Reconciliation Act of 1985) requires employers who provide group health plans to allow individuals who leave the employer to elect continuation of coverage under certain circumstances and for a limited length of time, typically eighteen months. This is a temporary solution and not inexpensive, but it gives you time to arrange other coverage.

2. *Participation in a plan provided by your spouse's employer.* This is likely to be the lowest-cost, highest-benefit choice for those who have the option of choosing it.

3. *Purchase of an individual policy.* This is expensive, but it may be your best option if you can't participate in employer-provided group coverage through your spouse. If you have a preexisting medical condition, you may find that insurance companies will write an exclusion for that condition into your coverage, or refuse to insure you at all. If you find yourself refused coverage, phone your state insurance commissioner and find out whether your state has a high-risk pool where you can get coverage.

   To shop for insurance, look in the yellow pages, talk to friends, contact insurance agents. But before you do, read up on what to look for. Two excellent magazine articles are: (1) "Are Health Care Costs Killing Your Business?" *Home Office Computing*, January 1992, pp. 30–37. Provides very specific information about what to look for in an individual health insurance policy. (2) "Which Policies are Best," *Consumer Reports*, August 1990, pp. 538–549. Provides an excellent explanation of the different types of health insurance and rates different policies.

4. *Participation in a group plan sponsored by a society or professional association.* The *Home Office Computing* article cited above indicates that there are some professional associations like National Writers Union that sponsor group policies in which you can participate if you join the association. In many cases, these policies are very good and save you money. However, the article cautions that some associations for the self-employed have been formed for the express purpose of marketing insurance to people like you and me, and in many cases their products are seriously flawed. If you want to pursue this option, read the *Home Office Computing* article and investigate any policy thoroughly before you sign up.

Disability Insurance

This is income protection and, in the case of a long-term disability, also protects your assets from being drawn down to replace lost income. Disability coverage is expensive but worthwhile. Actuarial statistics from the Health Insurance Association of America and other benefits consultants indicate that between the ages of thirty-five and seventy you are seven times more likely to get a disabling injury or sickness lasting three months or longer than you are to die. So buying disability insurance may be a higher priority than life insurance.

Buy only what you need, and get it before you leave your job if you can, because the amount you are able to purchase is determined by your earnings.

How much coverage do you need? Enough to fill the gap between the minimum income you need in order to live and any income you can count on receiving if you were unable to work. You don't need to pay income tax on disability insurance benefits, so figure after-tax dollars.

Other Considerations

- *Definition of disability.* Buy a policy that insures your ability to perform your *own occupation* as opposed to insuring your ability to earn an income at *any occupation*. The reason: if you are unable to practice your occupation but can perform a lower-level job, a policy that insures *any occupation* will reduce or terminate benefits.
- *Coverage for partial disability.* Buy a policy that covers you for *total and residual* disability. A policy that covers only total disability will not pay benefits unless you are totally unable to work.
- *Elimination period.* Consider a policy where benefits don't kick in until you have been disabled ninety days. This is like having a higher deductible in a health or auto policy: it reduces your premium.
- *Benefit period.* Look for a policy that will continue to pay benefits until you reach age sixty-five, at which time Social Security and Medicare benefits begin.
- *Guaranteed renewable and noncancellable.* Look for a policy with this feature, meaning the company can't drop you as long as you pay your premiums, and your premiums can't be raised above the levels stipulated in the contract.
- *Level premium.* If you can afford it and plan to hold the policy for a long time, you will do better to opt for a level premium over a rising premium, which starts lower but rises over time. Your agent should be able to illustrate both options.

Most disability policies will only insure you up to 60 percent of your income because they don't want to create an incentive for you to file a claim. Since the benefits are not taxed, you may not even need to insure at the 60 percent level. The objective is not to replace all lost income, but to insure the basic income you need in order to live without drawing down savings or other assets.

The problem for starting-out consultants is that you do not *have* an insurable income: no employer, no salary, no track record of self-employment earnings you can evidence through copies of prior-year tax returns. This is why you should buy disability insurance before leaving your job, while you have a salary the insurer can use to qualify your benefit. However, this raises another potential obstacle: insuring your own occupation, since your occupation will be changing. Work with your agent to solve this problem by defining your occupation by the skills required on your job that are similar to the skills you will need to function as a consultant.

For more information, read "What if You Couldn't Work Anymore?" in *Changing Times*, August 1990, pp. 53–56.

Retirement

The IRS provides two alternatives for self-employed people to build tax-deferred savings for retirement: a Simplified Employee Pension (SEP-IRA) and a Keogh. You can use either or both, and they can be powerful tools for building your retirement fund. Discuss with your accountant which plan makes the most sense for you, and have your accountant figure your annual contribution.

Both types of plans must be nondiscriminatory, meaning that whatever you set up for yourself must also be available to all other employees. This is not a problem when you are the only employee, but once you hire others, you should review your plan and perhaps amend it.

SEP-IRA

The advantage of the SEP-IRA is its simplicity and flexibility. You can contribute up to 15 percent of your pretax earnings in any given year, although your contribution may not exceed $30,000. You can skip a contribution during lean years without jeopardizing the tax status of the account. You can direct how the funds are invested. You pay no taxes on the funds until they are withdrawn. You may begin withdrawing funds at age 59½ and pay ordinary income tax on the amounts withdrawn. Any amounts withdrawn prior to age 59½ are taxed as income and subjected to an additional 10 percent penalty tax.

Keogh

Keoghs are more complex than SEP-IRAs and require more paper-work to establish, but offer two advantages. (1) With a "money-purchase plan" (see below), you can contribute up to 25 percent of your pretax earnings each year, not to exceed $30,000. This may seem unreachable when you're starting out, but prove very attractive as your earnings grow. (2) When you take withdrawals from a Keogh you can average them over a five-year period for income tax purposes. Disad-vantage: in a money-purchase plan, you may not forgo contributing during lean years or reduce your contribution without amending your plan.

A Keogh can take two forms. One is a defined contribution plan. The other is a defined benefit plan.

Defined Contribution Plan   There are two kinds of defined contribu-tion plans: profit sharing and money-purchase.

A *"profit sharing" plan* is like a SEP-IRA in that you can contribute as much or as little each year, up to a maximum of 15 percent.

A *"money-purchase" plan* requires that you contribute the same per-centage every year, and that percentage may be as high as 25 percent. In order to change the rate at which you contribute, you must file a plan amendment, and the amended plan must remain nondiscriminatory, meaning that if your business has other employees, the amendment must apply to them as well. If you fail to make the required contribu-tion without amending the plan, the plan may lose eligibility for tax deferral and be subject to penalties.

Defined Benefit Plan   The IRS says that a defined benefit plan is any plan that is not a defined contribution plan. (Right.) Under this plan you determine the retirement benefit you want the plan to pay, and then you calculate and remit the contributions necessary to build a fund adequate to provide that benefit. The IRS says, "You may need profes-sional help to establish a defined benefit plan," and who am I to dispute that?

The current trend is away from defined benefit plans because they lock you into funding even if you're losing money, and plan administra-tion requirements under IRS rules are especially burdensome.

You may have both a Keogh and a SEP-IRA, provided the combined contribution does not exceed 25 percent of your pretax income or $30,000. Therefore, if you set up a money-purchase Keogh plan for, say, a 10 percent annual contribution, you have the flexibility in good years to contribute another 15 percent to your SEP-IRA, and not to fund your SEP-IRA during lean years.

Computing your maximum contribution is not as straightforward as you might like to think. You have to deduct your retirement contribution from your income before you apply the 15 percent or 25 percent multiplier to figure your retirement contribution. Neat trick. You also are allowed to add back into your income for purposes of the calculation half of your self-employment tax. This means your maximum SEP-IRA contribution works out to be 13.0434 percent of your net income, and your maximum Keogh contribution works out to 20 percent of your net income.

For more information, read:

- "10 Basics About Keogh and SEP-IRA Retirement Plans," *Home Office Computing*, February 1991, pp. 26–67.
- "Retirement Plans for the Self-employed," IRS publication 560.

It's best to build health insurance premiums, disability insurance premiums, and contributions to your retirement plan into your financial projections when estimating the costs of going on your own.

Deductibility

A further note is in order on which benefits are deductible business expenses and which are not. A corporation may deduct as a business expense premiums for group health coverage for employees, group term life insurance, group disability insurance. To be deductible, the benefits must be available to all employees.

Sole proprietors, partners in a partnership, and owners of more than 2 percent of an S corporation generally may not deduct as a business expense the cost of their own fringe benefits, with one exception: 25 percent of health insurance premiums were made deductible under the Omnibus Budget Reconciliation Act of 1993, but you will want to check whether this provision has been extended beyond 1993. Fringe benefits provided to employees are deductible.

When to Rely on Consulting Contracts

Few consulting engagements involve fees that would be worth the costs of litigation to collect, and few consultants expose themselves to significant liability when they go to work for their clients. For these reasons, most consulting contracts are informal and take the form of a letter or proposal spelling out what you propose to do for the client, what you will charge, and when you will get paid. I believe it is important to put this information in writing because doing so forces you to be specific and establishes that you and the client share the same understanding and expectations.

Occasionally I will ask a client to indicate acceptance of a proposal by signing and returning a copy for my files. For example, I will do this when I feel for some reason the client may not be with the organization through the end of the contract, and I want a record of his having made a commitment to me on behalf of the organization. I have never had to produce such an agreement in order to get paid.

Formal contracts are almost always initiated by clients who have official procedures that must be observed for the hiring of consultants. In my world, these are usually government agencies and large corporations, and their contracts often run to many pages.

Terms and Conditions of Formal Consulting Contracts . . .

- Obligate the consultant to fulfill duties and deliver products stated in the contract (usually described in very general terms).
- Obligate the client to pay an agreed fee and establish the terms and conditions of payment.
- Establish the contract period and completion dates.
- Provide terms for cancellation.
- Protect the confidentiality of the client's information.
- Protect ownership of intellectual property (copyrights, patents, trademarks, etc.) and establish who owns the consultant's product and has rights to its use and resale.
- Limit the liability of the client and the consultant.
- Assure the client that the consultant complies with relevant laws and regulations, such as requirements for affirmative action compliance or workers' compensation insurance coverage.

I always feel at a disadvantage when asked to sign these contracts, knowing they've been written by a team of lawyers whose aim is to protect the interests of the other party, not mine. Nonetheless, I usually accept such contracts as a necessary evil of doing business with large organizations, but I don't hesitate to mark them up. I strike out and initial passages that do not apply (for example, if I am required to warrant that I carry workers' compensation coverage), then sign the contract and send it back. I can't think of a time when a client has objected to my changes.

Two areas where I get particularly uneasy with a client's contract are those dealing with ownership of intellectual property and with liability. If my work for the client will draw on processes and methods of my own and I feel there is a risk that the client might claim ownership, I make sure to spell out the items for which I expect to retain the rights. Recent changes in US law have extended copyright protections to consultants by requiring corporations to forfeit ownership of works produced by consultants unless the corporation's ownership of such works was specifically established at the time the work was commissioned. With respect to liability, I am uneasy if it appears that I can be held liable for damages in an amount in excess of the fees paid to me by the client. Where ownership issues or liability limits are unclear or not suitable, I may reword and initial the relevant paragraphs, or attach an addendum that incorporates my position into the contract. If the stakes are big enough, I will have my lawyer help me.

My Advice on Consulting Contracts

- Always summarize your understanding in writing, even if only in a letter or memo to the client that captures the basics concerning what you have agreed to do, what you will charge, how you will handle unforeseen changes, and how you will be paid.
- Get the client to acknowledge and return your letter with his signature at the bottom.
- Be sure the person who has committed to hire you has the authority to make that commitment on behalf of the client organization.
- If you have doubts about whether the client will pay your bill, you can (1) ask for part of the fee up front, or (2) break the job down into phases and make the start of each successive phase contingent on receipt of payment for the one preceding.
- Have your attorney draft a formal contract for consulting agreements that involve large fees that cannot be broken down into progress payments. For example: commission or equity-sharing arrangements where you will invest significant time without being paid until the project reaches fruition, such as helping broker a joint venture or acquisition. Unlike typical consulting engagements, where going to court would cost more than sustaining a

bad debt, these kinds of agreements can be worth litigating, and you want a solid contract to back up your rights and remedies.

- If you are delivering services or products where there is potential for liability (for example, a human-resources manual), have your attorney draft a written agreement that includes liability limits and advises the client in writing to review the product with his attorney.
- When a client sends you a formal contract: (1) make sure that your obligations and compensation are correctly presented; (2) see that your liability is limited to amounts paid to you by the client; (3) eliminate warrants that do not apply to you or you cannot in good faith sign; (4) make sure that your intellectual property rights are safeguarded. If your concerns and the size of the stake justify doing so, hire your attorney to help redraft the agreement.
- If you are sent a long, complex contract and you do business by yourself, ask whether the client has a simplified contract for engaging individual consultants or sole proprietors. Some do.

When to Cover Yourself for Liability and Casualty Losses

Liability Insurance

As a general rule, I believe in carrying $1 million or more in umbrella personal liability insurance that will kick in where homeowner's, auto, and other insurance policies leave off. Umbrella liability is commonly sold in tandem with homeowner's and automobile coverage at a nominal additional cost. Check with your insurance agent.

If you have your office at home and meet clients in your office, consult with your insurance agent about amending your homeowner's policy to cover your liability for business visitors injured on your premises.

If you rent commercial office space, it is common for lease contracts to require you to carry tenant's insurance, which includes liability insurance, naming the landlord as an additional insured. Check your lease. If this is not required, check with your insurance agent to discuss whether you should have this coverage anyway.

Your attorney can advise you on whether you need product liability, malpractice, or libel insurance.

In some fields there are forms of insurance unique to the risks of the field. For example, Pattie Garrahy carries advertising insurance for protection in circumstances where she places an ad insertion order with a magazine and the client changes its mind, leaving PGR Media with $50,000 or $100,000 of ad space on its hands. Find out what special forms of insurance may be appropriate in your field.

Casualty Insurance

You can cover your office equipment for fire and theft as well as business interruption and data recovery. Premiums are not high. Check with your insurance agent. It is possible that your homeowner's policy can be revised to provide this coverage, or that you can get a separate office contents policy. My premium for 1992 was only a hundred dollars.

Ideas to Take Away

- Financial security means protecting your assets and income and building for retirement.
- Consider using an attorney to file for incorporation, reduce liability, review contracts, protect your intellectual property.
- Consider using an accountant to help make financial projections, set up a record-keeping system, structure a retirement plan, handle tax filings.
- Include health insurance, disability insurance, and retirement savings in your financial projections.
- Don't buy richer insurance coverage than you need. Buy health and disability coverage. Ask an attorney about liability exposure. Buy fire, theft, and business interruption.
- Review your retirement plan when you hire employees.
- Always summarize your understanding with a client in writing.
- Before you sign a contract, make sure it limits your liability and protects your intellectual property.

14   **RECORD KEEPING AND TAXES**

Basics to keep you on track

Simple Systems for Tracking Time and Expenses

In my version of hell we sit at gray steel desks under naked forty-watt bulbs reading IRS instruction booklets aloud and penciling mysterious figures into a maze of interconnecting tables that march across worksheets so vast they drape over the edges of desks and mate in dark corners.

That's why I don't spend more than a whit of time at bookkeeping and taxes on this green earth; the opportunity may soon be more than ample. My financial record-keeping system consists of a two-sided ledger. On one side I record every penny that flows into the business and whence it came; on the other I record every penny that flows out and its purpose. At year end, I give a one-page summary to my accountant who plugs it into Schedule C ("Profit or Loss from Business—Sole Proprietorship") on my wife's and my joint tax return. Done.

You can make record keeping far more complicated than I do. If complication is your game, the most effective step you can take is to hire employees. Once you are an employer, there will be a host of state and federal people taking an unwholesome interest in your business, and the only way to hold them at bay will be to make your business a fortress of detailed records and to lob forms at them over the parapet.

There are two questions to ask in designing a record-keeping system: (1) What information do I need in order to manage my business? (2) What information does the government require?

Records to Manage Your Business

To manage your business you need information that reveals where your earnings stand compared to what you had hoped, accrues time and expenses for each project or client, alerts you to significant variations in cash flow, and helps you plan for them. You need a record-keeping system that can answer these kinds of questions:

- What are my overall expenses? Revenues? How do they compare with my financial projections? If they differ, why?
- How much money do I have in the bank?
- Who can I send a bill to? Who is overdue in paying me?
- For each client or project, what are my revenues and expenses and how do they compare to my bid?
- To whom do I owe money?
- What business expenses have I paid out of pocket that I need to reimburse myself for?
- What significant upcoming revenues or expenses do I need to plan for?

The level of complexity and the specific kinds of information you need will depend on what kind of consulting you do and how you organize your business. For example, Eric Mitchell needs a different kind of information system to manage his newsletter, seminars, and conferences than I need to manage my consulting practice. Pattie Garrahy needs a system that enables her to distinguish between the time-and-materials media planning work she does for a client and the commission-based media placement work. If you have any kind of profit sharing plan in place, you will need a system to track it.

Records to Satisfy the Government

To keep the government happy, you need a record-keeping system that tracks revenues and expenses in categories that correspond to the tax laws, enabling you or your accountant to calculate your taxes and fill out forms that must be filed. The kinds of questions you need to be able to answer include:

- How much money have I taken in? What were the sources by tax category (consulting, interest, royalties, and so on)?
- How much have I spent? How have I spent it by tax category: operating expenses, meals and entertainment (50 percent of which are not deductible under current law), capital investments (assets that you will use for more than one year), personal draw, taxes, etc.?

- Who are my employees and how much have I paid them?
- What payroll taxes have I withheld and paid?
- What contract workers have I used and how much have I paid them?

The records you need will depend on what kind of consulting you do and how you have structured your practice: as a sole proprietorship, partnership, S corporation, or C corporation (see chapter 11).

Four Approaches to Record Keeping

You can take one of four approaches to setting up and maintaining a record-keeping system:

1. *Hand-kept records.* This is how I keep records, using nothing more than a glorified check register where I can record income and expenses by category.
2. *Simple computer-based records.* This could consist of good, simple bookkeeping software like Quicken (published by Intuit) and user-friendly software like Timeslips (published by Timeslips Corporation) to track your time and expenses on a project-by-project basis.
3. *Sophisticated computer-based record system.* There are many systems available, and your accountant can help you select one that fits your needs.
4. *Part-time bookkeeper.* You can bring somebody in part-time, as Pattie Garrahy and Brizius & Foster have done, to set up and maintain a record-keeping system, freeing you to spend your time on marketing and consulting.

If you are doing business as a sole proprietor, you may not need a record-keeping system any more complex than mine. If you set up your books on computer using a program like Quicken, you can save yourself the nuisance of reconciling your checkbook and adding up columns of revenues and expenses at year end. In addition, the category, subcategory, and class breakdowns offered by programs like Quicken automatically enable you to track expenses and revenues both by type and by project or client.

Taxes: What You Are Liable for, and How to Keep Your Nose Clean with the IRS

Nothing that follows should substitute for the advice of a tax professional. My intent here is simply to sketch out in broad terms how your tax filing requirements vary from sole proprietorship, partnership, and corporation.

Though the tax situation is very complicated, here are two considerations worth noting:

1. The tax consequences of going on your own are greatly simplified by:
   - Not having employees, and . . .
   - Doing business as a sole proprietor or S corporation, which enables you to report your business profits and losses in your personal tax return.

2. You pay more taxes when you go on your own.
   - When you do business as a sole proprietor, you must pay self-employment tax, which is the same as paying FICA twice.
   - If you do business as a corporation, you pay half the FICA as the employer and half as an employee. Any earnings you do not pay out as wages will be taxed twice: once as profits to the corporation, and again as dividend income to you.

Tax Consequences of Differing Organizational Forms

Tax consequences and paperwork vary, depending on what form your business takes. Following is a top-line summary. Note, however, that no matter what form your business takes, if you have employees you will be required to withhold their state and federal income taxes and FICA contributions, and to pay federal unemployment taxes and any equivalent tax in your state.

Sole Proprietorships

If you do business as a sole proprietor, you and your business are one entity in the eyes of the law and the IRS.

- Any income tax liability incurred by your business is incurred by you personally and reported on Schedule C ("Profit or Loss from Business, Sole Proprietorship") of form 1040, your personal tax return.
- You will be liable for self-employment tax (see below), which is reported on Schedule SE ("Social Security Self-Employment Tax"), form 1040.
- You get a deduction on your 1040 for half of your self-employment taxes.

Schedule C income is being highly scrutinized by the IRS because of the growth of self-employed taxpayers and the tendency among some to bury personal expenses in their business books. Don't deduct expenses that are not allowed under current tax law. And don't assume tax law follows the rules of logic. Two examples: (1) Only 80 percent of expenses for business meals are deductible. (2) Business costs of certain electronic devices like cellular phones may not be deducted *at all* unless at least half of the device's total usage is for business purposes.

Partnerships

A partnership is not a taxable entity, but it is required to file an annual information return, form 1065 ("US Partnership Return of Income"), which tells the IRS and state department of revenue what the partnership earned during the year, and how those earnings have been allocated to the partners. The partners report the earnings on their personal tax returns.

- Your share of the partnership's earnings are reported as income on Schedule K-1 ("Partner's Share of Income, Credits, Deductions, etc.") of form 1065, and on Schedule E, page 2 ("Income or Loss from Partnerships and S Corporations"), of your personal tax return, form 1040.
- Self-employment tax is reported on Schedule SE, form 1040.

S Corporations

- Earnings are reported on Schedule E, form 1040.
- Self-employment tax is reported on Schedule SE, form 1040.

C Corporations

If you do business as a regular (or "C") corporation, you and your corporation are two different entities, and each must file a return.

- You will be liable for income tax on wages and dividends you receive from the corporation, and for paying Social Security tax, by filing form 1040 the same as you would as an employee of any other organization.
- Your corporation will be liable for income taxes on profits, which are reported by filing form 1120. (At the time of this writing, taxes on corporate earnings are somewhat lower than taxes on personal income.)

Estimated Tax Payments

As a sole proprietor, partner in a partnership, or owner of an S corporation, you are required to make estimated tax payments if your income tax (on all sources of income) and your self-employment tax will exceed taxes paid through withholding and credits by $500 or more. A penalty may be imposed on underpaid taxes. An unexpected surge in income at year end could put you into the penalty category; work with your accountant to manage your revenues and tax payments to avoid a penalty. Your estimated tax payments are due April 15, June 15, September 15, and January 15. For more information, get IRS publication 334, "Tax Guide for Small Business," and IRS form 1040-ES, "Estimated Tax for Individuals."

Any C corporation whose estimated tax is expected to be $500 or more is required to make estimated tax payments. The tax payments are due on the fifteenth of the following months of the corporation's fiscal year: fourth month, sixth month, ninth month and twelfth month. For more information, get IRS publication 334, "Tax Guide for Small Business," and IRS worksheet 1120, "Corporation Estimated Tax."

FICA and Self-Employment Tax

FICA stands for Federal Insurance Contributions Act, and it is the tax that funds Social Security. When you are an employee, you and your employer each contribute to your FICA. The FICA tax rate for 1994 was set at 7.65 percent of the first $60,600 of wages, plus 1.45 percent of all additional wages.

When you are a sole proprietor, you must pay both the employee and employer shares of the Social Security tax. This is the self-employment tax, and the rate in 1993 is, logically, exactly double that of the FICA tax for employees: 15.3 percent of earnings up to $60,600 and 2.9 percent of all additional earnings. You are allowed to deduct half of the self-employment tax from your income in figuring your income tax. The maximum income exposed to FICA and self-employment taxes is raised almost every year, and may be higher at the time you are reading this book.

Unemployment Taxes

You are liable for unemployment taxes only if you have employees. The federal unemployment tax system, along with the state systems, provides unemployment payments to workers who have lost their jobs. At the time of this writing, FUTA (Federal Unemployment Tax Act) taxes are payable on the first $7,000 in wages paid to each employee during the tax year. The tax is imposed on the employer and may not be deducted from employees' wages. The gross federal rate at this time is 6.2 percent, with a credit of up to 5.4 percent for the state unemployment tax you pay, making the net federal rate 0.8 percent. States often reduce the unemployment tax rate for employers with low turnover rates. FUTA rates are subject to change, but have remained constant for several years.

Workers' Compensation Insurance

Requirements for workers' compensation are set by state statute. Contact your secretary of state's office to find out the requirements in your state.

Other Taxes

Other taxes for which you may be liable include sales taxes, real estate taxes, personal property taxes, registration fees, use taxes, and corporate franchise taxes. Ask your accountant whether any of these apply in your situation.

Checklist for Hiring an Employee

Here's a checklist for hiring an employee and keeping square with state and federal tax withholdings and filings required of an employer in Minnesota. Every state is different. Contact your accountant or the office of the secretary of commerce to find out what your state requires. (The following is adapted from "Checklist for Hiring an Employee," *A Guide to Starting a Business in Minnesota,* published by the Minnesota Small Business Assistance Office, copyright 1991, Minnesota Department of Trade and Economic Development, pp. 138–144.)

1. Determine whether the worker will be deemed an employee in the eyes of the IRS.
    *   Get Form SS-8, from the Internal Revenue Service, "Information for Use in Determining Whether a Worker is an Employee for Federal Employment Taxes and Income Tax Withholding." (For a definition of what constitutes an employee, see chapter 7.) Form SS-8 provides worksheets for computing income tax withholding, FICA, and FUTA (federal unemployment tax).
    *   State unemployment compensation. Contact the office of your secretary of state or department of revenue for worksheets in computing state unemployment compensation.
    *   Workers' compensation. Call your state's department of economic development or labor and industry to find out what rules apply to workers' compensation in your state, and the conditions under which workers will be considered employees or independent contractors for workers' compensation purposes.
2. Obtain federal employer identification number.
    *   Form SS-4, "Application for Employer Identification Number," available from IRS.
3. Obtain state taxpayer identification number.
    *   From your state's department of revenue and taxation.
4. Obtain state workers' compensation insurance. You can obtain it through your own insurance company.
    *   In Minnesota, coverage is required for the entire time you have employees.
5. Obtain state unemployment compensation employer identification number.

- Required in Minnesota within thirty days of establishing a business. Contact your state's department of revenue and taxation or department of labor and industry.

6. Verify compliance with immigration law.

   - Form I-9, "Employment Eligibility Verification," and Form M-274, "Handbook for Employers with Instructions for Completing Form I-9." A new form I-9 must be filed each time you hire. Available from US Immigration and Naturalization Service.

7. Obtain employee withholding information (Form W-4; child support and spousal maintenance obligations).

   - Form W-4, "Employees' Withholding Allowance Certificate," is used both for federal and state withholding and is available from the IRS.
   - Employers are required to ask individuals who are hired whether they have court-ordered child support obligations that are required to be withheld from income, and to ask the terms of the court order, and follow its terms.

8. Notify employees of eligibility for Earned Income Credit tax refund.

   - The Earned Income Credit (EIC) is a refundable tax credit for certain low-income workers who maintain a household and have dependent children.
   - Use Notice 797, "Eligibility for Refund Because of Earned Income Credit," and Form W-5, "Earned Income Credit Advance Payment Certificate," both available from the IRS. Notice 797 is a printed notice that the employer must give the employee within one week before or after the employer provides the employee with Form W-2. An eligible employee must file a Form W-5 with the employer each year.

9. Withhold federal income tax and employee share of FICA, and . . .
10. Withhold state income taxes.

    - These are accounting entries on the employer's books. The amounts also must be listed on each employee's pay statement.
    - Tables showing the amounts to be withheld are provided by the IRS and your state's department of revenue and taxation.
    - The taxes are withheld each time wages are paid, and the taxes are paid through periodic deposits and quarterly tax returns (see steps 12 and 14).

11. Account for employer's share of payroll taxes.

- Payroll taxes include the employer's share of FICA (Social Security) tax, FUTA (federal unemployment tax), and SUTA (state unemployment tax).
- These are also accounting entries made on the employer's books each time wages are paid.
- The amounts of these taxes are shown in the tables for steps 9 and 10.

12. Deposit withheld federal income tax and FICA tax, and
13. Deposit FUTA tax.
    - These deposits are made with form 8109, "Federal Tax Deposit Coupon," which is sent to the employer after the IRS receives the application for an employer identification number.
    - For federal income tax and FICA, the amount of accumulated undeposited taxes determines how often deposits must be made.
    - FUTA tax deposits are made quarterly, unless the amount owed is less than $100, in which case it is carried over to the next quarter.
14. Deposit withheld state income tax.
    - Contact your state department of revenue and taxation. Odds are they will have contacted you when you filed for your state taxpayer identification number (step 3).
15. File federal quarterly withholding return.
    - File form 941, "Employer's Quarterly Federal Tax Return," quarterly with the IRS.
16. File state quarterly withholding return.
    - Obtain the appropriate form from your state department of revenue and taxation.
17. File state unemployment compensation tax report.
    - Obtain the appropriate form from your state department of revenue and taxation. This is a quarterly filing.
18. File FUTA tax return.
    - Form 940, "Employer's Annual Federal Unemployment Tax Return," or "940-EZ Simplified Form." (Har, har.)
    - Obtain these from the IRS and file annually by January 31.
19. Provide form W-2 to employees and others.
    - Form W-2, "Wage and Tax Statement."
    - Obtain these from the IRS and file annually by January 31.
20. File state reconciliation of income tax withheld.
    - Obtain from your state's department of revenue and taxation.
21. Information returns, pensions, and other payments.
    - Employers who make payments to consultants and independent contractors who are exempt from withholding will be required to

file form 1099 Misc. (provided to payee) and 1096 (summary form filed with the IRS) if the amount of funds paid exceed a designated level. Obtain the forms and instructions from the IRS and file annually by January 31.
- Employers who pay pensions are required to issue form 1099R. Obtain these forms and accompanying rules from the IRS. Also contact your state department of revenue and taxation for any special rules pertaining to these filings.

The biggest problem in following these procedures isn't the difficulty of getting them right, it's the time they take that you could otherwise spend marketing and consulting. As I see it, you have four alternatives to following these steps yourself: (1) avoid hiring employees by using contract workers and associates (see chapter 7); (2) require the first employee you hire to take care of all the paperwork as a condition of employment and part of the job description; (3) investigate hiring the servies of a payroll firm like Paychex, Inc. or Ceridian, Inc. For a modest fee, they will handle the paperwork; (4) hire a part-time bookkeeper.

For more information on tax issues affecting your business and a list of helpful publications, get IRS publication 334, "Tax Guide for Small Business."

Ideas to Take Away

- Your record-keeping system must help you: (1) manage your business; and (2) meet your tax and legal obligations.
- Your accountant can help you set up a system that fits your needs.
- A simple hand-kept or computer-based system will be adequate if you have a simple business. Many sophisticated computer-based programs are available for more complex businesses.
- The tax and paperwork consequences of going on your own are simplified by doing business as a sole proprietor or S corporation and by not having employees.

Skip Pile, profiled below, went on his own from a senior position at a large advertising agency where he was responsible for finance, operations, and new business. He blended two strengths: an understanding of the nuts and bolts involved in organizing and running a successful business, and an insider's understanding of how the advertising industry works. He has put these strengths to work in two significant ways. First, he has built a niche helping corporations streamline their communications functions to cut costs and negotiate to get more value out of their advertising agencies. Second, he has structured his own business to grow in value as an asset he can someday harvest to finance his retirement.

MAKING SURE THERE'S A PROFIT AT THE END OF THE DAY
Profile
WALTER M. PILE, JR.
Marketing Communications Consultant, Boston, MA

In the spring of 1987, at age thirty-nine, Skip Pile, surrendered to office politics and left his position as executive vice president of Boston's largest advertising agency to explore other options. Today he's president and majority stockholder of Pile and Company, a consulting firm on Newbury Street in Boston's upscale Back Bay, whose fees in its fifth year totaled nearly $900,000.

Many things are striking about Skip Pile. One is the financial success of his consultancy. Not only did he suffer no pay cut when he bailed out of the executive suite, but he's grown his income 12 to 15 percent a year since then—despite the fact he was forced to make a significant course correction early in his entrepreneurial journey, when the market for his services as they were originally conceived was blindsided by the Wall Street crash and recession in the advertising industry.

Another striking fact about Skip is the care with which he has structured and run his business to grow it as an asset, which he can harvest when the time comes for retirement. This is not a story about leaving the rat race and big bucks for quality of life and financial compromise. This is about taking what you've learned from years of growing somebody else's business, and putting it to work to build a business that's got your own name on the door.

Skip entered the advertising and marketing communications industry in the late sixties at a New York agency where he did media planning and buying for consumer products companies like Gillette, Procter & Gamble, General Foods, and Post. He was recruited to Boston in 1972, age twenty-four, to become media director at Hill, Holliday, Connors, Cosmopulos, Inc., which had billings of $10 million at the time.

Hill, Holliday grew like mad. In only two years during the early eighties, as the high-tech revolution took hold in New England, billings doubled from $75 to $150 million. In 1981, Skip was promoted to EVP in charge of the business side of the agency with responsibilities for finance, operations, and new business. It's the position he held until his departure six years later. When he left, billings had reached $320 million, up more than 3,000 percent since he hired on.

Skip had had firsthand exposure to the kinds of problems involved in structuring and running a successful business, and the initial focus of Pile and Company was to provide consulting services to firms in advertising, design, public relations, and related fields. His services focused on nuts and bolts finance and operations issues like pricing, profit forecasting, merger and acquisition work, and incentive compensation. His business, he likes to say, is the *business* of marketing communications—not advertising strategy, creative development, or media planning. He formed a corporation and set out to dominate this niche.

He did well enough so that by the late summer of his first year he was able to bring in a partner, Rick Hooker, to take a minority interest in the firm and share in the consulting work. But on October 19, 1987, the day their first employee started work, the stock market crashed and changed the course of Pile and Company's business. The crash triggered a pullback in spending by major advertisers, throwing cold water on demand for Pile and Company's services.

"I found myself proposing to design an incentive compensation system for an agency prospect, and it would take two months and three board meetings to get a decision," Skip told me when we met. "Then one day the director of marketing for Lotus Development Corporation called." He was an associate of another client of Skip's and had recently taken the position at Lotus. "He said, 'There's ninety-five people here in marketing communications. I don't know what they all do. I've got a $4-million payroll and three outside agencies, and my understanding was we have all these people in-house to save money. Can you help me?' "

It's apparent that Skip enjoys telling this story. He folds his hands behind his head and rocks back in his chair.

"So I said, 'It's going to cost you *x* dollars and take ninety days,' and the Lotus guy said, 'Can you wait 'til Monday to get the check, because my accounts payable department shuts down early on Fridays.' Well. That's when I knew we were on to something."

Five years later Pile and Company is consulting primarily on the *client* side of the marketing communications business, helping companies structure the function internally, helping them to select advertising agencies and design firms, managing the review process from beginning to end, structuring agency compensation, and negotiating the contract with the agency they select. "We work with companies in the same operational business areas we set out to address, but on the other side of the equation. We're one of four or five firms nationally that work in this niche, and we prosper."

A typical client of Pile and Company might spend $10 million a year on advertising, although some spend well over $200 million. His biggest client at the time we talked was the computer firm Groupe Bull located in Paris. Groupe Bull had forty-three ad agencies in seventeen countries before Pile and Company helped them consolidate. Bull consolidated these into two agencies globally, and one worldwide media-buying consortium headquartered in Paris.

"Even where you can't consolidate agencies, you can standardize contracts and compensation practices around the world. The Belgians and the Australians and the French would all have you believe that their indigenous country situations are unique, but in fact from a lot of experience working both on the agency side—and now on the consulting side—we've learned that it's one world in this business, and you can write a single contract that'll fly just as effectively in any country of the globe. Sure you have to be careful in France about artistic ownership, be careful in Italy about payment terms, be careful everywhere about foreign currency exchange exposure, but the general legal provisions work."

Pile and Company wrote a handbook for Bull for each of their country managers on advertising agency compensation and contractual standards, laying out all the alternative methods of paying and what method is recommended and why. The booklet takes Bull's managers through a paragraph-by-paragraph explanation of a good contract and where they have latitude.

Pile and Company's clients include Hewlett-Packard, NYNEX Mobile Communications, Reebok International, Dun & Bradstreet Software, and Zenith Data Systems, to cite a few. About 40 percent of their business comes from helping clients streamline and integrate their marketing communications functions, and the balance comes from helping them select ad agencies, structure compensation, and negotiate contracts.

In addition to a minority partner, Skip has brought on a salaried associate to share in the consulting, and three support staff. Skip does 75 percent of the marketing, and their clients are 75 to 80 percent New England–based. One of Skip's goals is to position Pile and Company as the best in its niche nationally within the next three years. A cornerstone to his marketing strategy is maintaining close relationships with the trade press, people who get wind of change in the ad business first. "Half our business comes from referral, and the other half comes from chasing rumors—agency relationships that are in trouble, and so on." Skip's relationships with trade journalists also help Pile and Company get a lot of publicity, which in turn helps build their perceived position as a leader in the market.

The typical agency review contract is an eight-week undertaking, billed on a fee basis, half up front and half on completion. Organizational consulting is billed on an hourly basis at rates ranging from $95 to $210. Pile and Company typically has two or three agency reviews in progress at any time. The critical question facing Skip at present is how to turn these successful client *projects* into long-term *relationships*.

"I'm making this up as I go along. The big problem with our core business is that it's projects. We do a good job for Kao Infosystems to hire their agencies, but then we haven't figured out the next product to sell them. They're happy, they refer others to us, but we need to find a way to sign them up for the next phase of work."

A natural is to segue into organizational consulting, but that poses a problem. The problem is that the person in the client's organization who makes the buying decision for Skip's agency review service is usually the director of marketing communications, but the buyer for organizational restructuring is at a higher level, maybe his boss. "The director of marketing communications can feel threatened pretty quickly when someone's talking to his boss about reorganization."

Skip is looking for what he calls "annuity" products, something he can offer a client that generates sustained revenues. In a joint venture with *Adweek* magazine, Pile and Company conducts an annual survey of advertisers' and agency executives' perceptions of and attitudes toward the top fifty ad agencies. The study is called PACTS (Pile and Company Tracking Study). Pile and Company packages and sells the detailed, proprietary findings to agencies who subscribe to PACTS. *Adweek* provides the subscriber list, publishes the top-line results of the study every year, and lets Skip market PACTS on *Adweek's* letterhead.

Pile and Company has also developed a software product called Marcom Manager to help large-scale, multidivisional companies manage their marketing communications function: budgets, agency compensation, media spending by brand and market, and so on. "These are deceptively complex questions that are unanswerable in most companies."

He hired Arthur Andersen's Business Systems Consulting Group to write the software, and at the time of our interview was in the process of rolling it out to initial prospects. "Marcom Manager is a way of taking something we've learned and leveraging the value by turning it into a product that we can sell over and over. And it becomes another entree into consulting to help the client improve operations."

Skip looks the part of an ad agency exec: graying hair, trim mustache, navy suit, suspenders, crisp blue-and-white-striped shirt. His office is in the heart of the advertising and graphic arts section of town. He has an expansive cherry desk and a matching credenza-cum-bookcase that climbs the wall behind him, and opposite an enormous bay window takes up an entire wall three floors above Newbury Street.

He commutes from Concord, where he lives with his family. He's an avid gardener and has taken up woodworking (latest project at the time we talked: building a puppet theater.) With the exception of Sunday afternoons during winter, he has given up working nights and weekends the way he did when he was in the ad business. His typical schedule runs from 7:00 A.M. to 7:00 P.M., he travels three times a month, and goes to Europe every six weeks or so.

Every Thursday morning at 8:30 is an all-staff meeting, "the receptionist, everybody that works here. They put up the agenda, I add my own items." The six of them sit down and review current projects. They discuss and rate every prospect. They review the P and L for the month, and discuss aged receivables. "Everybody discusses everything. I do that to avoid the political problems that come up when some people have information and others don't."

Skip says what he likes best about being on his own is the feeling of not having to work with people he dislikes. "There's never so much money involved that you can't walk away from it. In the advertising business, maybe it's a $25-million account, families depend on it, you've got to do it no matter what. Here, I have the freedom to work with good people. The other thing is, I waited until I was forty to do this, and a lot of the illusions about what it means to have your own business are behind me. I don't want to be famous, run a huge organization. What's important to me is family and making some money. If you know what you want, everything else gets easier."

His goal is to retire in ten years, and the way he intends to get there is by building a company that can be turned into cash when he's ready to leave. He's been very methodical in laying the groundwork, his credo being to run a company with a balance sheet and to make that balance sheet sing.

"Don't lease anything; fund it out of cash flow. Buy and depreciate—it adds substance to the balance sheet and controls internal torque. And don't pledge personal assets."

He incorporated Pile and Company from the beginning, and hired Arthur Andersen as his corporate accounting firm because he wanted their name on the financial statements. He capitalized the business out of savings, and his expansion has been funded entirely out of retained earnings. Even his line of credit for working capital is secured by retained earnings held as certificates of deposit. He makes sure to show a profit, even though that exposes the company to corporate income tax, because the ability to demonstrate uninterrupted years of profitability "opens other options," whether those involve selling the company, attracting investors, or securing credit.

Two keys to building a salable practice are still eluding him and consume much of his creative energy these days. One is building those annuity products that provide more leverage and sustain client relationships. Another is coming up with a way to make himself dispensable: stand-alone products that don't require Skip, or what he calls a "horizontal business," where others do the selling.

Skip's formula for success is simple. "Treat your consulting practice as something other than yourself. It's business, not you. Make sure you have a plan that has you making a profit *every month*. At the end of the year, you'll have made money."

EPILOGUE

The Uniqueness of You

When I was interviewing for jobs fresh out of college, it was fashionable for personnel managers to ask you where you wanted to be in your career five years down the road. It was a zeal test—did you really, really want this job, this company, this career? If we let you onto a rung here, are you the sort who's going to climb or the sort who's going to thank his lucky stars he got aboard and just hang on for the ride? It's a dilemma any employer faces: how to tell the strivers from the deadbeats.

Careers, in the sense we knew them twenty years ago, are not so prevalent now. We are reportedly in an era of such change that most of us will have five different careers before we kick off our work boots for good. Which raises the question, what exactly is a career if you have to change it five times?

My best boyhood friend was so keen on becoming a doctor, he was skinning and mounting road kill at thirteen just to get the hang of the trade. Today he is an arcane specialist, head of his department, caught up by the restructuring of health care, spending far too much of his rare talent trying to manage budgets and far too little in the research that thrills him.

He surely always had an answer to that gnawing interview question. I never did. He was a person of goals, where I have always been a person of appetites. Today, we are all improvisers. We will become what the times and our talents and the risks that we take conspire to make of us. Career goals for many are being supplanted by quality of life goals. The questions to ask, it turns out, seem to be more like, when I am eighty-eight and taking stock of my life, how do I want to have lived it?

What is security? If the significant rewards have been, nearly always, the fruits of risks I have taken, what risks will I take to enrich the balance of my life?

Working independently is license for breaking rules and redesigning your life. But you can grow just as stale working on your own as in any job, and you probably won't see it coming. It happens when you stop taking risks. Having grown very good at what you do, you develop a reputation and a following. Demand for your time outstrips the hours available. You raise your rates to slow demand. The problem, of course, is that this is also a formula for sticking to familiar territory. To stay challenged and relevant, you need to strike off into uncharted realms. Be willing to earn less to learn more. The same daring and humility with which you entered consulting, lo and behold, are the keys for escaping the snare of your own success. It's that zeal test again, but there's no personnel manager sitting across the desk to administer it. Are you going to mount your compass on the office wall as an artifact of past glories, or take it down and use it?

When you are comfortable, taking risks is not the obvious choice. The world, after all, is overbooked with smart people. Just the same, none of them approaches a problem the way you do. For every foray you take into unfamiliar territory—feeling your heart quicken and your instincts stir, wondering how you're going to make a success of this and asking why you ever took it on—you invoke methodologies that are yours alone, honed through countless consulting encounters since the road kill of those dim early years. In doing so, you bring the world something special: the wonderful uniqueness of you. The problem may turn out to be as old as the hills, but your solution has an elegance all its own. What you get in exchange, as a friend used to say, is another lump on your head to run your fingers across and smile about in your declining years.

It is a fair trade. Take it.

INDEX